God Has A Plan For You!

52 Bible Study Sessions

Robert D. Prescott-Ezickson

CSS Publishing Company, Inc., Lima, Ohio

GOD HAS A PLAN FOR YOU!

Copyright © 2001 by
CSS Publishing Company, Inc.
Lima, Ohio

All rights reserved. No part of this publication may be reproduced in any manner whatsoever without the prior permission of the publisher, except in the case of brief quotations embodied in critical articles and reviews. Inquiries should be addressed to: Permissions, CSS Publishing Company, Inc., P.O. Box 4503, Lima, Ohio 45802-4503.

Scripture quotations marked NRSV are from the *New Revised Standard Version of the Bible*, copyright 1989 by the Division of Christian Education of the National Council of the Churches of Christ in the USA. Used by permission.

Scripture quotations marked NIV are from the *Holy Bible, New International Version*. Copyright © 1973, 1978, 1984 International Bible Society. Used by permission of Zondervan Bible Publishers. All rights reserved.

Scripture quotations marked RSV are from the *Revised Standard Version of the Bible*, copyrighted 1946, 1952 ©, 1971, 1973, by the Division of Christian Education of the National Council of the Churches of Christ in the USA. Used by permission.

Library of Congress Cataloging-in-Publication Data

Prescott-Ezickson, Robert D., 1955-
   God has a plan for you! : 52 Bible study sessions / Robert D. Prescott-Ezickson.
     p. cm.
   ISBN 0-7880-1804-3 (alk. paper)
   1. Bible—Study and teaching—Baptists. I. Title.
BS588.B35 P74 2001
220'.71—dc21   00-065113
                                                                                       CIP

For more information about CSS Publishing Company resources, visit our website at www.csspub.com.

ISBN 0-7880-1804-3   PRINTED IN U.S.A.

God's plan for me has certainly been an adventure. This book is the latest installment on that adventure and plan.

This book is dedicated to my Lord and Savior, Jesus Christ, that those who read it will be inspired to read the Bible and put it into action in their lives.

I express my gratitude to my wife Barbara and my daughters, Megan and Kristen, for their support and encouragement as this book was written, submitted, and eventually accepted. They have prayed with me all the way and celebrated with me when the book was accepted for publication.

I also want to thank the congregation of First Baptist Church in Meriden, Connecticut, for allowing me a place to minister and preach. My time with them has helped me grow as a preacher and a pastor.

I also want to express my gratitude to Mr. Robert Coote of the Overseas Ministries Studies Center and a member at First Baptist. Bob read the first draft and offered invaluable corrections and suggestions that were certainly essential in getting this book published.

Robert D. Prescott-Ezickson
Meriden, Connecticut

Table Of Contents

Introduction	11
Chapter 1 God Has A Plan!	15
Chapter 2 A Vision For Greatness	19
Chapter 3 Joseph: A Lesson In True Forgiveness	25
Chapter 4 I Have Come Down To Rescue — Through You	31
Chapter 5 The Power Of Intercession	37
Chapter 6 Between The Lines: Genesis And Exodus	43
Chapter 7 The Necessity Of Sacrifice	45
Chapter 8 Lessons From The Wilderness	49
Chapter 9 Between The Lines: An Overview Of Deuteronomy	55
Chapter 10 Transitions Of Leadership	57

Chapter 11   61
Samson: He Could Have Been Great

Chapter 12   69
God Uses Women Too!

Chapter 13   75
A Lesson In Spiritual Warfare: Beware Of The Occult

Chapter 14   81
Between The Lines: Don't Forget To Pray

Chapter 15   85
The Zenith Of Israel: The Reign Of Solomon

Chapter 16   89
Contest On Carmel

Chapter 17   95
Resurrection Previews

Chapter 18   101
Music In Worship

Chapter 19   107
The Power Of Praise

Chapter 20   113
The Titan Prophets: Elijah And Elisha

Chapter 21   117
The Heart Of Revival

Chapter 22   121
Esther: For Such A Time As This

Chapter 23   127
A Peek Behind The Curtain

Chapter 24   133
   The Forgiveness And Restoration Of Job

Chapter 25   139
   Ezra And Nehemiah: Coming Home From Exile

Chapter 26   143
   Just How Bad Is Sin, Anyway?

Chapter 27   149
   May I Help You?

Chapter 28   153
   God Knows Me, Do I Know God?

Chapter 29   159
   Wisdom For Everyday Living

Chapter 30   165
   Is All In Vain?

Chapter 31   167
   This Is Not Logical, Captain!

Chapter 32   173
   Higher Thoughts And Higher Ways

Chapter 33   179
   Do Not Pray?

Chapter 34   185
   Between The Lines: The Prophets

Chapter 35   187
   How To Treat Your Bible

Chapter 36   193
   A Tale Of Three Cities

Chapter 37 God Has A Plan	197
Chapter 38 Ezekiel: A Lesson In Personal Responsibility	203
Chapter 39 Dreams And Visions: Reflections On My Fortieth Birthday	207
Chapter 40 Concern For The Great City	211
Chapter 41 Malachi And Matthew: Elijah Comes Back	217
Chapter 42 The Rich Man And The Poor Widow	223
Chapter 43 Jesus: The Fulfillment Of The Old Testament	229
Chapter 44 One Small Offering	233
Chapter 45 Stewardship In The Early Church	237
Chapter 46 God Has A Plan: Jew And Gentile	243
Chapter 47 The Center Of Christianity	249
Chapter 48 Born Of A Woman	257
Chapter 49 We're On The Way	261

Chapter 50 267
 The Christmas Test: Jesus Has Come In The Flesh

Chapter 51 273
 Full Circle: God Has A Plan For You

Chapter 52 281
 The Story Continues

Index Of Referenced Scriptures 283

Introduction

God Has A Plan for You!

God has a plan for you! That is a bold claim, isn't it? Yet it is true. God's plan for you is written in the Bible. God says in Jeremiah 29:11-13, "For I know the plans I have for you, declares the Lord, plans to prosper you and not to harm you, plans to give you hope and a future. Then you will call upon me and come and pray to me, and I will listen to you. You will seek me and find me when you seek me with all your heart."

I believe the Bible is the written Word of God. I believe the Bible should not only be read, but obeyed as well. I believe the Bible is the true authority for Christian faith and practice. I believe the Bible reveals God's plan for humankind. I cannot claim originality for this idea, though I can't remember specifically who inspired me for it either. Nonetheless, God not only has a plan He has revealed that plan, and called us to be a part of that plan.

We are ever learning more about God and about ourselves through the leading of the Holy Spirit. One of the primary methods the Spirit uses to lead us in these new directions is through a new appreciation for the message and mind of God revealed through the Holy Scripture.

Christian history has also shown that relying solely on the leading of the Spirit, without consulting an objective authority, has led to excesses and perversions of the faith. Nearly every denomination is guilty of some excess. While the wineskin of Christianity has stretched with a myriad of practices and teachings, some have gone astray from the true orthodox Christian faith. People, "led by the Spirit," have started cults, initiated inquisitions, and perverted the true will and message of God. We need a book like the Bible to be the objective authority that acts as the time-tested standard by which every leading of the Spirit can be measured and approved as in line with God's historic revelation.

In the summer of 1994, I was inspired to try an idea to motivate my congregation to read the Word of God, and to challenge myself to preach through the parts of the Bible on which I didn't normally preach. We all have our favorite sections and books. I am guilty of neglecting certain books in my preaching ministry for a variety of excuses which, in the long run, won't hold water. The idea was simple: Challenge people to read through the Bible in a year. Each Sunday, I would bring the sermon from the previous week's reading. It averaged out to 22 chapters per week. I put only one condition on myself: the Easter sermon had to have something to do with the resurrection.

The next year, 1995, was an excellent year to make this challenge. The 1995 church year was laid out in such a way that I found an excellent message for Easter in the Old Testament. The communion sermons were easy to make from that week's readings. I also used my newsletter articles to fill in some of the gaps that the sermons couldn't cover. These are the "In Between the Lines" chapters you will find throughout the book.

Preaching in the church must always take the context into consideration. My context is First Baptist Church in Meriden, Connecticut. Context, of necessity, will bend the preaching and the applications in certain directions. I pastor in New England and have pastored in Southern New Jersey and Southern Indiana. I would not say the same things the same way in each context. Each audience hears things and interprets things differently. I pastor an American Baptist Church. I would not say some of these things in a Southern Baptist or Methodist or other denomination church. First Baptist Church is primarily middle class. I might have to say things differently to a different socio-economic group.

First Baptist is a moderate-sized church in central Connecticut. The people are generally conservative in their theology and practice. In 1994, First Baptist Church experienced a renewal from God that I still praise Him for and marvel at. Having been through a time of conflict and consultation, we had just completed a process of writing a vision statement. In January, 1995, we were preparing to vote on a vision statement for the church. That context provides the background for the sermon on Abraham and the need for vision. That vision helped to bring us together and give us direction. Working through the Bible helped us to understand our place in the plan of God for the ages and how we could fulfill our part of that plan.

Meriden is a blue collar, medium-sized city of 60,000 people. Like several cities in Connecticut, Meriden was experiencing urban decline and decay, though the situation was not to the point of hopelessness. Meriden is a city of diverse cultures, mainly white and Hispanic, with a smaller representation of African-American people. The general attitude towards Meriden at the time was negative. Businesses and people were moving out. Meriden is the mission field God has called me to and I believe it has a lot of potential. Since 1995, God has blessed Meriden with a more positive attitude and new businesses moving in.

Beginning in 1995, thirty people took the challenge to read their Bibles through. Fourteen ended the year having completed the course. While we might lament that all thirty didn't make it, I rejoice that fourteen people did in fact read their Bible through. I sent regular encouragement letters. At the end of the year, I presented them with a certificate to celebrate their accomplishment. And to a person, they all expressed their appreciation and awe for the Bible. Several began reading it again, "to see all the things we missed the first time through."

I offer this book first of all to lay people to help them and motivate them in their reading of the Bible. Between the sermons and the newsletter articles, you should be able to find a reasonable explanation of what you are reading. I also offer this to fellow preachers as an encouragement to preach the whole counsel of God. I hope this helps you in that endeavor as we labor together for Christ. I offer this to Bible study groups and Sunday school classes. The various questions throughout each chapter are designed to help personal and group study. I also offer this to the academic setting as a series of biblical sermons that will help strengthen biblical preaching in the churches.

Chapter 1

God Has A Plan!

Genesis 1:31; 3:15; Ephesians 3:6, 10

The Bible has been described in many ways. It is a love story between God and His creation. It is the story of God and human beings. It is the instruction manual for human living. It is the written word of God. All of these are accurate.

When reading the Bible through, it is best to use some kind of overall framework. This framework needs to give us reference points and structure to our reading so that we can see how the various parts fit together as a whole. There are many ways we could design our framework. We could look at the theme of sacrifice and see how that theme is presented in the Scripture. We could try the dispensational system of how God has related to humankind. We could look at the progressive nature of God's revelation. The framework for this book I will call, "God has a plan."

God has a plan. What is that plan? Why was a plan needed? The need for the plan becomes clear in the first three chapters of Genesis. Genesis 1 and 2 are somewhat different accounts of the creation story. Genesis 1 portrays God's orderly creation of the heavens, earth, and creatures. God does a day's work and takes a night's rest. Each day brings something new, different, exciting, and wonderful. Each day, God looks at His work and says it is good. The sixth day is the crowning day of creation as He creates human beings, male and female. Both male and female are needed to mirror the full image of God. Both male and female are given dominion and stewardship over all the earth. On the seventh day, God rests. The seventh day becomes God's day off, which he extends to all His creation as well.

- **How do you think God views the hustle and bustle of modern life?**

- **What does the sabbath command say about the human need for rest, vacation, or "just taking a break"?**

Genesis 2 presents things in a different order and with a different emphasis. Man is formed first from the dust of the ground. He is given the breath of life, that is, God's Spirit breathes God's life into the man. Then the animals are formed. Adam's dominion over creation is shown by his naming all the animals. Adam notices that all the animals come in pairs, but there is no single's ministry for Adam in the Garden of Eden. Eve is created from Adam's rib. God brings Eve to Adam — the Father giving away the bride in the very first wedding ceremony. This shows that women are God's gift and to be treasured and cherished, not abused or oppressed or enslaved. Marriage is blessed as the best relationship between a man and a woman.

In both accounts, at the end all is well. The man and woman are in charge of the garden. They are allowed to eat from any tree except the tree of knowledge of good and evil. Everything is just fine until ... "the serpent is crafty" (Genesis 3:1). In Revelation 12:9, John identifies the serpent of the garden with God's enemy, Satan. Satan hated God. Satan had rebelled in heaven and had been thrown out. Satan was hoping the earth would be his own little kingdom, but now these humans have been given charge over creation. Satan wanted to hurt God and he chose to do that by hurting God's children. We could debate all day about why Eve did what she did and why Adam did what he did. The bottom line is that Eve believed a lie and of her own free will ate of the fruit. The bottom line is that Adam believed a lie and of his own free will ate of the fruit. Nobody put a gun to their heads. They chose to disobey God.

- **Suppose you had the chance to persuade Adam and Eve not to eat of the fruit. What would you say to them?**

They suffered the consequences of their actions. When they ate, they became aware of each other's nakedness. In their purity and innocence, their nakedness hadn't bothered them. Nakedness shows the purity and innocence of their relationship. They had nothing to hide from each other, but now that they knew about evil, they had secrets. They had things they wanted to hide. They could no longer be comfortable being naked. They lost their purity. They lost their innocence. In the spiritual sense of the word, they died.

The punishment for sin is death. Death here is best described as separation. They were separated from God because they had disobeyed His command. They had obeyed (worshiped) Satan instead of God. They were also alienated from each other. Before they ate the fruit, they could be skin to skin. Now they had fig leaves separating them. It symbolizes their lost intimacy with each other. How could Adam ever trust Eve again? How could Eve ever rely on Adam for leadership again? Not only that, but also they had given up control of the earth to Satan, who now became the prince of this world. Everything and everybody were lost because of sin.

If the story ended here, it would be heartbreaking. But God had a plan. God knew it would happen, so He planned ahead. He gives the first inkling of His plan in Genesis 3:15: "He will crush your head, you will strike his heel" (NIV). Jesus was bruised on the cross, but when he rose again, he crushed Satan completely.

What was God's plan? In Ephesians 3:10, Paul says God's intention was to show to the various authorities and powers the manifold wisdom of God. I wonder if Satan's rebellion caused a lot of questions in heaven. Who is better? Who is wiser? God created the world as a contest ground saying, "Whoever can rule wisest on this planet is the best." Satan rules now through sin, death, lying, fear, and murder. God has invaded and rules His people through righteousness, life, truth, confidence, and hope. Who is the wiser? Who has been shown to be the best?

The zenith of God's plan is Jesus. Jesus came to earth to take away sin and crush Satan. Isaiah tells us that Jesus was bruised for our iniquities. His bruised and beaten body was the ultimate sacrifice of atonement for us. He shed his precious blood for us on the cross. It is through that sacrifice and shed blood as an atonement for sin that Satan was vanquished and sins are now forgiven. That was God's plan all along, to forgive us of our sin through Jesus

Christ. God's plan is infinitely wiser and superior. We should remind ourselves that we are now a part of God's plan. You are part of the plan to show God's wisdom to the heavenly authorities. You are now a part of God's plan that sin should be forgiven through Jesus Christ.

For Further Reflection

Read 1 Peter 1:20 and Revelation 13:8. When did God make His plan?

What is God's plan for your life?

What is God's ideal for male/female relationships?

Chapter 2

A Vision For Greatness

Genesis 12:1-7; 15:1-6; 21:1-5

As we read through the early chapters of Genesis, we see the consequences of Adam and Eve's sin multiply without restraint. Cain kills his brother Abel out of jealousy and anger. The story of Cain's grandson, Lamech, is the story of the first man to take more than one wife and a man who took retribution beyond what was reasonable. By the time we get to Genesis 6, humankind is so evil, so sinful, so enslaved to Satan that God is grieved to His heart that He even created them. He determines to wipe out everything with a flood, which He does. Yet one man finds favor with God — Noah. Noah and his family become the new progenitors of the earth's population.

Even so, sin continues. Noah gets drunk on the wine he makes and utters curses on his grandson. The people of the earth rebel against God's command to spread across the earth. They try to maintain unity through their great building project, the Tower of Babel. God sees their intentions and confuses their languages. Even through all this, God had a plan. He was working to fulfill His plan.

- **Is world unity a bad thing? Why does God judge this effort?**

As we come to Genesis 12, we see that God has found a man with whom He can work and who will work with Him. His name is Abram and he lives in Haran, in what is today far eastern Turkey or Western Iraq. Haran had an urban atmosphere and was considered a center for idol worship. Abram received a vision from God. The only question is whether the vision would be enough for Abram to move from Haran. God says to Abram, "Come to a land I will show you and I will make you a great nation. I will bless you and make you a blessing to all nations" (Genesis 12:1-2). While the exact meaning doesn't become clear for several hundred years, it is enough for Abram. At this point, Abram and his wife Sarai, have no children. In that promise to become a great nation is the promise of children. The promise to be a blessing is a bit more nebulous, but it can't be bad, can it? So Abram packs up his entire household and sets off not really knowing the destination. He doesn't know he is there until he gets there. When he does arrive, God appears to him.

Now I wish I could say everything went fine, Abram did perfectly, he had a son, and they all lived happily ever after. But the Bible is not a fairy tale. It shows human beings at their best and at their worst. The story of Abram is the story of a person who is constantly learning new things about walking with God and waiting patiently for God to fulfill His promises. Abram was 75 years old when he left Haran. Once in the promised land he stayed until a famine came. Then he went to Egypt, where things didn't go well. Out of fear for his life, Abram lied about his relationship with Sarai. Sarai was nearly taken into the Pharaoh's harem. Abram was essentially kicked out of Egypt, but while he was in Egypt, he increased in wealth.

Back in the promised land, God appears to him, and Abram questions the promise. In Genesis 15:5, God reiterates His promise concerning Abram's descendants. The ritual in chapter 15 is a covenant ritual whereby God swears His promise to Abram. In Genesis 15:6, Abram believes God, that is he puts his faith in God, and God credits his faith as righteousness. They go from the mountain top to the valley as Sarai tries to force God's promise by persuading Abram to have a child through Sarai's Egyptian slave girl. This brought tension into the household.

Finally, when Abram is 99 years old, 24 years after coming to the promised land, God appears again and promises Abram a son. He changes Abram's name to Abraham. He changes Sarai's name to Sarah. The name change shows that Abraham has matured in his faith and patience. God seals His personal covenant with Abraham and all his descendants through circumcision. The miracle happens. When Sarah is ninety and Abraham is 100, they have a son and name him Isaac. Isaac is the child of God's planning and timing. Isaac is the one through whom the promise will continue.

- **Imagine parenting at 99 or 100. Imagine being a teenager with parents who are 113 or so.**

Now in all this, Abraham kept the vision. Certainly, he stumbled. He misinterpreted. He tried to force God's timing, but he never lost sight of the promise or the vision. The vision of what God could do kept Abraham trusting in what God would do. He owned the vision, and never gave up hope or faith that God would do exactly as He had promised. Not only did Abraham live to see his son, but he lived long enough to see his grandsons Jacob and Esau. God fulfilled His promise.

God has given the Church a vision and a mission. We have it written in the Bible. It is a vision that gives us purpose and energy and enthusiasm. In addition to the Bible, we have a vision from the Holy Spirit of what the Church can become and accomplish. Like Abraham, we could have many spiritual descendants. The people we bring to Jesus could number as many as the stars. We will be blessed, and we can be a blessing to many others, even to the whole world.

New Christians typically mention two things that attract them to the Church and increase their desire to join. First is the preaching and worship. They hear the Bible preached and they understand. The worship is not only exciting, but they sense the presence of the Holy One. The second thing mentioned by people who join the Church is the friendliness of the congregation. If churches continue with both of these elements, we should be able to expect many more people to believe in Jesus and join the Church. There can be a new attitude of love, cooperation, acceptance, patience, communication, concern. The Church can be an exciting place to worship, serve, and fellowship. All this can happen if we will focus on the vision God has for us as His people.

- **Do an informal survey of your class or group. What attracted people to your church?**

The important question in all of this is, why are we doing this? What is our real motive? Whatever your answer was, the best answer is this: We are doing this in obedience to God to glorify Jesus. Like Abraham, we will have our ups and downs, but don't lose sight of that number one priority.

I can only imagine what will happen at the judgment on the last day. Jesus says in Matthew 25 that nations will be judged. In Revelation 1-3, churches are judged. So it is reasonable to assume that churches will be judged, perhaps divided by pastoral tenures. Some day, in heaven, God will call us forward as local congregations. Jesus begins to read the record for all of heaven to hear. "This congregation heard the message, owned the vision, and obeyed my Word. They turned around and started listening to my Spirit. They embraced the vision for their church that I sent to them. They became a premiere church in all of their region. They were a model of obedience in renewal, in mission, and in ministry. They grew in their stewardship until all of them were tithers and beyond. They all used their gifts in ministry to build up the church and spread the gospel to the entire community and surrounding towns. Their worship services were a steady stream of praise and glory to God and a time where I could speak to the people and they would listen. They were people of constant prayer, and their prayers were answered. They were people who revered my book and read the Bible until they knew it by heart. They truly loved one another and loved the world as much as I did. Let all of heaven know that this congregation is a faithful and loving church and they did my will. They are welcome in my Father's kingdom and shall have positions of honor and authority because they were faithful to me."

- **How would Jesus evaluate your church at this time?**

All the saints and angels break into harmonious praise to God for working such a wonderful work. They break into wild applause for us, for being obedient and faithful. For all eternity, your name tag in heaven says, "Hello, my name is _____." People will come up to you and say, "How exciting it must have been to be in that church at that time. God really worked miracles through you." You will respond, "Jesus blessed us and he deserves all the glory. I thank him that he allowed me to have a part in his plan."

Now, I have a question. Do you want to be that church on that day? Then you need to own this vision on this day. Not only own the vision for the Church, but own the vision for yourself as a Christian. Commit yourself to be an active part of God's plan in this time in history. Not every declining church turns around. Not every dying church gets another chance at life, but God will do that for you. You can see it. You can be a part of it. This is God's plan. This is God's vision for you as a Christian. This is God's plan for your church.

Do you want to be that church on that day? Then own the vision He has given us today, and let's fulfill it together with God's help.

For Further Reflection

Read Isaiah 40:30-31. What does God have you waiting for?

Read Romans 4 and Hebrews 11. What is faith according to the Bible? How did Abraham demonstrate his faith?

What is the vision God has given for you? Your family? Your church? Your community?

Chapter 3

Joseph: A Lesson In True Forgiveness

Genesis 45:7, 8; 50:15-21

I find the story of Joseph to be the most fascinating in Genesis. It has all the elements of the oppressed hero winning the final victory. At age seventeen our hero comes across as a spoiled son who flaunts it in front of his brothers. He tattles on his brothers. He dreams about his superiority and rubs his brothers with it. He is his father's favorite. Small wonder his brothers are jealous and less than loving.

Nonetheless, what the brothers do is cruel and inexcusable. They sell Joseph into slavery and deceive Jacob, their father, into thinking he is dead at the hand of some wild animal. The brothers here cause more heartache than they bargained for. They didn't really care about Joseph. Even though they could see Jacob was grieved to his heart about Joseph, the brothers were not bothered enough to go to Egypt to attempt to buy Joseph back. While Joseph comes across as a wiseacre, the brothers come across as cruel and heartless.

- **Imagine that you have the opportunity to talk the brothers out of selling Joseph. What would you say?**

Joseph is sold to an official of Pharaoh. While most people would be cursing the lemons, Joseph begins to make lemonade. He shows himself to be skilled at administration and organization. He runs Potiphar's house efficiently, and God blesses the whole household for Joseph's sake. Almost like the story of Eden, everything was going great until.... Rather than a serpent, this time temptation comes through Potiphar's wife, who doesn't really care if she remains faithful to her husband. She tries to get Joseph to compromise his morals with her, but Joseph remains pure. Finally, she tries to force herself on Joseph, but he gets away. To save her own skin and reputation, she accuses Joseph of rape. Potiphar is angry and has Joseph thrown in prison.

- **How would you or how do you react when people wrongfully accuse you of something?**

Again, most people would curse the lemons. Joseph begins his lemonade business all over again. His administration skills are noted by the jail keeper. Joseph is put in charge of the whole jail. There is an opportunity for Joseph to get his case to Pharaoh when he correctly interprets the cup-bearer's dream. But the cup-bearer forgets. Two years later, when Pharaoh has a mysterious dream, the cup-bearer remembers Joseph. Joseph is brought before Pharaoh. All those years of lemonade making, and the stock is set to skyrocket. Joseph correctly interprets Pharaoh's dream. There will be seven years of plenty and seven years of famine. Joseph counsels Pharaoh to make plans and prepare for the famine. Pharaoh sees Joseph's wisdom and makes Joseph crown prince over all Egypt. Joseph wins wonderful cash and prizes: A brand new wife, a brand new house, a brand new chariot, and a brand new job.

Joseph has finally come into his own. Yet with all this, there is still a deep pain in his heart. We can see that pain in the names of his children. Manasseh means forget. "God has made me forget all my trouble hardship and my father's household" (Genesis 41:51 NRSV). Ephraim means fruitful. "God has made me fruitful in the land of my suffering" (Genesis 41:52 NRSV). Make no mistake, the pain is there. Funny thing about pain and hurt, they don't just go away. They refuse to be buried and forgotten.

By the time Joseph becomes second ruler, he is thirty years old. He has been away from home for thirteen years. Most commentators would put Joseph in prison for ten of those thirteen years. The old saying is, "Time heals all wounds," yet that is not always true. Hurts of this nature can be healed only after they are acknowledged, confronted, apologized for, and forgiven. Current studies in psychology and psychiatry bear this out. The more we try to bury hurt, anger, guilt, or shame, the more it eats away at us. Another old saying is, "Confession is good for the soul." That is because confession of these feelings is a way of letting them out so they can't eat away at us anymore.

Eventually, these hurts have to come out in the open. The story of Joseph certainly illustrates that God thinks that way as well. Jesus says in Matthew 5:23-24, "If you are offering your gift at the altar and remember that a brother or sister has something against you, leave your gift and go be reconciled to your brother and sister" (NRSV). When our relationship with another person is at odds, our relationship with God is at odds. If our brother or sister will not be reconciled, we can rest because we attempted to make things right. With all his power and prestige, Joseph could certainly have left Egypt and found his father and family. But he didn't. For all the seven years of plenty, he didn't. Joseph needed to be reconciled to his brothers just as much as his brothers needed to be reconciled to him. Until then, there would always be pain and no lasting peace.

- **If you had been Joseph, would you have let all this time slip by without contacting your family?**

The seven years of famine begin, and it hits Canaan as hard as Egypt. Two years into the famine, Joseph's brothers come to Egypt to buy food. Guess who is in charge of selling food? That's right, our hero, Joseph. About 22 years have passed. Joseph recognizes his brothers, but they don't recognize him. Joseph devises a plan to see if his brothers have learned how to love and care for each other. He imprisons Simeon. He commands them to bring back Benjamin if they want more food and to see Simeon alive.

- **If you had been Joseph, how would you have handled this opportunity?**

You would think they would come right back, but they wait until the food runs out and the situation is desperate. Much of that is Jacob's fault because he is very protective of Benjamin and wouldn't let him go. But hunger forces him to let Benjamin go and they come to Joseph in Egypt. Joseph can scarcely control himself when he sees his own brother. He releases Simeon and feeds them. But he doesn't reveal his true identity. He gives them food. He also sets Benjamin up to take a fall for theft.

The brothers prove they have learned their lesson when they return and offer themselves in Benjamin's place. No longer will they abandon their brother to slavery. Now they would give themselves. When Joseph sees this, he reveals his identity to them. Even as he reveals himself, we see Joseph's spirit of forgiveness and his understanding that God has been at work in his life all along. "Don't be angry or distressed. God sent me here to preserve your lives. It was not you who sent me here, but God" (Genesis 45:5). Now hear this! Joseph is not charging God with cruelty, but crediting God with bringing good out of human evil. This is clearly demonstrated in Genesis 50:20 when the brothers come begging for mercy after the death of Jacob. "You meant it for evil, but God meant it for good." The only way it could turn for good is if Joseph cooperated with God and learned to forgive.

Sometimes we focus on the evil that is done to us and figure God was in on it. God is present, but not in sending the evil. In trial and tribulation, God always designs good for us. Sometimes we get in the way with our own sin and mess it up. We cannot blame God for our sin. Sometimes others refuse to act according to God's will and mess it up. We cannot blame God for the sin of others. The amazing thing about God's grace is that even when God's will gets messed up, God brings good out of it. That does not justify or excuse the evil. Rather, it exalts God's grace and goodness. The fact that Joseph takes no revenge or retribution is the sign of his complete forgiveness of his brothers.

We all have hurts and pains, caused by someone else. We have all caused someone else hurt and pain. The only way we can stay in a relationship with those people is through forgiveness. The only way a marriage lasts for years is by mutual forgiveness. The only way for parents and children, brothers and sisters, to stay close is by mutual forgiveness. The only way to have longtime friends is by mutual forgiveness. The only way to be a strong, vibrant, and loving church is through mutual forgiveness. Forgiveness is the glue we need to repair broken relationships. That is why the New Testament emphasizes forgiveness from the heart. Jesus calls us to be forgiving people. Paul says forgive others just as God through Christ has forgiven us. Forgiveness is the final healing of the pain we carry. The story of Joseph is the story of true healing of relationships through the power of forgiveness. If we want this kind of healing in our relationships, we must also forgive as God has forgiven us in Christ Jesus.

For Further Reflection

Read Matthew 18:21-35. What pains and hurts do you have in your life? Whom do you need to forgive?

Who needs to forgive you for the hurt and pain you have caused?

Name the times in your life when God has turned bad into good.

Chapter 4

I Have Come Down To Rescue — Through You

Exodus 3:7-12

Between Genesis 50 and Exodus 1, about 300 years have passed. There has been a change in the Egyptian dynasties, and the current royal family has no loyalty to Joseph or his descendants. The Hebrews occupy Goshen, which was a fertile farm and grazing area. As they lived in peace, they multiplied from the original seventy to a very large population, large enough to cause anxiety among the Egyptians. Rather than try to make an alliance, the Egyptians enslaved and oppressed the Hebrews. After 50-100 years of this oppression, God comes to rescue them.

As in the case of Abraham and Joseph, God again chooses a man to work with, a man who will work with God, even if somewhat reluctantly. The man is Moses. Moses spends his early life as part of the Egyptian royal family. He was adopted by Pharaoh's daughter, who found him as a baby, floating in the river in a basket. Moses enjoyed all the privileges of the royal court. He was thoroughly educated and trained in the Egyptian culture. At some point, he became aware of his Hebrew heritage and was distressed by the injustice of the Egyptian oppression. He decides that the oppression and slavery of the Hebrews must end. He tries to do it all himself by killing one Egyptian taskmaster. His crime is discovered and Moses flees from Egypt to Midian.

- **How many people can you name in the Bible who committed murder, but are also biblical heroes? What does that say about God using us in spite of our sins and weaknesses?**

Moses is a real lesson in the difference between trying to do things in our own strength and doing them with God's power. Moses wants to free his people. He wants to teach them how to live together, but when he does that on his own, he fails. Killing one Egyptian made no difference to the oppressed Hebrews or the oppression by Egypt. All it did was get Moses exiled. I find a strong parallel to those today who would like to end abortions. Some believe they need to take it on themselves through murder and killing. Like Moses they have a good cause, but they have used ungodly means to achieve their ends. As in Moses' case, the murders are tragedies, but they haven't made any difference in the war against abortion. Whenever we try to do things in our own strength, we make wood, hay, and stubble. When we do things with God's strength, we have gold, silver, and precious stones (1 Corinthians 3:12).

- **Think about the times you did something in your strength and something you did in God's strength. What were the differences?**

Moses flees to the wilderness of Midian and is welcomed into the house of Jethro. Moses becomes a shepherd. We need to emphasize that Moses' time as a shepherd in the wilderness was not wasted time, although I'll bet Moses had a different opinion. Gershom, meaning "alien," tells me a lot about Moses' pain as Manasseh did about Joseph's pain. Yet, God was using this time to teach Moses about life and survival in the wilderness. This experience would be essential later when Moses would lead Israel into the wilderness. You may think of yourself as being in some kind of dead zone or dead time. Let Moses' experience remind you that whenever you are with God and God is with you, there is no such thing as dead time.

- **Think about your wilderness experiences. What was God trying to teach you in the wilderness?**

When God sees that Moses is ready, God appears to Moses through the burning bush. There is so much in this passage that we could take a month on this, but today, I want to underline two things. First, God says He has seen the misery of His people (Exodus 3:7). God sees. God observes. God knows.

Now, we can ask why it took God so long to get around to the problem, but I think the problem was with the people. Until their oppression, the Hebrews lived comfortably. There were no problems. Their propensity for idolatry in the wilderness leads me to wonder just how much the Egyptian religion influenced their thinking. Once they are oppressed, they start crying out to God. Funny how we always want God around in our pain but not in our pleasure. God has always been aware of His people and their situation, but they have not always been aware of God, until they come into hardship. God can now come to deliver them, because they are asking for help.

All of us go through hard times sooner or later. The true measure of faith is when we keep close to God during the happy and fun and up times as well as the sad, painful, and down times. Rest assured that God is aware of your situation. Are you aware of God in your situation?

Second, God says to Moses, "So come, I will send you to Pharaoh, to bring my people the Israelites out of Egypt" (Exodus 3:10 NRSV). Don't you hear Moses saying something like, "God, you've got all the power in the universe, why do you need me?" While he doesn't say that specifically, he does try to get out of the assignment with various kinds of excuses. God accepts no excuses. Moses argues with God so much that the Bible says God gets angry with Moses. Basically, God says, "Moses, you're the guy I chose, and your options are limited. Now get on with the mission." God uses human beings to accomplish His plan. This is very important. God has a plan, but that plan, to redeem human beings from sin, uses human beings in the process. God has no intention of just using His mighty power and doing it. God insists on using us frail, weak, sinful human beings. Even when it came time to take away sin, God came in human flesh rather than just snapping His fingers. God calls all of us to serve Him in one capacity or another. Like Moses, you may not feel gifted or talented, but God calls you anyway. Whatever you lack, God will make up. In fact, I think God likes it that way so that you *know* you did it with God's power instead of your own. When you serve God, excuses really don't work very well.

Moses goes back to Egypt and confronts Pharaoh. I'll bet the first time he walked in he was nervous. God confirmed Moses' call by performing the miracles through Moses. From the earthly viewpoint, it was Moses stretching out his rod. From the faith viewpoint, God was behind Moses working the miracles. Look at what God did through Moses! The ten plagues on Egypt came and went at Moses' command. The Israelites were freed. The Red Sea parted and Israel walked on dry ground while the Egyptian army was drowned. They found water in the wilderness, water from the rock, and manna and quails. They defeated Amelek in battle. They received the Law. All this God did through Moses. God did it, but Moses was there as God's agent and representative.

For his willingness to serve, Moses has become the pivotal figure of Jewish religion. Moses is honored as the Lawgiver and leader of Israel. Moses appeared to Jesus at the transfiguration. Moses lives in many hearts through the Ten Commandments.

What does God have in store for you if you obey His call? Not everything will be a picnic. Moses certainly had his hassles, but Moses was faithful. He saw the form of God. God talked with Moses face to face. Moses' face shone with the glory of God. Think what can happen in your life if you will draw close to God as Moses did. Moses became an honored member of God's hall of fame. All because he obeyed God's call.

What does God have in store for you? You are part of God's plan just as much as Moses was. Are you trusting in your own strength or in God's power? Are you savoring your time in the wilderness, letting God teach you what you need to know? Are you willing to serve God without making excuses? Moses wasn't made perfect in a day, and neither will we be. If we will be faithful as Moses was faithful, God promises to honor those who honor Him.

For Further Reflection

Read James 1:2-4 and 1 Peter 1:3-9. How did Moses' trials refine and mature his faith?

Name the times where God has refined your faith. What lessons did you learn?

What has God called you to do? With what abilities has God gifted you to accomplish His task?

Chapter 5

The Power Of Intercession

Exodus 32:7-14

I am always amazed at the Israelites after their exodus from Egypt. How quickly they abandoned the Lord. Moses had a preview when they started whining at the Red Sea. "Weren't there enough graves in Egypt that you brought us out here in the wilderness to die?" (Exodus 14:11). Every time they complained, God gave them what they asked for. They asked for bread, God gave them manna. They asked for meat, God sent the quail. They asked for water, God sent them water. They asked for guidance, God led them by the pillar of cloud and pillar of fire. Add to this the fact that they witnessed all the plagues on Egypt. Add to this the miraculous delivery at the Red Sea, their victory over Amalek, and the awe-inspiring presence of God at Sinai.

- **In your view, has the Church behaved better, worse, or about the same as Israel in the wilderness?**

You would think that having personally witnessed God doing all these things, they would have faith in God. Wouldn't you believe after all this? But look what happens when Moses stays on the mountain forty days and forty nights, just over a month. In that short time, Israel becomes impatient. The people say to Aaron, "Make gods for us to lead us. We don't know what happened to Moses." So Aaron — yes, Aaron, in line to be high priest, Moses' brother, coworker of all the miracles — makes a golden calf. "These are your gods, O Israel who brought you up out of Egypt" (Exodus 32:4 NRSV). God is so awesome, so unique, how can they possibly think a calf could adequately represent God? Beyond that, verse

6 says they sat down to drink and rose up to revel. You need to think of this as a wild drunken orgy.

- **Suppose you had the opportunity to talk Aaron out of making this calf. What would you say?**

God had a plan. His plan was to make the descendants of Abraham, Isaac, and Jacob into a mighty nation. Here we see that God's plan requires human cooperation, participation, and obedience. If the people do not obey, God is always willing to find a new plan. God tells Moses that He is considering wiping out the entire lot of them and making Moses into a great nation. God always has Plan B.

Put yourself in Moses' place for just a moment. You have done God's will and delivered Israel from Egypt. You're the guy through whom God sent all those plagues. You're the guy who parted the Red Sea. You're the guy who got water from the rock. You're the guy who got the manna and the quail. You're the guy that God talks with face to face. On the other side, you're the guy who gets all the hassle. The people constantly complain about you and your leadership. You don't do enough, at the right time, in the right place. All you hear is complain, complain, complain, and no thank yous.

The Israelites knew better than to practice idolatry. They had heard the first ten commands directly from God just a few weeks earlier. Now this bunch of whiny, complaining, nagging people have sinned a great sin. God says to you, "Leave me alone while I wipe them out, and I will work my plan through you. I will make you a great nation" (Exodus 32:10). What do you say to God? For me, I would really look at this as a "no brainer." "Let me get this straight, Lord. I leave you alone. You wipe out a whole nation of whiny, complaining, unappreciative people who have hassled me from the beginning, and then you make me into a great nation. Is that the deal you have put on the table? What's the catch? Where is the fine print? Where do I sign? I'll be back in an hour or two, will that be enough time?"

- **If you were Moses, what would you say to God at this point?**

Moses doesn't take the offer. Can you believe that? He refuses it. Instead, he prays for the nation. He prays for God's forgiveness. He prays that God will change His mind. Is he crazy? Maybe a little, but I think that the more reasonable possibility is that he truly understands God's Plan A. Moses knows that Plan A is always better than Plan B. In this action of Moses we see true patience. No matter how the Israelites will treat him, he will pray for their well being and safety. In this action of Moses we see true humility. He does not seek his own glory. He seeks God's glory. In this action of Moses, we see true self-control. He doesn't let himself get carried away by his emotions. He keeps God's plan in front of him.

The kind of prayer Moses offers here is called intercession. It comes from the verb to intercede. To intercede means to plead for a favor or request on behalf of another. Usually intercession takes the form of a righteous person pleading to God to forgive the sin of an unrighteous person or persons. We saw Abraham intercede for Sodom and Gomorrah, that God might spare the cities. Judah interceded with Joseph on behalf of Benjamin. Now Moses intercedes for the Israelites, that God will forgive their idolatry.

I wonder if the people of Israel realized how close they came to annihilation. One man stood between them and God. One man kept them alive, to continue to be God's Plan A in spite of their rebellion. We often hear, "I'm only one person. How can I make any big difference?" Look at the difference Moses made to Israel, and you will realize how big a difference you can make for your family, your neighborhood, your city, your state, your country, your world, and your church. One person, willing to intercede with God, can make all the difference in the world. That is why we should consider prayer such a priority. Your prayer makes a difference in our world. Your lack of prayer can also make a negative difference.

As we watch Moses practice the art of intercessory prayer, we can learn some lessons for our own prayer. First, Moses appeals to God on the basis of God's Plan A. God's Plan A was for Israel to be a great nation and a blessing to all nations. God's Plan A was for the exodus to be such an extraordinary miracle that God would be known for all time as the God who parted the Red Sea and overthrew the Egyptian army. Look at Moses' prayer in Exodus 32:11-14. "Lord, if you wipe the people out, the Egyptians will gloat. Your plan A for your glory to be known will have a big dent in it." Remember Abraham, Isaac, and Jacob — the beginning of God's plan A. God made certain promises to the patriarchs. If God wiped out the people, the world could conclude that God isn't always able to keep His promises.

When we intercede, we need to pray in line with God's will, God's plan, and God's promises. God's Plan A is for every human being to be saved through Jesus Christ. We are always in God's will when we pray for the salvation of someone else. This is again why it is important to know our Bibles. God's plan is revealed in the Bible. God's promises are written down in the Bible. If we are to appeal to God on the basis of His plan or promises, we better know what we are talking about.

- **What promises do you rely on when you intercede for others?**

Second, Moses is totally selfless. He seeks nothing for himself, but only God's glory. In Exodus 32:30-34, Moses goes back to God to plead forgiveness for the people. In verse 32 he says, "But now, please forgive their sin — but if not, then blot me out of the book you have written" (NIV). Moses was willing to give up his share in eternal life in order for God to forgive the people. Here Moses foreshadows Jesus, the one who truly gave his life as a ransom for sinners. To intercede for others, we must be willing to put ourselves out. We must be willing to give ourselves, to sacrifice ourselves on their behalf. Paul also made this same offer to God for the Israelites — his salvation for their salvation. Fortunately for them and us, God doesn't work that way. His ransom was Jesus and that is the only ransom we need. To be a true intercessor before God for another person, we must really care about that other person.

Third, Moses is bold, almost audacious, in his requests. He does not come to God timidly, cowering in fear. He looks God in the eye and says, "Here are the prayers I want you to answer." He doesn't let Israel's sin or his weakness cause him to back down. In

Exodus 33:18, we see Moses being so bold as to ask to see God's glory. The amazing thing is, God says, "Okay." Jesus says, "Ask and you will receive, seek and you will find, knock and the door will be opened" (Matthew 7:7). If you don't ask, you won't receive. The book of Hebrews says that we may approach the throne of grace boldly and ask for what we need (Hebrews 4:16). This doesn't mean to come in a disrespectful or irreverent attitude. It means to come in with confidence and courage that you have a request that God needs to hear and God needs to act upon. It means to come in with your case prepared. It means being prepared to hound God until He finally gives you the answer.

Fourth, Moses knew God's character. When God appeared to Moses, He declared the Name of the Lord. We read in Exodus 34:6-7:

> *And he passed in front of Moses, proclaiming, "The Lord, the Lord, the compassionate and gracious God, slow to anger, abounding in love and faithfulness, maintaining love to thousands, and forgiving wickedness, rebellion and sin. Yet he does not leave the guilty unpunished; he punishes the children and their children for the sin of the fathers to the third and fourth generation."* (NIV)

Later, Moses used this as his basis of his intercession when the people refused to go into the promised land (Numbers 14:13ff.). If we know what God is like, how He acts, we can more accurately and faithfully pray. Keep drawing closer to God and your intercession life will improve.

Intercession is a high and holy calling. God is always searching for someone to stand and pray for people so that He can turn aside from His wrath against sin and forgive. All of us as Christians are called to the ministry of prayer and intercession at some level. Some have a real gift for intercession and prayer, but whether gifted or not, all of us are called. Learn from Moses about how to carry out your ministry of intercession. Know God personally in His character. Know God's plan and pray for it to be accomplished. Know God's promises. Be bold and hold God to His promises.

One man or one woman can make a significant impact on our world through prayer. We will never know that impact until heaven. We see what Moses was able to accomplish. What can God accomplish through you?

For Further Reflection

Discuss why intercession is necessary. God knows what we need, why do we need such prayers?

Discuss aspects of God's character that will help our intercession. For example: How does God's love impact our intercession for others?

Name some times in your life when you think you settled for God's Plan B instead of Plan A.

Chapter 6

Between The Lines: Genesis And Exodus

Having read the Bible through Exodus, we realize there are several stories and lessons that were not highlighted. What have we missed between the lines? There wasn't space to talk about Isaac and Jacob in great detail. Isaac is known as the man of peace. He settled all his differences out of court. He made an effort to get along with all of his neighbors. He and his wife had two sons, Esau and Jacob. I like noticing the family dynamics and systems we find in the Old Testament. The family of Isaac is a classic lesson in why not to have favorite children. Isaac favors Esau, Rebekah favors Jacob. Their favoritism is a contributing factor to the problems that lead to the rift between Jacob and Esau. That problem of favoritism is passed on through Jacob as he favors Joseph. That favoritism is a contributing factor to the brothers' jealousy of Joseph and why they sold him into slavery.

Jacob is a classic lesson of growing in the Lord. All of us are growing in faith and have not been made perfect. God accepted Jacob even when he was totally selfish, immature, and relying on his own cunning and strength to get what he wanted. God worked with Jacob through the years. God knew that eventually Jacob's bag of tricks would run out. Jacob would have nowhere to turn except God. God waited patiently for that time.

That time came at the ford of the Jabbok as Jacob is returning to Canaan and is anxious about meeting his brother Esau. Jacob wrestles with God that night, which is a good picture of wrestling in prayer. Jacob desperately needs a blessing from God, and he wrestles with God until he prevails. The lesson for us is that sometimes we need to cling to God until He blesses us. Notice that the blessing comes with some pain. Jacob limps from that day onward, a physical sign of his night in prayer. That is also the night when God changes Jacob's name to Israel, "One who has striven with God and humans and has prevailed" (Genesis 32:28 NRSV).

The name change shows how Jacob has matured. He is no longer relying on his own wit and strength; he now relies on God alone. He meets Esau and they are reconciled. Jacob has become a new person. Paul says that we become new creations when we come to Jesus Christ (2 Corinthians 5:17). We can cooperate with God in that new creation if we follow the lesson of Jacob and learn to depend on God and not on our own insight.

- **What new name would God give you at this point?**

- **Discuss further the family dynamics in Abraham, Isaac, and Jacob. Do you see any patterns passed down through the generations?**

- **Name some of the times you wrestled with God for an answer to prayer.**

Chapter 7

The Necessity Of Sacrifice

Leviticus

The writer of Hebrews puts it as clearly as any: "Indeed, under the law almost everything is purified with blood, and without the shedding of blood there is no forgiveness of sins" (Hebrews 9:22). Leviticus, with all its sacrifices, can be a difficult book. But if we look deeper than the regulations, we see the reason for the sacrifices, and the ultimate sacrifice for all sins.

Sacrifices had two important lessons to teach the people of Israel. First, a sacrifice had to come from your own wealth. Sacrifice meant you had to give up the best of your flock or your wealth when bringing an offering to God. Notice how often God says that the offering had to be without defect. It would not be a sacrifice if we were getting rid of something we didn't want in the first place. Sacrifice happens when we give to God something that is truly valuable to us. When we give to God, we need to give the best we have to offer.

- **Examine your own giving to God. Would sacrifice best describe your giving? Have you brought your best?**

Second, a sacrifice was a substitution for the person making the offering. Especially in terms of the sin offering, this is very important. God says that everyone who sins deserves to die (Ezekiel 18:4). By God's grace, God gave the Israelites a system whereby their guilt could be transferred to the animal. Then the animal was killed for the guilt of my sin instead of me. That is why Moses stated they were "to lay his hand on the head of the burnt offering, and it will be accepted on his behalf to make atonement for him" (Leviticus 1:4 NIV).

We sing about being washed in the blood of the lamb. In Israel, the blood was used to make atonement for the sinner. The life of an animal or human was thought to be in the blood. While the thought of so much blood may make us squeamish, it was a very moving and holy sight for the faithful of the Old Testament. They may not have understood the "how" anymore than we do, but they had faith that God accepted the blood as a sacrifice, and used the blood to purify them of their sins. The sprinkling of the blood made things holy, set apart to God for special use. The priests were also sprinkled with blood, setting them apart for God's service. When they saw the blood, they didn't think about whether they were going to use Tide or Oxydol to get the stain out. The stain was a badge of honor. It was a sign of cleansing and wholeness. It was a symbol of their cleansing from their sin.

Some people have a negative reaction when they hear about the blood of Jesus. Yet that blood is the blood that cleanses us from all unrighteousness. That blood is power and protection over evil. Because we have washed our garments in the blood, they have become white as snow. Our souls are completely clean.

In Jesus we see the fulfillment of all the levitical sacrifices. Jesus is our sin offering who takes away our guilt. Jesus is our peace offering who brings us close to God. Jesus is our burnt offering, who atones for our sin. When God sent Jesus, He sent his very best. God sent a male, unblemished by any sin or defect or mistake. He gave Jesus willingly, as a substitution for our sin. When we lay our hands on Jesus our guilt and sin is transferred to him, and he takes it away. Jesus' blood, shed on Calvary, takes away our unrighteousness and brings us into the presence of God. Now we are set apart by Jesus for service to God.

The celebration of the Lord's Supper reminds us of Jesus' sacrifice for us. The bread symbolizes Jesus' unblemished body, sacrificed for us. It was God sacrificing his very best, his only Son. It was Jesus sacrificing his very best, his perfect life. It was the fulfillment of every Old Testament sacrifice. From here on, sacrifices were no longer necessary, because Jesus' sacrifice brings full atonement. The cup symbolizes Jesus' blood shed for us. Just as the Old Covenant was introduced by the shedding and sprinkling of blood, so the New Covenant is brought in by the shedding of Jesus' blood. In partaking the cup, we partake of Jesus' blood. It is a symbol of our covenant with God for the forgiveness of sin. As we partake of the Lord's Supper, reflect on this. God gave His best. Jesus gave his best. What should we return to God?

For Further Reflection

What can you bring to God that would symbolize your best?

When you partake of the Lord's Supper or communion again, reflect on the awesome sacrifice God made for your sins.

Chapter 8

Lessons From The Wilderness

Numbers 14

It is hard to believe that a whole nation could be so rebellious. If Numbers had a subtitle, it would be, "The Book of Rebellion." After the census, the Israelites leave Sinai, presumably on their way to conquer the promised land. This two week journey will take forty years, all because of rebellion.

The first rebellion is found in Numbers 11 where the people crave meat. God provides for their desire by sending the quail. Some of the people die because in their craving meat, it became their idol, their all-consuming goal. In their desire to fill their bellies, they forgot God. Sometimes the very thing you crave, the thing you can't live without, brings your destruction. We could find interesting parallels to tobacco, alcohol, illegal drugs, unsafe sex, and so on.

The second rebellion is a leadership contest among Moses, Aaron, and Miriam. Aaron and Miriam were in a tiff because Moses married outside his race. God settles this by proclaiming Moses his confidant. Miriam is punished with one week of leprosy.

But the biggest, most devastating rebellion comes when the spies return from looking over the promised land. Twelve spies go out, one from each tribe, to reconnoiter the land and its fortifications. They come back with a divided opinion. They all agree that the land is good and worth inhabiting, but they disagree on Israel's chances of conquering the people of the land. The vote is 10-2 not to attack. The congregation follows the majority, which is their tragic error. You see, doing God's will is not really a matter for a vote, it is a matter for obedience. For those who are used to congregational polity, majority rule, and a democratic system, this is a difficult lesson to hear. But the lesson here is that the majority is not always right. The majority is wrong if they are refusing to do God's will. This rebellion is the last straw that consumes God's patience. In the words of Popeye, "That's all I can stands, and I can't stands no more." He pronounces judgment on the whole nation. Every person, twenty or older, will die in the wilderness over the next forty years. The ten spies die immediately — so much for the majority. The people try to come around the next day, but by then it is too late.

- **Suppose you were there. What would you say to try and convince the Israelites to go into the Promised Land?**

The rebellion continues in Numbers 16 with Korah, Dathan, and Abiram. "Everybody is called of the Lord, who are you, Moses, to boss us around? Why does Aaron get to be High Priest? Anybody can do that job." It is hard for me not to cast this in terms of churches complaining about their pastors. "Why does the Pastor get to do this. Anybody can do that. Pastor, where do you get off telling us how to live our lives? Let us run the church and you just preach nice and soft 'feel good' sermons." Again, God demonstrates that Moses and Aaron are His chosen ones. His demonstration is quite convincing. The earth swallows these rebels whole.

Baptists, along with several other reformed traditions, believe in the priesthood of every believer. Indeed, we believe that all are called of God to do the mission of God. But we must also recognize that God calls certain people to lead, and these leaders should be obeyed. Leaders aren't necessarily perfect, or spiritually superior, they are just chosen. Moses was a murderer and had a speech impediment, but God chose him. Aaron was easily swayed by crowds and made the golden calf, but God chose him. God chooses those who are pastors, denominational executives, and staff ministers. God also chooses church moderators, board chairpersons, and Sunday school teachers. The lesson of Numbers 16 is to respect the leadership God has chosen. In Numbers 17, God settles all the questions by having Aaron's staff bud and give fruit.

- **Suppose you had the chance to speak to Israel and persuade them to not rebel against Moses. What would you say?**

An interesting study at this point is to contrast Israel in the wilderness with Jesus in the wilderness. Israel craves food in the wilderness. They give in to their craving and rebel against God. They demand meat. The manna is not enough for them. They want meat. When he was in the wilderness, Jesus fasts for forty days and is hungry. When the Devil comes to tempt him at his physical hunger, Jesus says, "No. We do not live by bread alone, but by every word of God" (Matthew 4:4). The devil succeeded in making Israel sin through physical cravings and passions. Jesus was victorious over the devil by not giving in to physical cravings and appetites.

In the wilderness Israel questions God's leaders. That is tantamount to questioning God's leadership through his leaders. Satan tempts Jesus to jump off the temple. Jesus refuses, saying, "You shall not put the Lord to the test" (Matthew 4:7). Israel tested God, Jesus trusted God. In the wilderness, Israel is afraid to die. They refuse to enter the promised land because they don't think they can survive the battle. Jesus, in the garden of Gethsemane, agrees to die for the sin of the world. Every time Israel met temptation in the wilderness, they met with defeat. Every time Jesus met temptation in the wilderness, he was victorious.

In all this, I am amazed that so many people would risk missing out on God's plan. God's plan for Israel was for them to march into Canaan and take the land and live happily ever after. Israel doubted God's goodness. "If only we had died in Egypt! Or in this desert! Why is the LORD bringing us to this land only to let us fall by the sword? Our wives and children will be taken as plunder. Wouldn't it be better for us to go back to Egypt?" (Numbers 14:2-3 NIV). Israel also doubted God's power. "But the men who had gone up with him said, 'We can't attack those people; they are stronger than we are'" (Numbers 13:31 NIV). Israel doubted God's chosen leaders. "They came as a group to oppose Moses and Aaron and said to them, 'You have gone too far! The whole community is holy, every one of them, and the LORD is with them. Why then do you set yourselves above the LORD's assembly?' " (Numbers 16:3 NIV). Several times God was ready to wipe them all out. Had it not been for Moses' intercession, the story would have ended quite differently. The lesson for us is not to doubt God's plan for our lives. God has designed good for us. That does not mean that we will never have pain or suffering. It does mean that God's ultimate plan will be for our good — eternal life in heaven. God has the power to accomplish His plan. The resurrection of Jesus is proof enough of that. God has given us leaders who are called to be the guides and player-coaches who help us to accomplish God's will and plan.

Many in our world are missing out on God's wonderful plan for their lives. Some are in open rebellion, hating God and worshiping Satan, but their numbers are relatively few. Many are in ignorant rebellion, not knowing or understanding what God actually wants them to do or to avoid. Many churchgoing people are wrapped up in the things of the world that dilute their effectiveness for the Kingdom of God. Some are addicted to their cravings: tobacco, alcohol, drugs, immoral sex, power, popularity, material goods, money. Some are engaged in behaviors which society approves but which God disapproves — psychics, horoscopes, pornography. Most of these people need to see real Christians living real lives of discipleship and truth. We must stand for what the Bible says is truth and not back down or give in.

The Bible says that God has a plan, a wonderful plan for our lives. That generation of Israel missed out on the plan because of its rebellion. Like Moses, we must continue to pray and live lives of exemplary integrity that people will see in our own lives that God's plan is the best. Like Israel, we have choices to make. Like Jesus, we will be tempted. Will we satisfy our cravings, or listen to every word of God? Will we question God's goodness and power, or trust God for every need? Will we question God's leaders, or support them with our prayers and actions? Will we obey God's orders, or cower in fear for what it means to us personally? Jesus won the victory for us at Calvary. We have no reason to fear and every reason to follow.

For Further Reflection

Read Hebrews 13:17. Discuss leadership and obedience in the church.

What are your points of rebellion? Where are you learning to trust God more?

Can you name other times in the Bible where it was too late to repent?

Discuss the advantages and disadvantages of a democratic system within the church.

Chapter 9

Between The Lines:
An Overview Of Deuteronomy

By now you know that the Ten Commandments, which were first recorded in Exodus 20, were written down several times and in several formats. We find different compilations of the major commandments in Deuteronomy. The name "Deuteronomy" comes from the Latin, *deutero* — meaning second, and *nomos* — meaning law. The title of the book tells us that this was the second giving of the law as Moses makes his various farewell speeches. Deuteronomy, rather than Exodus, came to be the foundational book of the Law for Israel.

In 2 Kings 22, during the reign of Josiah, a book of the Law is found while they are cleaning up the Temple. When Josiah reads the book, he is very upset because he realizes that Israel has not kept the Law. Josiah institutes several religious and political reforms based on the Law he heard. Judging from the description of those reforms, we believe that the book was Deuteronomy. Josiah burned down the high places and celebrated the Passover in Jerusalem, as mandated in Deuteronomy.

When Jesus is tempted in the wilderness, Jesus uses the Law as written in Deuteronomy to defeat the temptations of the devil. "Man does not live by bread alone" is Deuteronomy 8:3 (NIV). "Do not put the Lord your God to the test" is Deuteronomy 6:16 (NRSV). "Worship the Lord and Him only" is Deuteronomy 6:13. If Jesus defeated the devil with his knowledge of Deuteronomy, then knowing the Law as found in Deuteronomy can be helpful for us as the Spirit leads us to victory in our times of temptation.

We also find a prophecy about Jesus in Deuteronomy 18:14-19, where Moses predicts the coming of a great prophet. We do not often consider the prophetic ministry of Jesus, but Jesus was the greatest of all God's prophets. The major job of the prophet is to bring God's message to God's people and the world. Certainly, Jesus was faithful in that task.

The description of the prophet in Deuteronomy 18:17-19 shows that the person being described is more than the ordinary prophet. This prophet will be like Moses. This prophet will have the very words of God. Those who do not listen to the prophet will be called to account by God himself. Jesus is the one who totally fulfills this description.

I know that as you read through the Bible, the reading can be dry in places (pun intended). But the first five books of the Bible, known as the Pentateuch, form the basis for everything else that we read in the rest of the Bible. Only as we appreciate the experiences of the patriarchs in Genesis, the formation and experiences of Israel, the Law and the commands of God, will we appreciate what comes later as we read about Israel and Jesus.

- **Jesus used the Law for spiritual victory over Satan's temptations. Compare Paul's view of the Old Testament in Romans 15:4.**

- **What other teachings from Deuteronomy can help us in our spiritual battles?**

Chapter 10
Transitions Of Leadership

Joshua 1

One would have to figure, even with the hardship, that the people of Israel got used to living in the wilderness. After forty years living one lifestyle, with the same leaders, you would get used to how things were. You would get used to the manna falling every night and gathering it every morning. You would get used to the quail every night for dinner. You would get used to the pillar of cloud and pillar of fire. You would get used to living in tents, out in the wilderness. You would get used to Moses being God's appointed leader and doing what he told you. Especially so because, as the older generation dies off, those who are left have grown up knowing only the wilderness life. You get used to it.

But now the time has come for a major, radical, and drastic change in the lifestyle of the Israelites. They will go from nomads living in tents to sedentary people living in cities, towns, and villages. They will go from being rather close-knit in the wilderness to being spread out over the entire territory of the promised land. They will go from being wandering shepherds to being settled farmers. They will go from having Moses as their leader to a man named Joshua.

Joshua is not an unfamiliar person to the Israelites. All these years, he has been Moses' assistant and commander of the army. He was halfway up the mountain when Moses received the Ten Commandments. He was the elder for the tribe of Ephraim. He was one of the two spies who voted to go into the promised land. For his pro-God vote, God preserved him through the years so that he would live in the land he spied out.

He was not unknown to the Lord either. The Bible says that many times after Moses left the Tent of Meeting, Joshua would still hang around, presumably talking with God (Exodus 33:11). Joshua was the natural choice as successor to Moses, yet there is always some question about the new guy on the block. It is like the vice-president becoming president. It is like the sports team after the superstar retires or there is a new coach. Yes, he did great as an assistant to the previous one, but how will he do when he is the one in charge?

- **Think of a similar transition period in your church or job. What were your feelings about the situation?**

Joshua has one distinct advantage: "No one will be able to stand up against you all the days of your life. As I was with Moses, so I will be with you; I will never leave you nor forsake you" (Joshua 1:5 NIV). Joshua has God on his side, completely and unreservedly. "As I was with Moses." No one can question that God was with Moses in everything. Now Joshua has that same promise. "No one will stand against you." God was giving Joshua every encouragement.

However, there is one thing God requires of Joshua:

> *Be strong and very courageous. Be careful to obey all the law my servant Moses gave you; do not turn from it to the right or to the left, that you may be successful wherever you go. Do not let this Book of the Law depart from your mouth; meditate on it day and night, so that you may be careful to do everything written in it. Then you will be prosperous and successful.*
> — Joshua 1:7-8 NIV

We hear a lot about how to be successful and prosperous in our day and time. Some time back, there was the Dale Carnegie course, "How to Win Friends and Influence People." Our gurus today include: Donald Trump, *Making the Deal*, William Bennett, *The Book of Virtues*, and L. Ron Hubbard, *Dianetics*. There is a whole market of how-to books aimed at helping us to be successful whether it be by improving our memory, making us more assertive, or teaching us how to invest correctly.

But if we look closely at what God says to Joshua, all of these formulas are second and third class. God doesn't tell Joshua to memorize everybody's name, or get in touch with his feelings, or be more assertive or whatever. God's formula for success is to keep the book of the Law and never depart from it. Then you will be prosperous and successful. If you want the best book on how to win friends and influence people, how to win the deal, how to be virtuous, how to tap into your inner spiritual strength, how to be more assertive, and even how to invest wisely, then you want the Bible. To win friends — love your enemies. To influence people — those who would be great must be servant of all. To win the deal — trust in the Lord with all your heart and lean not on your own understanding. To tap into your inner strength — trust God in your weakness and He will make you strong. To be more assertive — stand firm against the devil.

From our vantage point, Joshua was working at a deficit, because all he had was the Law while we have the whole Bible. However, Joshua was responsible for obeying what God had given to him. We are responsible for obeying what God has given to us. Joshua was obedient to the Law. God kept his promise. Joshua prospered. No one was able to stand against him. Because he was obedient, the time of transition went smoothly for Israel. They followed Joshua and conquered the land and lived there.

Churches also experience times of leadership transition. Older generations of leaders step down or are called home to heaven. A new generation arises. We have anxieties about such transitions. How will the new leaders act? Will they be faithful to the vision and the lessons from our past? In times of transition like this what should we be doing?

First, to the new leaders, do you want to be successful and prosperous? Then follow the Joshua formula. Meditate day and night on the words of the Bible. Do not let the lessons of Scripture depart from your heart. If you do that, then God will be with you. You will be able to lead, because we will see God's influence in your life. Trust in God and He will guide you.

Second, to us who follow, we need to be faithful followers. Notice how the Reubenites and Gadites encourage Joshua in his task: "Then they answered Joshua, 'Whatever you have commanded us we will do, and wherever you send us we will go. Just as we fully obeyed Moses, so we will obey you. Only may the Lord your God be with you as He was with Moses. Whoever rebels against your word and does not obey your words, whatever you may command them, will be put to death. Only be strong and courageous!' " (Joshua 1:16-17 NIV).

- **Have you encouraged your boss, pastor, or other church leader in their leadership lately?**

Keep praying for your leaders, board members, Sunday school teachers, your music director, and your pastor. Your prayers help them to be better leaders. We should expect some bumps in time of transition. It is part of the territory. But if leaders and followers will work together according to God's principles, the bumps will not be anything to worry about, but instead, they will be learning experiences for all of us.

For Further Reflection

Name some other self-help and success books and programs. How do they compare to the Bible?

Discuss some ways to make leadership transitions within the church a smooth process.

Chapter 11

Samson: He Could Have Been Great

Judges 13-16

Reading through the book of Judges, there is the sensation of being on a long roller coaster ride. Israel quickly forgot their heritage and their God. Joshua's generation remains faithful, but the next generation lapses into idolatry. The words in Judges 2:10 are an indictment on both generations. "And all that generation also was gathered to their fathers; and there arose another generation after them, who did not know the Lord or the work that He had done" (Judges 2:10 RSV).

The church is always one generation away from extinction. There is a two-pronged aspect of our mission of telling the Good News. We must tell those who have not heard about Jesus so they have the opportunity to make a decision of faith. We must also raise up our children in Christian homes so that they will declare their faith in Jesus at the appropriate time. The older generation of Israelites evidently did not teach the younger generation about the Lord. That is why the younger generation had no anchors. If we want our children to make right decisions, we need to model good decision-making skills before them. We need to teach them the ways of the Lord. The church contributes to this mission through Sunday school, worship, service, discipleship, and fellowship activities. While many churches may have excellent programs, these alone are not sufficient. Christian living must be our everyday lifestyle throughout the week, not just on Sunday. It must be modeled in the home, in the workplace, and in the school, as well in the church. If we neglect one or the other, then we risk that our next generation will not know the Lord.

- **What programs in your church are effective in teaching the future generations about the Lord?**

Israel lapses into a pattern of idolatry, followed by God's judgment, followed by God raising up a hero-type leader, who leads Israel back to the Lord and conquers the enemy of the day. It is a broken-record litany throughout the book: "Israel again did evil in the sight of the Lord and worshiped idols. So the Lord delivered them into the hands of _____ who oppressed them for _____ years. Then God raised up _____ who delivered them for _____ years." You would think they would learn their lesson, but they don't.

The sad conclusion of the book of Judges is 21:25: "In those days there was no king in Israel; all the people did what was right in their own eyes" (Judges 21:25 NRSV). The problem is that what they thought was right wasn't always correct according to God's Law. They worshiped idols. They fell into civil war over a brutal rape and murder. There were mass murders and insurrections. The bottom line is they did not keep the Law. One could easily call this the dark age of Israel.

- **"People doing what they thought was right in their own eyes" is an apt description of America today. Do you agree or disagree with that statement? Why?**

The story of Samson, one of the better-known judges, mirrors the roller coaster spirituality of Israel during this period. His story begins in Judges 13. Like Israel, Samson had a great beginning. His birth was foretold by an angel. His parents had been childless, emphasizing the miraculous nature of the birth. He is a Nazirite, committed to God by the Nazirite vow. The major features of this vow were the abstinence from alcohol and the growing of the hair. This vow was usually temporary, but by the Lord's instruction it applied to Samson for life.

In the birth announcement, however, we also see something troubling. "It is he who will *begin to deliver* Israel from the hand of the Philistines" (Judges 13:5 NRSV, emphasis mine). Why only begin and not complete? As Samson matures into manhood, his major weaknesses also come to the light. He had a problem controlling his temper. He had a problem controlling his lust. Because of his lust, he did not exercise good judgment in his choice of women. This was by far the most serious problem.

Samson's problem with women mirrors Israel's problem with idols. Frequently, the prophets condemn idolatry as spiritual adultery. Israel was supposed to be married to Yahweh. When they were worshiping other idols, they were giving the love due Yahweh to another god. His parents thought that Samson should have found a good Jewish girl and settled down. Instead, he is attracted to the heathen Philistine women. Judges 14:4 makes the point that the Lord was in Samson's first marriage to a Philistine woman. God wanted Samson to make trouble. Samson makes trouble. Samson gets in trouble. His downfall came at the hands of Delilah, another Philistine woman. If we ask, "Why did he stay with her?" the answer is, "He had a weakness for women which he did not control."

The epitaph I want to give Samson is, "He could have been great, but ..." He could have been great. He was born into a good and faithful family. They were obedient to the Nazirite vow until Samson was old enough to keep it himself. He had a great gift, being anointed of the Lord with incredible physical strength. He judged Israel for twenty years, so evidently he had some leadership capabilities. He began the deliverance from the Philistines. God was with him. That is enough to make anyone great. He could have been great, but ... He was ruled by his passions. His anger ruled him sometimes; his lusts ruled him other times. Ruled by his passions, he lacked wisdom, patience, and self-control in his life. In the end, these became his undoing and downfall. And that is why he does not complete the deliverance of Israel from the Philistines. He ends his life in captivity, dying with his Philistine captors who were mocking him. He began the mission of deliverance from the Philistines, but he did not complete the mission.

But let's not join the Philistines in laughing at Samson until we examine ourselves. All of us who have faith in Jesus Christ could be great. God wants us to be great, for Him. God is with us. He sent Jesus to die for our sins. The Holy Spirit lives inside us.

God has made every provision for us to reach our potential greatness in Jesus Christ. But all too often, Christians are undone by following their own desires instead of God's will.

- **What else has God done for us or said to us that shows He wants us to be great?**

Think about it. There are many, in secular and religious life, who could have been great, but they lost their greatness by giving in to their lusts and desires. Think about Richard Nixon. He is applauded for his world leadership capability and political wisdom. He was undone by his lust for absolute power. Think about Jim Bakker. In his ministry, he helped thousands turn to the Lord. He was undone by his lust for money and sex. Think about Jimmy Swaggart. Certainly, God has used him around the world to bring thousands to salvation. He was undone by lust and his unwillingness to repent. Think about Pete Rose. In my opinion, he is the greatest baseball player that ever played the game. Yet he was undone by his lust for gambling. Think about Dick Morris, advisor to President Clinton. He was undone by his lust which led him to be unfaithful to his wife. Think about Dexter Manley, at one time a star with the Washington Redskins, or any number of almost-great sports personalities undone by drug abuse. I could go on with a long list of secular and religious heroes who qualify for the "almost great." While some do get a second chance and make a comeback, most have slipped into the pages of the record books with the footnote of foolishness permanently attached.

The point is, if it can happen to them, it can happen to me and it can happen to you. Temptations abound everywhere. We must constantly be on our guard. When we yield to temptation, we lose the greatness God wants for us. The temptations that brought down the almost-greats listed above are the same temptations every person faces, day in and day out. Temptation often comes through good things. But we sin when we pervert that good purpose of God and use that thing to satisfy our own lusts and desires.

Sexuality is a gift from God, but if we misuse it, we sin and fall from greatness. Our society today holds a double standard concerning sexual behavior. Hollywood movies and television glorify all kinds of immoral sex. If we were to follow Hollywood's rules, unmarried sex, prostitution, adultery, and homosexuality would be acceptable behaviors. Yet as several of the people mentioned above found out, if we behave that way in real life, there are tragic consequences.

Pornography is a subtle way the devil can entice us into lust and sin. Pornography is available through more sources now than ever before. With the availability of pornography on the Internet, the only way to stay pure is to exercise self-control. We cannot rely on government or on-line servers to control this flood of filth. If you want to be great in the Lord, then you must find the power in the Holy Spirit to resist the various sexual temptations in our world today. God's standard for sexual purity is abstinence until you are married. Marriage is to be between one man and one woman until death parts them. Following God's standard for our sexuality is the only way to find true greatness in this area of our lives.

Power and popularity come from God, but if we become proud and arrogant, we sin and fall from greatness. Power comes in many forms besides political power. We are well aware that there are often power plays and power groups within churches. Having power is not a sin, but when that power is misused or abused, then we fall from greatness.

Jesus' standard for those who would be ruler of all is that they are to be the servant of all (Mark 10:43). Leaders in church and in society are accountable for their use of the power God has given them. Leaders must lead by setting the highest possible example of godly Christian behavior. Misuse of power comes in many forms: sexual harassment, improper use of funds entrusted to our care, using our influence to benefit friends and cronies rather than the people we are called to lead. If God has given you power, then consider it a privilege and don't misuse your authority. Use what God has given you for His glory, and greatness will come as another gift from God.

Money is a gift from God, but if we idolize it and make gaining money our priority, we sin and fall from greatness. Again, our society has brainwashed us into believing that money solves the world's problems. When government wants to solve a problem, what do they do? Throw money at it. We think that if we could just have enough money, we can be happy, cure cancer, find world peace, feed the poor, and still have enough left over for our luxury items.

It is especially in the area of money that people fall short of greatness. Many Christians compromise their greatness by their stingy giving habits. The average donation level to churches in the United States is still less than two percent of income. The biblical standard of faithful giving begins with tithing ten percent of our income. When we take what belongs to God and spend it on ourselves, we fall from greatness. Faithful sacrificial giving to the church is one way to show that money is not an idol in our lives; it moves us toward greatness in the kingdom of God.

Closely related to money is how we use our material wealth. God has gifted us with many good things. We are called to be faithful stewards of those gifts. If we misuse our gifts, we sin. We fall from greatness.

If we would be great, we must be people of impeccable integrity. We must uphold and live by the biblical values of truth, honesty, justice, fairness, compassion, love, kindness, and righteousness. If we compromise ourselves in any of these areas, we compromise our potential for greatness in the kingdom of God. We need to be on our toes against the various forms of temptation that would compromise our integrity. Gambling can quickly become a snare that entraps us. Dishonesty, even in small amounts, will eventually bring us down. Gossip, slander, and foul language will compromise our witness for the gospel. Uncontrolled anger or jealousy can lead us to do things that will bring us down. We must avoid illegal drugs and excessive use of alcohol. If you want to be great, you have to be wise to avoid these temptations. Trusting in the Lord is the only way to obtain that kind of wisdom. Don't do what is right in your own eyes. That is how Israel got into a whole lot of trouble. That is how a whole generation grew up that did not know the Lord. That is how they compromised their potential for greatness.

As we look at Samson's end, we see the tragedy. Instead of dying peacefully, having delivered Israel from the Philistines, he dies violently with his Philistine captors. He is buried by his brothers, but there is no mention of a national mourning. He slips into the pages of the forgotten. He is mentioned in Hebrews 11:32 as a hero of faith, but he is more of a footnote than an example. Except for his life as recorded in Judges, he slips into anonymity, with the footnote of foolishness permanently attached. He could have been great, but....

Don't let this become your epitaph, "He or she could have been great, but ..." Stay on your guard against temptation, sin, and the devil. You can be great in the eyes of the Lord if you will stay faithful to Him. Stay faithful to Him in your sex life, in your financial dealings, in your positions of authority and power, and in your personal integrity. Don't trust in your own sense of right. Certainly, do not listen to world's standards. It is our mission to raise up a generation that will stay faithful to the Lord. If we want to raise a generation that knows the Lord, then we must seek the greatness that God desires for us. It is up to us to set an example of greatness that they will want to imitate. Listen to the Word of God. If you truly want to be great, "Trust in the Lord with all your heart and do not rely on your own insight. In all your ways acknowledge Him and He will make straight your paths" (Proverbs 3:5, 6 RSV). You can be great for God. The path of doing God's will is the path to true greatness.

For Further Reflection

How would you like your epitaph to read?

What are the ways in which you can fall from greatness? Think about some ways you can resist those temptations.

When someone falls from greatness, is it possible to be restored? Under what circumstances?

Chapter 12

God Uses Women Too!

1 Samuel 1:19-20

I like browsing bookstores. Many times I go in just to look over new titles, to see what people are writing about, and what people are reading. For several years I have noticed many books about male and female relationships. Some have humorous titles, *Men are from Mars, Women are from Venus.* In Christian bookstores there are shelves of books about how Christian men and women ought to relate to each other, such as *What Wives Wish Their Husbands Knew About Women* and *What Husbands Wish Their Wives Knew About Men.*

A few years ago there was an open anti-male movement, coincidentally timed with the Clarence Thomas-Anita Hill fiasco. Several female comediennes got their start during this period with their anti-male monologue. On the television comedy channel, many routines have to do with the uneasiness, mutual anxiety, and frustration of male-female relationships. We learn about this animosity at a young age as boys learn to compete with girls. Remember the nursery rhymes? What are little boys made of? What are little girls made of? We grow up hearing how boys are better than girls or girls are better than boys. No wonder that when we reach adulthood, we don't know how to relate to each other.

Gender competition, animosity, oppression, abuse, and division can be traced back to the earliest pages in the Bible. Not all the oppression was male to female; remember Joseph and Potiphar's wife. Nonetheless, by the time of Abraham, we are dealing with an extremely patriarchal society where men were everything and women for the most part were considered property. One of the *avant garde* features of the Israelite Law was how much power and status were given to women. The daughters of Zelophed were allowed to inherit their father's land. The many laws governing sexual behavior reveal God's will that women should not be abused, mistreated, or taken for granted. The commands to watch out for the widows and orphans reveal God's compassion on women in a patriarchal society, that they not be taken advantage of. In spite of the Law, we saw in Judges how a woman could be treated as property, abused, and killed. When things like this happen, they are not God's will.

Unfortunately, the Church's treatment of women throughout history has been less then ideal. In some denominations, notably the Catholic and Southern Baptists, women are not allowed to be ordained to priestly or pastoral ministry. Joan of Arc was martyred in part for how she expressed her faith as a woman. The witch trials of New England, in the early history of this country, betray a prejudice against women. Often these trials went against women of means so that the men could gain their property and wealth.

- **What is your church's position on women in authority? On women working outside the home? On husband and wife relationships?**

In our society today we still have progress to make in terms of equality of the sexes. Typically, women are paid less than men in equal positions. Sexual harassment usually has to do with women being harassed, although men are sometimes the victims. If the bookstores and comedy routines are any indication of our national mood, we still have our mutual frustrations and anxieties when it comes to dealing with the opposite sex. Even in that term, opposite sex, we are supposing a relationship of differences and animosity. Is this really what God wills?

Our story of Hannah gives us a starting point for looking at various women throughout the Bible and seeing the truth about what God thinks of women.

> *In bitterness of soul Hannah wept much and prayed to the Lord. And she made a vow, saying, "O Lord Almighty, if you will only look upon your servant's*

> *misery and remember me, and not forget your servant but give her a son, then I will give him to the Lord for all the days of his life, and no razor will ever be used on his head." ... So in the course of time Hannah conceived and gave birth to a son. She named him Samuel, saying, "Because I asked the Lord for him."*
> — 1 Samuel 1:10-11, 20 NIV

In Genesis 1, God created humankind in His image, male and female He created them. And he gave them dominion over all creation. It takes male and female, together, to create the image of God.

Male is part of the image of God. We see this male image in God as Father, provider, protector, warrior, explorer, and teacher. The male image is perceived predominantly as logical, rational, concrete thinking. Female is a part of the image of God. We see this female image in the maternal images of God (Isaiah 66:13), as nurturer and teacher. The feminine image is perceived predominantly as emotional, feeling, tender, caring, supportive, abstract thinking. These are not exclusive characteristics, but they are some broad generalizations that show the image of God is not all male, nor all female. It takes both together. Because of this joint creation in the image of God, and the joint stewardship over the earth, I would prefer to refer to complementary genders instead of opposite sexes. Complementary means we are supposed to go together, work together, and help each other fulfill God's will for our lives. The Bible implies that was God's original intention.

Although sin has wounded that partnership, through God's power it can be restored. We see several men and women in the Bible who work more as partners, even in a patriarchal society. Abraham and Sarah, Isaac and Rebekah, Jacob and Leah and Rachel, all seem to work as partners in the running of the family and in their spiritual commitments. They talk to each other, consult with each other, listen to each other. The men were the heads of the house, but it was never a dictatorship of oppression, always a partnership that worked together.

We see several women heroes of the Bible, women who were used of God to accomplish God's purposes for Israel. Miriam is described as a prophetess. Deborah, the judge, leads Israel into victory. Jael becomes the hero of the day by killing general Sisera. Manoah's wife raised Samson in the knowledge and fear of the Lord. Ruth showed uncommon loyalty to her mother-in-law, Naomi. In 1 Samuel, Hannah is presented as a woman of faith and prayer who has her prayers answered. David's wife Abigail, whom we will meet soon, shows herself to be a woman of wisdom and reconciliation. In the New Testament, we encounter Mary the mother of Jesus, the women disciples of Jesus, Phoebe the deaconess, and so on. The point is that since we have the stories of these women in the Bible, we can draw certain conclusions about God.

- **Name some Christian women in history who have lived a positive witness for Christ.**

First, God speaks to women. Women are created in the image of God and part of that image is the spiritual capacity to communicate with God. Second, God speaks through women. Huldah the prophetess spoke God's word to King Josiah (2 Kings 22:14-20). Mary Magdalene proclaimed to the apostles about Jesus' resurrection (John 20:18). Third, God works through women to build His kingdom. Men and women are partners in the sharing of the gospel. Women can and should preach the gospel in the power of the Spirit. Women have several role-model heroes in the Bible they can look to as examples.

Men and women are equal, but not the same. Equality does not mean sameness. We are not meant to do certain things. Men certainly cannot bear children. Though there are exceptions, we don't typically think of women as being cut out for physically demanding tasks. God created us to be different, but complementary. We can celebrate the differences without using them as an occasion for oppression, animosity, or competition.

As the Church, we are called to be at the forefront of living the way God wants people to live. The history of the Church in gender relations has hurt our example to the world. When the Church still has turf wars based on gender, our example to the world is compromised. The Church needs to be the number one place where men and women work together sharing the love and message of Christ with a hurting, dying world. We will be able to work together only as we trust and respect each other as human beings created in God's image. We will trust and respect each other only as the hurts of the past are confessed and forgiven.

In the spirit of reconciliation, I would like to offer my apology on behalf of men, to women. I apologize for our oppression, abuse, and harassment. I apologize for all the ways this oppression has been manifested: in the family, in the workplace, in society, in sexuality. On behalf of men, I ask your forgiveness of these sins. I pray that with God's strength, we will work together as partners to accomplish the mission God has given us, jointly. As the Church, we can be the place where men and women love each other as brothers and sisters in Christ while keeping sexuality under godly control. As the Church, we can be the place where men and women have equal opportunity to serve God without getting distracted by elements of competition between the genders. As the Church, we need to model the truth of the Bible that male and female compose the image of God. We can avoid the harassment and oppression that is all too common in the secular world. As the Church, God has called men and women to work together to fulfill the vision and accomplish the mission He has given us. We can affirm that God speaks to men and women, through men and women.

For Further Reflection

Realizing this chapter is potentially controversial, how do you react to this view of how God uses women?

If you disagree, how does God use women from your reading of Scripture?

Chapter 13

A Lesson In Spiritual Warfare: Beware Of The Occult

1 Samuel 28

In our reading of the Bible, we are now about to come to the age in Israel that really is the high point of its national existence, the time of David and Solomon. The last official judge of Israel is Samuel, who was a faithful prophet and leader of the people. Yet we see again that preacher's kids are not always perfect. Being raised in a godly home is no guarantee about how the children will turn out. Samuel tries to have his sons inherit the family business of judging Israel, but they just don't have the integrity for the task. So the people of Israel ask Samuel to appoint them a king. It was understood that God Himself was Israel's king. The sin in this request for a human king is that Israel wants to be like the nations around them, rather than being different because God rules in the midst of them. Under God's direction, Samuel reluctantly appoints a king.

- **If you were given the opportunity to persuade Israel that they didn't need a king, what would you say?**

The first king of Israel is a humble man from the tribe of Benjamin named Saul. Saul is a lot like Samson. He could have been great, but ... Saul starts out well but finishes up horribly. He starts humble. At first he is obedient to the leadership of Samuel. He wins a victory over the Philistines. But he has serious character flaws: impatience, lack of trust, weak leadership, and lack of confidence. He shows his impatience when Samuel is late for an appointed sacrifice. He shows his lack of trust when he makes the sacrifice himself. He shows weak leadership in not keeping his men together. He is disobedient when he takes some of the spoil from the battle with the Amelekites, contrary to the explicit instructions from Samuel. For his disobedience, God takes the kingdom away from Saul and plans to give it to another, namely, David.

Saul falls into depression; the Bible describes him as tormented by an evil spirit. He becomes jealous of David's popularity and military prowess. He tries to kill David. In his jealous anger, he swears at his son Jonathan. He obsesses about killing David, thinking that getting rid of David will preserve the kingdom for himself. Finally in his last hour, he has no word from God and he turns to occult practices for guidance.

> *Now Samuel was dead, and all Israel had mourned for him and buried him in his own town of Ramah. Saul had expelled the mediums and spiritists from the land. The Philistines assembled and came and set up camp at Shunem, while Saul gathered all the Israelites and set up camp at Gilboa. When Saul saw the Philistine army, he was afraid; terror filled his heart. He inquired of the LORD, but the LORD did not answer him by dreams or Urim or prophets. Saul then said to his attendants, "Find me a woman who is a medium, so I may go and inquire of her." "There is one in Endor," they said.* — 1 Samuel 28:3-7 NIV

Saul himself had put all the mediums out of the land. This is interesting since the Law was specifically clear that death was the punishment for those who practice the occult, not exile. "Do not allow a sorceress to live" (Exodus 22:18 NIV). "Do not turn to mediums or seek out spiritists, for you will be defiled by them. I am the LORD your God" (Leviticus 19:31 NIV). "I will set my face against the person who turns to mediums and spiritists to prostitute himself by following them, and I will cut him off from his people" (Levitcus 20:6 NIV). It is also interesting that they needed to be expelled in the first place. Evidently, the occult was a popular thing until the expulsion. Was the expulsion of mediums Saul's attempt to get back in the good graces of God?

- **Name some popular occult practices of our day. In what ways can we present a positive witness for Christ to those enslaved in these practices?**

Yet when it came down to the wire, there was no voice from the Lord. God does not talk to us when we have unconfessed sin in our lives. So in desperation, Saul seeks any kind of spiritual guidance he can get. Even though they are supposedly expelled from the land, everyone knows where a medium can be found if you need one. That is why the penalty was death.

> *So Saul disguised himself, putting on other clothes, and at night he and two men went to the woman. "Consult a spirit for me," he said, "and bring up for me the one I name." But the woman said to him, "Surely you know what Saul has done. He has cut off the mediums and spiritists from the land. Why have you set a trap for my life to bring about my death?" Saul swore to her by the LORD, "As surely as the LORD lives, you will not be punished for this." Then the woman asked, "Whom shall I bring up for you?" "Bring up Samuel," he said. When the woman saw Samuel, she cried out at the top of her voice and said to Saul, "Why have you deceived me? You are Saul!" The king said to her, "Don't be afraid. What do you see?" The woman said, "I see a spirit coming up out of the ground." "What does he look like?" He asked. "An old man wearing a robe is coming up," she said. Then Saul knew it was Samuel, and he bowed down and prostrated himself with his face to the ground. Samuel said to Saul, "Why have you disturbed me by bringing me up?"* — 1 Samuel 28:8-15 NIV

First, I find it instructive that the woman was surprised to see Samuel. She was used to dealing with a demonic spirit who would imitate the dead person being sought. Now she had the real person, not her demon friend. Second, I see evidence for life after death. Samuel did exist in the world of the dead. Third, I see another tragic ending to the life of one who could have been great, but ...

Saul will die in the battle the next day. The only positive point I see is that Saul will be with Samuel. Assuming Samuel was in the place of the righteous dead, it shows a God whose mercy is as powerful as His judgment.

- **What are some of the implications about the afterlife you see from this passage?**

This story is a powerful lesson about evil spirits and the war we wage against them. We can see from the Gospels that Jesus constantly fought demons. Demons are real. We can see that in every story of demon possession or oppression; they always do harm to their victims and never good. Satan's whole strategy is to deceive us into dishonoring God and ourselves. He deceived Saul through impatience and disobedience. He deceived Eve through lies. Today his web of deception is more widespread and systemic than ever. The main purpose of Satan's kingdom is to keep us from reaching our full potential as God's children. He wants us to fail, and fail miserably. He wants to keep us from greatness.

We are at war. Our very lives, physical and eternal, are at stake. The lives of all our loved ones, and every person in the world, physical and eternal, are at stake. Jesus came and won the crucial victory when he died on the cross. He defeated the devil by doing God's will perfectly throughout his whole life. The proof of his perfection is his resurrection. Satan has been dealt the victory blow; he is a wounded animal. Though he knows his end, he denies it and tries to deceive us into thinking it isn't true.

We live in a world of mediums, spiritists, occultists, and other servants in the kingdom of Satan. It is not incumbent upon us to put them to death as the Old Testament commanded. So we must wage the war in the heavenlies, through prayer.

The occult is all around us, in places we might not suspect. There are occult stores and psychic reading specialists open for business in many towns and cities. There was an article in our local paper about a girl who wanted Halloween off from school because as a witch, Halloween for her was a religious holiday. Many cases of child abuse have been linked to what is known as satanic ritual abuse, where children are molested and abused in the context of satanic rituals.

While that is overt occultism, there are more subtle forms. Astrology — guiding one's life by the stars — is an occult practice. Psychics — the heirs of the mediums and spiritists of yesteryear are involved in occult practices. Mediums — people still seek contact with the dead. Do you remember the movie *Ghost*? Lucky numbers, tea leaves, tarot cards, Ouija boards, crystal balls are all associated with occult practices. There are people who seriously guide their lives by the messages they get from these objects.

Some Christians unknowingly wear occult objects as jewelry: pentagrams, ankhs, crystals, and other things. These objects can be avenues for demonic influences. The demons don't care if you are overtly evil and perverted. They are perfectly willing for you to be a fine, upstanding, moral citizen, as long as you don't guide your life by God's Holy Spirit. Remember Ronald Reagan and astrology? Guided by the stars? Satan says, "Okay." Guided by your spiritual force within? Satan says, "That is good." Anything but God's power is fine.

You can say you don't believe in demons. You can say the occult won't affect you. Again, there is Satan's deception. It can happen to you, even if quite innocently. Satan is out to get you, with or without your consent; it doesn't matter to him. You can say you've never seen a demon, nor have any of your friends. I've never seen one either, but the Bible tells me demons exist. Story after story from the mission field and our own country testify to experiences of others in this realm of the spiritual war.

The lesson from Saul today is don't be deceived. We are supposed to follow God and God alone. Don't get wrapped up in these other things that are not from God. I'm sure Saul never thought he would be one of those who would consult a medium. But there he is, bringing up Samuel. Keep on your guard. Dabbling in the occult is but another way to lose your greatness. Like Samson, Saul joins the ranks of the almost great. His epitaph in 1 Chronicles 10:13 is not very flattering, "Saul died because he was unfaithful to the LORD; he did not keep the word of the LORD and even consulted a medium for guidance ..." (NIV). Don't be deceived in this. Keep your guard up. Don't lose your greatness. Trust in God and follow Him only.

For Further Reflection

Discuss times you have felt God's guidance in your life. What were the primary ways God communicated to you?

Discuss times you have felt the presence of evil. What did you do?

Some Christians pray to the dead. What does this passage say about that practice?

Chapter 14

Between The Lines: Don't Forget To Pray

The book of Joshua offers many lessons for Christians. The name Jesus is a derivative from Joshua, meaning, "Yahweh saves," or "Yahweh is salvation." Joshua is a type of Jesus in that he leads Israel into the promised land and conquers the enemies. He is the head of the Lord's army against sin and corruption.

Perhaps Joshua's most famous battle is Jericho, where "the walls came a tumblin' down." Can you imagine being Joshua and listening to God's instructions for the first time about how to take Jericho? March around the city once a day for six days, then seven times on the seventh day, then blow the trumpets. C'mon God, get real. This is a military battle, not an invitation to a band concert. Can you imagine General Shwarzkopf marching around the Iraqi desert during Desert Storm, then having the army band playing "When The Saints Go Marching In"? That is the functional equivalent. Some battles in our lives are far more complicated than our resources can handle. In those battles we must trust the Lord completely and follow His instructions to the letter, no matter how weird they may seem at the time. God gives the victory when we are completely obedient to His revealed will.

The story of Achan (Joshua 7) also presents a lesson concerning God's view of sin. Achan, of course, was the man who took some of the spoils from Jericho, when God told them not to take anything. The reason for that rule was because this first victory in the promised land was entirely dedicated to God. The city of Jericho was a whole burnt offering to God. In taking some of the booty, Achan stole from God. (I like to say he was Achan for a breakin'.) His sin is discovered, but now he has contaminated himself and the community of Israel. He must endure the consequences of his sin.

Not only Achan, but Achan's entire family. While it may not seem fair on the surface, we must remember that our sin affects more than just ourselves. The consequences of our sin ripple out to others in our lives, like ripples in a pond when you throw a rock in the water. Sin not only hurts us, but also the ones we love.

As Israel conquers more and more of the promised land, the people of Gibeon decide that if you can't beat them, you may as well join them. They devise a clever ruse, acting like people from a foreign country, wishing to make a treaty with Israel. The telling line is Joshua 9:14: "So the men partook of their provisions, and did not ask direction from the Lord" (NIV). *They forgot to pray!* Many Christians today treat prayer with some scoffing, doubt, or "in emergency only" attitudes. Prayer is our communication link with Jesus. We cannot afford to forget to pray. The consequences of this error reach hundreds of years into the future.

Years later King Saul, in his zeal, waged an extermination campaign against the Gibeonites. This violated the covenant Joshua had made with them hundreds of years earlier. Early in King David's reign, a famine comes upon the land which is connected with Saul's sin of killing the Gibeonites. To make atonement for the innocent lives of the Gibeonites, two sons and five grandsons of Saul are killed and their bodies exposed (2 Samuel 21). All this trouble could have been avoided, if the elders of Israel had not forgotten to pray when the Gibeonites first came to them.

Prayer is power with God. We need to take every decision to the Lord, major or minor, and understand the perfect will of God. In our Bible reading to this point, we can see that David was a man of constant prayer and seeking the Lord's direction and blessing. I notice that David was also very successful in everything he undertook. Could there be a connection? You bet. Prayer was the source of David's power and friendship with God. That isn't reserved for David alone. All of us can have that relationship with God, if only we will remember to pray.

- **Name some times your sin seriously affected those around you.**

- Have there been times in your life when you forgot to pray? What happened?

- Name some times God gave you some "offbeat" instructions. What happened?

Chapter 15

The Zenith Of Israel: The Reign Of Solomon

1 Kings 3-8

Our theme as we have been studying through the Bible is "God has a plan." God's plan is to redeem humankind from sin and death. He chose Israel as a nation to live out God's will according to God's law. They had a rocky start during the time of the Judges. Saul began to pull the people together but didn't have the leadership capabilities to complete the process. David was the perfect leader and politician. Through his military prowess, David was able to subdue all the surrounding nations that at one time or another had given Israel trouble. What made David such a great leader? He loved the Lord and did God's will. Though the human failures in David's family still carried their consequences, God worked through David to bring about a time of peace and prosperity previously unknown in Israel.

- **Discuss some of the consequences of David's sin on his family.**

David's son Solomon is the one who gets to enjoy all this peace and prosperity and make Israel the reigning nation of the period. If we are looking for types of Jesus in the Old Testament, Solomon represents what it will be like in the millennium when Jesus is King of all the earth. It will be a time of total peace. It will be a time of unprecedented economic prosperity and growth. It will also be a time of growth in knowledge, wisdom, and culture. Though his many political marriages get him in trouble, Solomon's reign also shows that in the millennium, people from every nation, tribe, and culture will be part of the governing power. Jesus will not discriminate. Solomon foreshadows Jesus' establishing the Church, the bride of Christ from many nations. The difference is that while Solomon was led astray by his wives into idolatry, Jesus brings his bride closer to God in true worship.

Solomon is the one who builds the temple of the Lord in Jerusalem. We can only imagine how beautiful and luxurious the first temple must have been. I have seen the foundation stones at the Wailing Wall. They are huge. Truly the original temple must have been one of the wonders of the ancient world. In building the temple, Solomon unites the religious life of Israel. Jesus also will make Jerusalem the religious center of the Messianic Age. In the reign of Solomon, we see a foreshadow of God's plan. All of redeemed humanity will enjoy the reign of Jesus Christ on earth. It will be a time of love, peace, prosperity, and learning.

What made Solomon so great? In 1 Kings 3:3, the Bible says, "Solomon loved the Lord and followed Him with his whole heart." That makes for a great person of God. Beyond that, it also shows that Solomon knew his limitations. When God gave him one wish, Solomon knew he didn't have the wisdom to rule as God would like. So he asked God for wisdom. Along with his gift of wisdom were other cash and prizes. Solomon ruled by wisdom. The basic definition of wisdom is to know right from wrong, good from bad, God's will from what is not God's will. Solomon was able to discern these things and rule accordingly. Solomon's wisdom has become proverbial. Listen to this description in Chapter 4.

> *God gave Solomon wisdom and very great insight, and a breadth of understanding as measureless as the sand on the seashore. Solomon's wisdom was greater than the wisdom of all the men of the East, and greater than all the wisdom of Egypt. He was wiser than any other man, including Ethan the Ezrahite — wiser than Heman, Calcol and Darda, the sons of Mahol. And his fame spread to all the surrounding nations. He spoke three thousand proverbs and his songs numbered a thousand and five. He described plant life, from the cedar of Lebanon to the hyssop that grows out of walls. He also taught about animals and birds, reptiles and fish. Men of all*

nations came to listen to Solomon's wisdom, sent by all the kings of the world, who had heard of his wisdom.
— 1 Kings 4:29-34 NIV

- **If God were to grant you one wish, what would you ask for?**

Solomon writes in the Proverbs that the fear of the Lord is beginning of wisdom. Once we know God in a personal relationship with Jesus Christ, we can know right from wrong, good from bad, God's will from what is not God's will.

The celebration of the Lord's Supper reminds us of what it cost Jesus to get wisdom for us. The bread symbolizes his body, broken for us as a perfect sacrifice. The cup symbolizes his blood, shed for us, inviting us into a new covenant. The celebration of the Lord's Supper is a special time of talking with Jesus and listening to him. As we listen to him we can get wisdom. He will tell us when we did right, and when we did wrong. He will tell us when we were good, and when we were bad. He will tell us when we were in God's will and out of God's will. As we confess our sins, and as we obey what he tells us, we can demonstrate that wisdom to others, and not leave it merely in the realm of the theoretical and intellectual.

In the Lord's Supper, we also celebrate our faith that Jesus will come back again. We should periodically remind ourselves of that facet of the Lord's Supper. Paul says, "We proclaim his death until he comes again" (1 Corinthians 11:26). Jesus is coming again. It is nearly 2000 years closer now than when Jesus first stated the promise. We can celebrate that we will be there during the 1000 year reign of Jesus Christ. The Bible says that those who serve faithfully now will rule with Jesus then. All of us who have put our faith in Christ will enjoy those 100 decades of peace, joy, love, prosperity, contentment, and growth. Whenever you partake of the Lord's Supper remember this fact: We will be there. By the grace of God, we will be there. Remember that God has a plan. That plan includes us at the millennial reign of Jesus Christ, King of kings, Lord of lords, and Ruler of heaven and earth.

For Further Reflection

While it was a golden age, Solomon's reign also sowed the seeds for the divided kingdom. What things about Solomon's reign do you think contributed to this rebellion?

What does Solomon's experience tell us about the importance of marrying a person who shares a similar faith perspective?

Imagine being in the millennial kingdom of Jesus. What do you want to do and where?

Chapter 16

Contest On Carmel

1 Kings 18:20-40

You can see by now that the history of Israel after the reign of Solomon was little better than the time of the judges — up and down. During the reign of Solomon's son, Rehoboam, Israel was divided into northern and southern kingdoms. The northern kingdom never has a king that is commended for good things. The north has coup after coup and change after change. The southern kingdom keeps the line of David intact with a few good kings, but that is about as much as we can say.

Starting with Jeroboam I in the north, Israel falls into idolatry, worshiping calves at Dan and Bethel. It goes downhill from there until Ahab, who is considered the worst of the Israelite kings in terms of morality and spirituality. He married Jezebel, a woman from Syro-Phonecia, who becomes the prototype of evil women throughout the Bible. Jezebel's god is Baal, and she is deeply devoted to making Baal worship the only worship in the northern kingdom of Israel. She kills the Lord's prophets and sets up Baal temples throughout the land. She imports Baal priests and prophets from her homeland.

Baal was a fertility god, closely tied to agricultural cycles. It was believed that Baal and Ashtoreth had to get together every spring in order for there to be rain and good crops. So, to send the clear message to the contrary, God sends a drought upon the land for three years. The prophet-hero of the day is a man named Elijah. We don't know much about Elijah's beginning but we know he is favored of God. Along with Moses, he appears to Jesus on the Mount of Transfiguration. The prophetic book of Malachi says that one like Elijah will come preaching, preparing the way for the

Messiah. God works through Elijah to command the drought to begin and, after three years, to pray for the drought to end.

As the drought is about to end, it is time for a showdown at the Carmel corral. Elijah presents himself to Ahab, who blames Elijah for the trouble in Israel.

> *Ahab went to meet Elijah. When he saw Elijah, he said to him, "Is that you, you troubler of Israel?" "I have not made trouble for Israel," Elijah replied. "But you and your father's family have. You have abandoned the LORD's commands and have followed the Baals."*
> — 1 Kings 18:16-17 NIV

- **Name some people who have tried to blame others for their troubles. Have you ever done this?**

Elijah counters that it is Ahab's unfaithfulness to the Lord as well as Jezebel's actions that have brought on this drought. How often we want to avoid our own responsibility and blame someone else for our troubles.

Elijah then issues his challenge:

> *"Now summon the people from all over Israel to meet me on Mount Carmel. And bring the four hundred and fifty prophets of Baal and the four hundred prophets of Asherah, who eat at Jezebel's table." So Ahab sent word throughout all Israel and assembled the prophets on Mount Carmel. Elijah went before the people and said, "How long will you waver between two opinions? If the LORD is God, follow him; but if Baal is God, follow him."*
> — 1 Kings 18:19-21 NIV

This challenge is still fresh for the people of the world today. If Allah is God, follow him; if Jesus is God, follow him. If Buddha is God, follow him; if Jesus is God, follow him. If Krishna is God, follow him; if Jesus is God, follow him. But we need to go beyond the realms of other religions. If money is God, follow it; if Jesus is God, follow him. If sex is God, follow it; if Jesus is God, follow him. If power is God, follow it; if Jesus is God, follow him. If popularity is God, follow it; if Jesus is God, follow him. If drugs are God, follow it; if Jesus is God, follow him. If alcohol is God, follow it; if Jesus is God, follow him.

- **What competes for full devotion to God in your life?**

There is only one God in the mind of Elijah and in orthodox Christian thought. There can be no rivals. There can be no split decisions. There is no tie score. There are no runners-up who will take over if God cannot fulfill his obligations.

> *Then Elijah said to them, "I am the only one of the LORD's prophets left, but Baal has four hundred and fifty prophets. Get two bulls for us. Let them choose one for themselves, and let them cut it into pieces and put it on the wood but not set fire to it. I will prepare the other bull and put it on the wood but not set fire to it. Then you call on the name of your god, and I will call on the name of the LORD. The god who answers by fire — he is God." Then all the people said, "What you say is good."*   — 1 Kings 18:22-24 NIV

Essentially, Elijah challenges the Baal prophets to a contest between their gods, while asking the people of Israel to act as judges, witnesses and referees. The rules are simple, yet challenging. The Baal prophets will prepare an altar with a sacrifice. Elijah will also prepare an altar with a sacrifice. The Baal prophets are to call on Baal to answer by fire. Elijah will call on the LORD. The god who answers by fire is the true God. Everybody agrees to the terms and Elijah lets the Baal prophets go first.

In this description of the contest, we have some really satirical and funny lines. The Baal prophets limp about the altar in a kind of dance and rhythm. They constantly repeat, "O Baal, answer us." (Didn't Jesus say something about vain repetition?) "There was no voice, there was no answer." The writer emphasizes that there was absolutely no sign of any action. There was no hint that Baal was even thinking about answering. There was total silence in response to the cries of the prophets.

- **What negative lessons about prayer do the Baal prophets teach us?**

At noon Elijah began to taunt them. "Shout louder!" he said. "Surely he is a god! Perhaps he is deep in thought, or busy, or traveling. Maybe he is sleeping and must be awakened" (1 Kings 18:27 NIV). Here we have the most insulting satire of pagan religion and idol worship penned in the Bible. When the text says that maybe Baal has gone aside, traveling or on a journey, most agree that Elijah is saying that Baal is in the bathroom with the door shut. So the prophets yell louder and slash themselves. But there is still no answer.

The time for the evening offering comes, and it is now Elijah's turn with Yahweh.

> *Then Elijah said to all the people, "Come here to me." They came to him, and he repaired the altar of the LORD, which was in ruins. Elijah took twelve stones, one for each of the tribes descended from Jacob, to whom the word of the LORD had come, saying, "Your name shall be Israel." With the stones he built an altar in the name of the LORD, and he dug a trench around it large enough to hold two seahs of seed. He arranged the wood, cut the bull into pieces and laid it on the wood. Then he said to them, "Fill four large jars with water and pour it on the offering and on the wood. Do it again," he said, and they did it again. "Do it a third time," he ordered, and they did it the third time. The water ran down around the altar and even filled the trench.* — 1 Kings 18:30-35 NIV

The contest has reached a crisis point. The Baal prophets have used all the time on the clock and Yahweh is getting his hands on the ball for the first time. Elijah proceeds to challenge God even more by pouring the water on the altar. Water in the midst of a drought is hard to come by. It represents a sacrifice of the thing they need the most. Elijah orders that twelve jars of water be poured on, to represent the twelve tribes of Israel. It increases the difficulty for Yahweh because now he has a very wet sacrifice to burn. It is going to take more than a match to light this sacrifice.

> *At the time of sacrifice, the prophet Elijah stepped forward and prayed: "O Lord, God of Abraham, Isaac and Israel, let it be known today that you are God in Israel and that I am your servant and have done all these things at your command. Answer me, O Lord, answer me, so these people will know that you, O Lord, are God, and that you are turning their hearts back again."* — 1 Kings 18:36-37 NIV

Notice Elijah's simple prayer in contrast to the ranting and raving of the Baal prophets. He reminds the people of who God is and of His special relationship to Israel. The purpose of the contest is not to defeat Baal, not to make the Baal prophets look stupid, not to put on a media event with the Lord's power. No, the purpose of this contest is that the heart of the people might be turned back to God. God displays His power to increase our faith, love, and devotion to Him.

- **Compare your prayers to the Baal prophets and Elijah. Which example do you follow?**

"Then the fire of the LORD fell and burned up the sacrifice, the wood, the stones and the soil, and also licked up the water in the trench" (1 Kings 18:38 NIV). You need to have this picture of lightning falling from heaven in a controlled, intelligent manner. It wasn't a lightning bolt that just exploded the altar and everything on it. This was a controlled tongue of fire that consumed everything in order: first the sacrifice, then the wood, then the stones, then the dust, then the water in the trench. The lightning acted as a living being. When all the people saw this, they fell prostrate and cried, "The Lord — he is God! The Lord — he is God!" (1 Kings 18:39 NIV). The Lord God, Yahweh, proved himself to be the only true God, and every other god is a false god. The LORD is God. Follow him.

How did Elijah do all this? How could he command the drought to come and prolong it for three whole years? How could he command the fire to come down with such a simple prayer, with no dancing or slashing? We find the answer in the New Testament. "Elijah was a man just like us. But he prayed" (James 5:17). Elijah was a man who experienced the power of prayer because he knew the God he was praying to.

One of the secrets to an effective prayer life is to know God. Our relationship with God through Jesus should strive for intimacy. Prayer is the primary way to do that. Many people know about Jesus, but there is a difference between knowing about Jesus and knowing Jesus. It is similar to knowing about the President and knowing the President. The difference is personal relationship.

You can know Jesus personally, today, just by talking to him in prayer. It isn't a body to body, physical relationship. Rather, it is a spirit to spirit relationship. Jesus is present, waiting to talk to you and for you to get to know him. When we take time to pray, we deepen our relationship with Jesus. When we take the time to pray, we understand what God's will is. Then when we need to call on the Lord, we won't need to limp, dance, slash ourselves, or keep on repeating our prayer over and over. We can pray a simple prayer like Elijah, and know that fire will fall from heaven. Then everyone will fall down and cry out, "The Lord Jesus, he is God," and they will be drawn closer to him.

For Further Reflection

Discuss how our time is similar to Elijah's time. How should we be praying?

If you could get into a contest like Elijah, who would you challenge and why?

Chapter 17

Resurrection Previews

2 Kings 13:21

God has a plan! God gave hints about what His plan is all about. God's plan is fulfilled in the life and death and resurrection of Jesus. Throughout the history of Israel, through prophecy, through foreshadows, through everything in Israelite history and life, God was pointing to Jesus. When Jesus came, he fulfilled over 300 Old Testament prophecies and allusions. Scholars say he will fulfill 300 more when he comes again. God has declared from the beginning what His plan entailed and how it would be accomplished. We see on Maundy Thursday that the betrayal and the trial were all a part of God's plan for Jesus. We see on Good Friday how Jesus fulfilled thirty prophecies in one day by his death on the cross. We see Easter Sunday, Resurrection Sunday. This was the ultimate zenith in God's plan. Truly He wanted to make sure that we understood His intentions.

- **Discuss the importance of fulfilled prophecy for establishing the reliability of the Bible.**

We are used to previews in our society. We go to the movies and we see previews of coming attractions. Certainly, they show us only the best scenes. Even the most boring of bombs has three minutes of exciting stuff to put in the previews to make it look worthwhile. Television also gives us previews to keep us loyal to that network or station. Television news gives us teasers. "Tomorrow will be a real interesting weather day, details at 11."

God also has previews and teasers. He gave several previews of the resurrection in the Old Testament, one of which we read in 2 Kings 13.

> *Elisha died and was buried. Now Moabite raiders used to enter the country every spring. Once while some Israelites were burying a man, suddenly they saw a band of raiders; so they threw the man's body into Elisha's tomb. When the body touched Elisha's bones, the man came to life and stood up on his feet.*
> — 2 Kings 13:20-21 NIV

Can you imagine their shock and surprise? They are carrying out the sad task of burying their friend. It was their last act of kindness to the departed. Yet the times were risky, and they were in an area where raiders came to plunder the land. Not only are they grieving for their friend, they also have to be on the lookout during the funeral procession. Their worst expectations are realized. They see a band of raiders. Now the corpse has become a burden that will hinder their escape. Quick, here's a tomb. Throw the body in here. He won't know the difference. "What? He's alive! He's alive!" Don't you wonder whether they tarried, or if they said, "Let's rejoice later, right now we have to outrun those Moabite raiders"? Or did the man upbraid them, "This isn't my tomb, what's the big idea?" How wonderful and awkward it must have been. I'm sorry, today's funeral has been canceled as the corpse has come back to life.

- **If you were the person brought back to life, what do you think your first words would be?**

- **If you were one of these friends, what would your first words be?**

But this incident is not the only preview clip in the Old Testament. Elijah and Elisha both raised young boys from the dead. Both boys were the only sons of their mother. In both cases, the prophet lies down on the body and prays. In both cases, the prophet presents the boy to the mother. Now in these previews, God is saying, when my Son, the Messiah, comes, he will bring people back from the dead, just like this, and many more like them.

The New Testament also offers previews as Jesus comes to earth. Jesus himself raised people from the dead, leaving no doubt that Jesus has the power to raise the dead. It is also clear that Jesus is greater than Elisha or Elijah, because he raises himself from the dead. Take notice of that. The man thrown in Elisha's tomb comes to life, but Elisha does not.

New Testament preview number 1: Jairus' daughter. The raising of Jairus' daughter is bursting with meaning and significance. First, it is a little girl, not a little boy, who is raised. This happens in a cultural setting where girls were not as valued as sons. Yet in raising the girl, Jesus is saying daughters are just as much a gift from God as sons. He is affirming that girls have a part in God's plan that they need to fulfill.

Preview number 2: the widow's son. In that society, without her son, this widow would become a non-citizen. Widows needed their sons in order to protect their property and their rights as citizens. Already bereaved of her husband, now this woman must endure the death of her son as well. As the funeral procession comes out of the town of Nain to bury him, Jesus is walking by. He touches the funeral bier, the young man sits up, back to life, and begins talking. Luke 7:15 reads, "The dead man sat up and began to talk, and Jesus gave him back to his mother" (NIV). Notice how those words echo the words of Elijah. He gave him to his mother. This is as much a resurrection for the widow as it is for the young man. She now has status and a protector in society.

Preview number 3: Lazarus. Here we have an adult who is raised from the dead. The emphasis of this miracle is that we know he is dead because he has been in the tomb four days. There is no way this could be a resuscitation. This was a resurrection. It also served to declare Jesus' power to the people. This miracle brought him many followers, but it also increased the drive of his enemies to have him killed. Jesus uses this occasion to declare, "I am the resurrection and the life. He who believes in me will live, even though he dies; and whoever lives and believes in me will never die" (John 11:25-26 NIV). Again, women are blessed in this resurrection — Lazarus' sisters, Mary and Martha.

- **If you could choose one person in your life to be raised from the dead for one day, who would it be? What would you do?**

Preview number 4: a number of saints at the death of Jesus. This is recorded in Matthew 27. When Jesus died, there was a great earthquake. Many tombs were opened and saints who had previously died came back to life and went into the city witnessing. Here we have a preview of how Jesus will raise all the saints when he comes again in glory. Paul says that when Jesus comes back, the dead will be raised first, incorruptible.

The main event is Jesus' own resurrection. Three days after his death, Jesus comes back to life and shows himself to his followers. The main support beam of our faith is the resurrection of Jesus Christ from the dead. Without his resurrection, our faith is useless.

Jesus' resurrection is different from all the previews. Every one of those resurrected by Jesus eventually died again. They did not ascend to heaven. Every one of the others was raised by someone else. They did not come back to life in and of their own power. Every one of the others resurrected came back in his same human body.

But Jesus' resurrection is different in all these respects. Jesus is alive today because he ascended into heaven. Jesus raised himself from the dead. "I have power to lay down my life and to take it up again" (John 10:18). Jesus came back in a new, spiritual body. It could go through walls and transport anywhere instantly. In Jesus, all the previews are fulfilled, and given their full detail as to how God intends to raise us from the dead.

That is the bottom-line message of Easter. God is in the resurrection business. He wants to raise us from the dead. When God came the first time in Jesus, he resurrected us from the death of sin. We have died to sin and we no longer have to be controlled by our sinful natures. He is now giving us his resurrection power, through the Holy Spirit, so that we can live our lives by his power, to do his will.

And he will raise us from the dead. We believe that when we die, our spirits go to heaven to be with Jesus. Paul intimates that at that time, we may receive our heavenly body. In other places in the

Scriptures it looks like we may have to wait in a temporary spiritual body until this body is resurrected. Whichever the case, God wants to raise us from the dead to be alive with Him in heaven forevermore. That is God's plan. He wants us to be alive forevermore through Jesus Christ His Son.

God has a wonderful plan of eternal life in heaven and abundant life now for all those who will put their trust in Jesus as Savior and Lord. Believe that Jesus died for your sins and that God raised him from the dead. Ask God to forgive you and give you eternal life. Follow Jesus every day in obedience as your expression of gratitude and love.

For Further Reflection

Read Isaiah 53 and Psalm 22. How many prophecies in these passages were fulfilled in the passion of Jesus? How many have yet to be fulfilled?

Imagine meeting one of those who had been raised from the dead in Matthew 27. What would you want to ask him?

What aspect of Jesus' spiritual body is most appealing to you?

Chapter 18

Music In Worship

1 Chronicles 15 and 25

The book of Chronicles emphasizes the value of praise and music in worship. The writer spends a lot of print detailing the duties of the Levites in the temple, with specific emphasis on the music ministries of the Levites. All of this is credited to David who organizes the priests in shifts to minister always before the Lord with sacrifices and with music.

That David would emphasize music comes as no surprise since he is credited with writing many of the psalms and was himself a musician. We find several places where David organized the music in the tabernacle and in the temple.

> *The leaders of the Levites are to appoint their brothers as singers to sing joyful songs, accompanied by musical instruments: lyres, harps and cymbals. The musicians Heman, Asaph and Ethan were to sound the bronze cymbals; Zechariah, Aziel, Shemiramoth, Jehiel, Unni, Eliab, Maaseiah and Benaiah were to play the lyres according to alamoth, and Mattithiah, Eliphelehu, Mikneiah, Obed-Edom, Jeiel and Azaziah were to play the harps, directing according to sheminith. Kenaniah the head Levite was in charge of the singing; that was his responsibility because he was skillful at it.*
> — 1 Chronicles 15:15, 19-22 NIV

> *David, together with the commanders of the army, set apart some of the sons of Asaph, Heman and Jeduthun for the ministry of prophesying, accompanied by harps, lyres and cymbals. All these men were under the supervision of their fathers for the music of the temple of the*

> Lord, with cymbals, lyres and harps, for the ministry at the house of God. Asaph, Jeduthun and Heman were under the supervision of the king. Along with their relatives — all of them trained and skilled in music for the Lord — they numbered 288.
>
> — 1 Chronicles 25:1, 6-7 NIV

Now that is a worship band — 288 musicians. David arranged all the Levites into choirs and bands on rotating monthly shifts. His reason? So that there would always be someone praising the God of Israel.

- **How important is praise in your walk with Jesus? What kinds of things get you in the "praise mood"?**

In the Bible, music is a critical component of worship and praise. Listen to some of the passages that command us to use music as a means of worship. "Sing for joy to God our strength; shout aloud to the God of Jacob!" (Psalm 81:1 NIV). "Come, let us sing for joy to the LORD; let us shout aloud to the Rock of our salvation" (Psalm 95:1 NIV). "Speak to one another with psalms, hymns and spiritual songs. Sing and make music in your heart to the Lord" (Ephesians 5:19 NIV). "Let the word of Christ dwell in you richly as you teach and admonish one another with all wisdom, and as you sing psalms, hymns and spiritual songs with gratitude in your hearts to God" (Colossians 3:16 NIV).

Now notice the balance between singing aloud and singing in your heart. God recognizes that there are some people who can't carry a tune in a bucket with a lid on it. I think David knew that too. That is why we have choirs. Choirs are those who are gifted in singing, using their talent and gift to help others in worship who do not sing so well. God's command to you who are less musically inclined is to sing with your heart. I don't think God means for you to keep silent during the hymns. God is simply saying that if you can't sing with your voice, you are not obligated to embarrass yourself. You may sing with your heart. If you would like to sing with your voice as well, your song is still sweet in the Master's ears.

What we see from these passages is the importance of music in worship and how music can be used in worship. We have different music for different parts of the worship service. The typical music we find in worship includes the prelude, which is a time to focus on Jesus before the service begins. The fellowship chorus is a time to join together in praise, having greeted one another. The hymn of praise helps us praise God as we enter His presence. The affirmation chorus affirms our faith commitment after the Lord's Prayer. The Doxology reminds us that what we have given to God He gave to us first. Choral amens add music to times of prayer. The hymn of preparation is praise to God for His written word and preparation to hear the preached word. The hymn of commitment or invitation hymn invites us to respond to the message with a song in our heart. Choir specials have their roots in the Old Testament as we have seen. It is a time which allows those with musical gifts to render a service to the congregation and to God. Sometimes individuals bring special music providing another opportunity for those with gifts and talents to present them to God and us. All of this music lends order to the worship and reflects the mood of the moment. That is the power of music in worship.

- **Discuss the kinds of hymns and songs in your worship service. How are they used? What kind of mood are they intended to set?**

Music plays an important role in the tone and atmosphere of the worship. That contribution is as vital as the friendliness of the church and the power of the preaching. All our friendliness, all the of the best preaching, can be undone by dull, lifeless songs and lousy music. Music has power. It has power to engage and unleash our emotions. It has power to set the mood of our being and service. It can affect us by its rhythm and sound: major or minor, slow or fast, hard-driving beat to easy rhythm. Music can help us express the inexpressible. When we find it hard to praise God or pray to God, a song can be just the thing to give expression to our thoughts and feelings.

We know the power of music in our society. Music defines generations. When we hear big band sounds, we think of the 1940s. When we hear Elvis, or Chuck Berry, we think 1950s. When we hear the Beatles or the Rolling Stones or Bob Dylan, we think 1960s. When we hear the Carpenters, America, Led Zeppelin, or Chicago, we think 1970s. When we hear Bruce Springsteen or Michael Jackson, we think 1980s. When we hear Smashing Pumpkins or Spice Girls, we think of the 1990s. Some have managed to span several decades like Crosby, Stills, and Nash or Neil Diamond or the Grateful Dead.

Christian music also has its generational links. Classical composers brought music alive for the church in their generation — Bach, Handel, and Haydn. Before 1700, the Psalms were used in church worship services. In the 1700s hymns were composed. These are the beginnings of gospel hymns. The period continues into the 1800s. Much of the music of this time came out of the different revival camps around the country. As contemporary music emerges in the Christian context, it first becomes popular in group meeting settings and then moves to a worship setting. Many of the Gaither hymns we sing, such as "Because He Lives," started as popular songs and then were published in hymnals. In our day and time, praise and worship music is the forefront edge of contemporary music in worship. We are also moving towards expanding the accompaniment of hymns beyond the traditional church organ. Churches are adding guitars, drums, horns, woodwinds, and various kinds of percussion to their music in worship. I say all of this to underscore how the music of the generation creates the mood of the generation. We are creating a mood of praise and rejoicing before Jesus that is significantly different than the mood created by traditional gospel hymns.

- **Name your three favorite hymns or songs. Why are they special to you?**

All of these music styles and moods should be a part of the worship life of the church, in accordance with the style preferences of the congregation and minister. I appreciate all these styles of music and I would not want to sacrifice any one to have another, and I'm not sure we need to. All of us are learning to respect and appreciate the musical tastes and desires of other generations and not insist on having all our own way all the time. This is a mark of maturity as Christian brothers and sisters. I want to encourage that attitude of mutual appreciation and learning from others.

We have all styles in the church. It adds to our variety of worship experiences and moods. Often, the organist will play a classical piece on the organ, or have the Worship Choir sing a classical piece. Those are quite difficult pieces. I know, I have sung them. But they have a certain beauty about them that cannot be found in other styles of music. We sing hymns from the 1800s. That was the golden era of hymn writing. The words are stirring and they are set to appropriate music: "Rock Of Ages" at a funeral. Christmas carols at Advent. Easter hymns at Easter. We have many contemporary choruses. While many are upbeat, there are several that are slower, more contemplative.

Music has been a part of the worship of God since the earliest of biblical times, and music will be with us in heaven. It has evolved through the ages so that each generation can have its own distinctive style that contributes to the next generation. We are the heirs of about five generations of Christian music, and we are blessed to be able to use so many different styles in our services. In the book of Revelation, John sees all kinds of music and singing. In Revelation 4:1, the cherubim never stop singing, "Holy, holy, holy is the Lord God Almighty." In Revelation 4:10, the elders sing to Jesus, "You are worthy." Revelation 5 has two songs to Jesus. Singing is mentioned nine times in the heavenly scenes. At least in heaven, everybody should be able to carry the tune. So whether you sing or not, let the music bear you on its wings to God. Let the music express your worship to God when you cannot find the words. Thank God for the gift of music and the many styles and moods it can create so that our worship may be pure, in spirit and in truth.

For Further Reflection

How do you and your congregation view Christian rock music? Can it be used in worship?

Discuss the advantages of worship services with exclusive types of music (contemporary or traditional) compared to a blended worship service.

How important is music in your worship tradition?

Chapter 19

The Power Of Praise

2 Chronicles 5 and 20

The situation was quite desperate for King Jehoshaphat and the kingdom of Judah. Jehoshaphat was considered one of the good kings of Judah. He made a couple of mistakes in his alliances with Israel, but in the long run, he followed God's will and led Judah wisely. Even so, good people have their share of trials and tribulations and Jehoshaphat was no exception. We see what people are really made of when trials and tribulations come their way.

- **What trials and tests in your life have made you stronger or revealed your character?**

The desperate situation is that a rather large army, combined from three nations, came against Judah to make war. What to do, what to do? Some people would panic and lose control of the situation. Some people would surrender without even considering whether they could win. Some people would rush into battle even if they had a losing cause. Jehoshaphat decided to call all the people together and pray. I hope by now in your Bible reading you have noticed how often people pray, and what they pray. We talked about Moses and the power of intercessory prayer. We talked about Elijah and the power of simple prayer. Jehoshaphat gives us a lesson in prayer and praise.

I love the form of Jehoshaphat's prayer. It is mostly questions.

> *"O Lord, God of our fathers, are you not the God who is in heaven? O our God, did you not drive out the inhabitants of this land before your people Israel and give it forever to the descendants of Abraham your friend?*

O our God, Will you not judge them?"
— 2 Chronicles 20:6, 7, 12 NIV

When we pray we must always be mindful of who God is, and who we are in relationship to God. These two things form the foundation of answered prayers.

God is enthroned on the cherubim. God is ruler in heaven and over the earth. He gives us our allotted spaces and places of service. God is in control. We are God's people. We are His inheritance. We are the bride of Christ. We have been invited into the heavenly places to make our requests known before God. In short, we have been granted the right to pray and to have our prayers answered.

Jesus has given us incredible authority in prayer. "Whatever you bind in earth will be bound on heaven, whatever you loose in earth will be loosed in heaven" (Matthew 16:19). "Whatever you ask in my name, I will do it for you" (John 14:13). The list goes on. We have authority in prayer, but it is authority granted by Jesus. There are limits. Jesus asks us to use his authority to accomplish his will. In the end, we must complete our prayer like Jehoshaphat, "We are powerless against this great multitude that is coming against us. We do not know what to do, but our eyes are on you" (2 Chronicles 20:12 NIV). When we don't know what to do, we must keep our eyes on Jesus. In his time, the answer will come.

- **Discuss the tension between the Christian's authority in prayer and "Thy will be done."**

This is a great prayer when we find ourselves in trials and tribulations. Those are the times we begin to think that God has lost control. It is time to remind ourselves that God is ruler in heaven and ruler on earth. Those are the times we begin to think we have no right to come to God. It is time to remind ourselves that we are the people of God and He has given us our place. Those are the times when we want to stay away from church. It is time to remind ourselves to come to the Lord's house and lift up our prayers in the company of brothers and sisters in Christ. In such times, if we keep looking at the enemy or the problem, we will be overwhelmed. We must remind ourselves to keep our eyes on Jesus. Those are the times we are tempted to think that we have to solve the problem ourselves and no one will help us. We must remind ourselves that we are powerless against the foe and we must rely on God for our strength.

A wonderful thing happens in response to Jehoshaphat's prayer; God speaks through his servant Jahaziel. "Listen, King Jehoshaphat and all who live in Judah and Jerusalem! This is what the LORD says to you: 'Do not be afraid or discouraged because of this vast army. For the battle is not yours, but God's' " (2 Chronicles 20:15 NIV). How difficult it is to stand still in the midst of problems and trials. We want to move. We want action. We want to get away. We want to solve it. How can we help? How can we hurry it up? Sometimes, we need to stand still. Our modern cliché is, "Let go and let God." The battle is the Lord's. We no longer have to fight in our own strength. God will fight for us. Jehoshaphat had to fight the battle in prayer, but now he has the victory through this revelation that God will deliver.

- **Can you name a time in your life when standing still and waiting on the Lord accomplished more than a flurry of activity?**

Now Jehoshaphat has a new problem. What shall we do while we are standing and waiting? He picks a very interesting activity. "Let's sing some songs." Can you imagine that? There is a vast army that we are going to face. God has told us to stand still anyway; that's a new military tactic. Now the king says, "Sing." Not only that, he put the choir at the head of the army. I've always felt that choir membership was above and beyond the call of duty, but this is getting a little extreme. But Jehoshaphat believes the word of the Lord through Jahaziel. The battle is God's. In that case, the battle is over before it even starts. What do you do after the battle is won? You praise God. So, let's praise God. As they begin to sing and praise, the Lord acts, utterly destroying the entire opposing army. Forget machine guns, nuclear bombs, napalm, chemical weapons, and missiles. Their power is negligible to the power of praising the Lord. If we really want to win the battles of life, then we need to learn about the power of praise and use it appropriately.

Praise is glorifying God. It is adoring, exalting God and telling His excellent greatness. Praise is found throughout the Bible in various contexts. The book of Psalms has all kinds of praises tailored to every situation in life. The word "psalms" translates as "praises" in Hebrew. Another good book in which to find praise is Revelation. Here we see the kind of praise going on in heaven, which means that would be a good thing to happen here on earth as well. Praise is an expression of trust in God's goodness and power. We can praise God for His goodness, His control, His grace, His love, His holiness, His righteousness, His deliverance, His awesome majesty.

Mighty things can happen when people praise the Lord. Paul and Silas were in deep trouble. They were in jail in Philippi. What to do when you are in jail? Let's see. I know, let's praise God! That sounds new and different. So Paul and Silas start singing unto the Lord. An earthquake occurs and every prisoner is freed. As events unfold, the Philippian jailer comes to Jesus in faith.

Mighty things can happen in worship when we praise the Lord. Solomon was dedicating the new temple. He appointed certain priests to sing and praise God on various instruments.

> *The priests then withdrew from the Holy Place. All the priests who were there had consecrated themselves, regardless of their divisions. All the Levites who were musicians — Asaph, Heman, Jeduthun and their sons and relatives — stood on the east side of the altar, dressed in fine linen and playing cymbals, harps and lyres. They were accompanied by 120 priests sounding trumpets. The trumpeters and singers joined in unison, as with one voice, to give praise and thanks to the Lord. Accompanied by trumpets, cymbals and other instruments, they raised their voices in praise to the Lord and sang: "He is good; his love endures forever." Then the temple of the Lord was filled with a cloud, and the*

> *priests could not perform their service because of the cloud, for the glory of the Lord filled the temple of God.*
> — 2 Chronicles 5:11-14 NIV

God came down in such a mighty way, the regular worship service had to be altered. The priests couldn't continue with their sacrifice. Makes you wonder what might happen in our churches on Sunday while we are singing and praising God. In fact, I believe God comes and fills us.

- **Recognizing that God is always present, what would you do if your church filled with the glory of the Lord next Sunday?**

So what troubles, trials, and tribulations are you involved in? In what way is Satan tempting you, taunting you, or troubling you? Financial troubles? Relationship troubles — children, parents, husband, wife, sibling? Health troubles — debilitating, annoying, or life threatening? What to do, what to do? Is God still in heaven? Does God still rule over the nations? Is Jesus still Lord? Did he die on the cross for our sins? Have we trusted in him? Are we forgiven? Are you powerless against the foe? Then who ya gonna call? Whose battle is it, anyway? Then stand still, pray, praise, and see the deliverance of the Lord. It may take time. This is the time to stick with your faith in God. The battle is the Lord's and He will bring the victory.

What to do, what to do? I know, let's sing praises to God.

For Further Reflection

Read through a few of the Psalms. How many different situations do you see where the Psalmist is praising God?

Discuss some battles you will have this week. Strategize how you will praise God for the victory.

Chapter 20

The Titan Prophets: Elijah And Elisha

Elijah and Elisha were two of the most powerful prophets in the history of Israel. It is a shame they never wrote a book like the other prophets. But I do thank God for the stories we have in 1 and 2 Kings.

Elijah bursts on the scene in 1 Kings 18. We really don't know much about his background. But did he wield the authority of God! He stopped the rain, he started the rain. He brought a dead boy back to life. He called down fire from heaven on two groups of army soldiers who had come to arrest him. We have read about his great victory on Mount Carmel over the Baal prophets. After that incident, he falls into despondency, wondering if he were really making a difference in the spiritual life of Israel.

He finally winds up on Mount Horeb, one of the mountains of God in the Sinai peninsula. There he meets God in the still small voice. He complains that he is the only one left of all of God's faithful people. God tells him that He has 7,000 faithful who have not kissed the image of Baal. Now there's a lesson. How often do we feel that we are the only true servant of God around. No one else really follows God as closely as we do. Right? Wrong! There are thousands of God's servants in every place, quietly living their lives according to God's will. We are not alone in our struggles or our mission.

- **Name the times you have felt "all alone" in the Lord's work. How did God encourage you?**

Elijah receives three new commissions on Mount Horeb (1 Kings 19:15-16). One of them is to anoint Elisha as his successor.

Elisha becomes the apprentice and servant of Elijah, to learn the ways of the prophet. After some time, it is time for Elijah to be taken into heaven. Elisha knows the day is at hand and he sticks to Elijah like glue. He needs to be there when Elijah is taken. As they walk along, Elijah asks, "What gift can I give you before I depart?" Elisha responds, "Let me have a double portion of your Spirit" (2 Kings 2:9). Now there is somebody who really wants to know God and have the power of God. The power of God does not come until we know God intimately. That is why Elijah responds, "You have asked a difficult thing." It wasn't entirely up to Elijah. Elisha would know that God would grant this request if he saw Elijah taken. When the chariot of fire comes, Elisha sees Elijah taken into heaven.

Elisha's miracles are numerous. They include raising the dead, providing for the widow's need, healing Naaman the leper, and bringing military victory to Israel. Elisha is a different prophet from Elijah. Elijah pretty much kept to himself. Elisha resided with a group of prophets. Elijah had animosity toward the king of Israel. Elisha forged a working relationship without compromising the Word of the Lord. Elisha is personable and compassionate. Elijah comes across as gruff and firm.

Together, they act as a brake on the wickedness of the northern kingdom. They are the Lord's witnesses in a place and time where that is not popular. Just as today, it is not popular to witness or be a servant of the Lord. Yet our world needs our witness just as desperately, maybe even more than Israel needed a witness from the Lord. Witness is more than going door to door or calling on the phone. Witness happens when we live a life of love and testimony so that people can see the light of Jesus shining within us. Witness is who we are, not just what we do.

Sometimes, the world around us needs a firm voice like Elijah, calling down fire from heaven so that people will turn back to God. We must not be afraid to stand up and speak our convictions on spiritual and moral issues that confront us in today's society. If something is wrong, or is a sin according to the Bible, then say so. If God says so, we should say so.

We also need the compassion and empathy of Elisha. Acts of kindness, such as when Elisha showed mercy on the Syrian army, also show people the love and message of God in a positive way. Jesus was the perfect mixture of both prophets. Jesus condemned sin and forgave sinners. To the woman caught in adultery Jesus says, "Neither do I condemn you." But he also challenges her, "Go and sin no more." That is the love of God. God challenges us to be better than we are, and forgives us for not being all we can be. God blesses us to meet the challenge and live according to His will.

For Further Reflection

Compare Elijah and Elisha. Does it seem that Elisha inherited a "double portion" of the Spirit?

Chapter 21

The Heart Of Revival

2 Chronicles 30-35

The reigns of Ahaz and his grandson Manasseh were down times. Ahaz became a vassal of Assyria during his reign. Not only did he submit politically, but he also submitted religiously. He set up Assyrian idols and altars in the temple of the Lord. He closed the temple eventually and made people worship at corner idols. The Bible says he made his sons pass through the fire. The account in 2 Kings 16:3 is more specific: "He burned his son as an offering according to the abominable practices of the nations whom the Lord drove out before the people of Israel." He was so bad that when he died, he was not buried in the tombs of the kings.

Manasseh was just as bad if not worse. In the book of 2 Kings, Manasseh is totally bad and shed much blood in Jerusalem. In Chronicles, we read that the Lord punishes Manasseh and he repents of his sin. Nonetheless, the damage is done. His bad example is passed on to Amon who tries to revive idol worship. He is killed in a revolt.

Now in between the bad times, there are some good kings, who bring about renewal and revival. Renewal and revival in the Bible are not supposed to be one-time events that come and go; they are to be ongoing processes as we keep growing in Jesus Christ. Romans 12:1-2 talks about being transformed by the renewing of our minds, an ongoing process. In 2 Corinthians 5:20, we read that our lives have been transformed in Christ. The old has passed away, the new has come. This is not just a one-time event, but an ongoing process that should happen day to day. God is working renewal in several ways in the Church today. We should not take this for granted. Let's not do like Israel and keep it only for one generation. Let's keep passing it on to our children and their children.

- **Discuss how we can keep revival and renewal ongoing.**

Consider how Hezekiah and Josiah brought renewal and revival for Israel during their reigns. There are some things that they have in common and there are some things that they did differently. Hezekiah's main emphasis, according to 2 Chronicles 29, was the restoration of worship in the temple. Ahaz had closed the temple. Hezekiah opened the doors, cleaned the place out, and held a worship service of consecration. He offered many sacrifices to show his recommitment and Israel's recommitment to the Lord as their only God. He brought back the Levites and assigned them their various duties, especially the music ministry of praise.

- **Discuss the importance of worship and church participation in keeping a healthy spiritual life.**

Not only did he reinstitute the regular worship, he celebrated the Passover as well. We should not overlook the significance of this. The Passover is the first feast of the Hebrew calendar. The Passover is the feast where Israel celebrates its creation as a nation by the deliverance from Egypt. The Passover reminds them of their common heritage, their common identity, and their common spiritual source.

If we want renewal and revival to continue and grow throughout the Church, then we need to be committed to the worship services and special activities of our congregations. In worship, especially in the service of the Lord's Supper, we are reminded of our common bond in the love and salvation of Jesus Christ. We are reminded that we all have been saved by grace and forgiven of our sins. Through faithful attendance to worship services, Sunday school, meetings, and activities, we forge relationships with one another that increase the bonds of love between us. For Christian people who want to stay renewed, church is not optional. Church worship and activity are potent sources of our strength and power from God.

Josiah had a different emphasis in his revival. Josiah ordered the temple to be repaired. The Bible tells us that while they were cleaning and repairing the temple, a book of the Law was found (2 Kings 22:8-10). When Josiah heard the words of the book (probably Deuteronomy), he tore his clothes and sent to inquire of the prophetess, Huldah. Josiah was sincerely grieved at how Israel had broken the covenant with the Lord. He was concerned about God's punishment to come. Josiah's revival consisted of following the commands of the Law to the letter. He broke down every idol and pagan worship pole and centralized the worship in the temple. He kept the Passover and renewed the covenant between Israel and God.

If we want revival and renewal to continue to grow in the Church, then we are going to have to keep growing in our knowledge and appreciation of the Bible. We need to be people who continually read through the Bible and study to understand its meaning. In the Bible, God tells us how to live for Him. God tells us the blessings that will happen if we follow His word. God tells us the punishments that will come if we don't follow His word. Our heritage as Christians is that of a people who believe in the Bible, read the Bible, love the Bible, and follow the Bible. The Bible is the only book where you can believe everything you read.

If we say the Bible is the written word of God, then it must become the most known and the most read book in our lives. As we read, study, and obey the Bible, God has a potent tool for renewing and reviving us on a day-to-day basis. When we come to the Lord's Supper, we come to a time of worship, covenant renewal, and obeying what the Bible tells us. The Bible tells us that Jesus instituted this Supper on the night he was betrayed. The Bible tells us that Jesus commanded us to celebrate this Supper in remembrance of what he did for us on the cross.

Jesus tells us that this is the Supper of the new covenant in his blood. We are here to renew our covenant with God. Confess your sins and repent. Ask forgiveness. Pledge yourself anew to Jesus and obeying him. We also do this in the context of a church worship service, with brothers and sisters of Christ all around us. This reminds us of the importance of being with one another as we renew our covenant. Each time you partake of the Supper, renew your covenant with Jesus that you may continue on the path of renewal and revival.

For Further Reflection

Consider what traditions or events can be used to stimulate revival and renewal such as revival meetings, hymn sings, etc.

Discuss some of our modern idols which need to be torn out of our lives.

Which method do you think will be more effective in bringing revival to your church or community, emphasis on the Bible, or emphasis on God-centered worship?

Chapter 22

Esther:
For Such A Time As This

Esther 4

Until now, life had been fairly routine and simple for Esther. Esther, whose Hebrew name was Hadassah, was a single woman living with her cousin, Mordecai. Her parents died when she was young and Mordecai took her in and raised her as his own daughter. Mordecai was faithful to God and the Mosaic Law and brought Esther up in righteous living. He was also a government bureaucrat. He was a mid-level official in the palace of Ahasuerus, the Persian king. As such, he rubbed elbows with the other government officials, but he didn't have ready access to the king, and he wasn't on the council or anything like that.

I'm sure Esther thought she would live a routine life of a Jewish woman of the time. Her marriage would be arranged at a certain point. She would have children and a loving husband. Life in exile wasn't easy, but the Persian government was far more tolerant than the Babylonians. Yes, life was routine and simple until, through a series of events, God threw the wrench into the gear works.

- **Discuss some of the "monkey wrenches" and disruptions that have happened in your life. How did things turn out?**

Life is like that. Disruptions come from all kinds of sources. The first monkey wrench begins a year or so earlier when Vashti is deposed as queen. The idea sounded great when the king was angry, but now he misses Vashti. A plan is devised to find the king a new wife. "We'll bring in all the beautiful single women of the kingdom, give them a one-night date with the king and the king will choose a new wife." That sounds like nice work if you can get it.

So on that day, Esther's life is changed forever as she is one of those brought to the palace to be presented before the king. The chief eunuch favors Esther over the others and she gets special treatment. Life is anything but routine now. Her night for her date with the king comes and the king falls in love with her and makes her queen of the realm. Now this is a high honor, but this isn't necessarily a Cinderella story. Women were viewed more as objects for the king's pleasure and entertainment. Esther certainly isn't going to exercise the kind of power that we would attribute to a traditional queen. Yet even though she has little political power, she does have the power of relationship with the king. She is his wife.

Now Esther has a nice routine life in the royal palace. Nothing to do but sit around and let the servants take care of her. This also sounds like nice work if you can get it. But here comes monkey wrench number two, in the form of a man named Haman. Haman is described as an Agagite. This contrasts with Mordecai who is from the tribe of Benjamin. Saul, the first king of Israel, was also from the tribe of Benjamin. Saul made war with the Amelekites under King Agag, so there could be a national rivalry playing here as well. Haman is a high level advisor to the king. In fact, Haman was so exalted that people were told to bow in his presence. Of course, Mordecai, out of his Jewish convictions, refused to bow down to Haman. That made Haman very angry. Haman decides that Mordecai's death isn't enough. All of Mordecai's people, the Jews, should be wiped out as well. He devises a plan to have all the Jews killed and gets Ahaseurus to approve the plan and make it law: big monkey wrench. Mordecai and the Jews begin to weep and mourn. The details become known to Esther. Mordecai tells her that she needs to go into the king and get this changed.

> *So Hathach went out to Mordecai in the open square of the city in front of the king's gate. Mordecai told him everything that had happened to him, including the exact amount of money Haman had promised to pay into the royal treasury for the destruction of the Jews. He*

also gave him a copy of the text of the edict for their annihilation, which had been published in Susa, to show to Esther and explain it to her, and he told him to urge her to go into the king's presence to beg for mercy and plead with him for her people. Hathach went back and reported to Esther what Mordecai had said. Then she instructed him to say to Mordecai, "All the king's officials and the people of the royal provinces know that for any man or woman who approaches the king in the inner court without being summoned the king has but one law: that he be put to death. The only exception to this is for the king to extend the gold scepter to him and spare his life. But thirty days have passed since I was called to go to the king." When Esther's words were reported to Mordecai, he sent back this answer: "Do not think that because you are in the king's house you alone of all the Jews will escape. For if you remain silent at this time, relief and deliverance for the Jews will arise from another place, but you and your father's family will perish. And who knows but that you have come to royal position for such a time as this?" Then Esther sent this reply to Mordecai: "Go, gather together all the Jews who are in Susa, and fast for me. Do not eat or drink for three days, night or day. I and my maids will fast as you do. When this is done, I will go to the king, even though it is against the law. And if I perish, I perish." So Mordecai went away and carried out all of Esther's instructions. — Esther 4:6-17 NIV

Who knows? Perhaps you have come to royal dignity for such a time as this. Have you ever asked yourself, "Why am I here? What is my purpose? What am I supposed to do to serve God and make this world a better place? What is life all about? What will make my life really meaningful?" Not all of us are in royal positions, but that line for Esther hits all people where they live. Whatever position we have come into, we have come to it for such a time as this. We are here to serve God and in every way possible make sure that His will is done through us.

Such a time as ours is as perilous a time as Esther's. Guns and bombs and violence threaten to tear our society, our nation, and our world apart at the seams. We in America can consider ourselves under the threat of senseless terrorist acts just like Israel, Ireland, or Colombia. Such a time as this is a time of drug and alcohol abuse as people think they can escape or improve reality by altering their mental processes. Such a time as this is a time of casting off the restraint of traditional sexual morals. Along with that come related problems such as teenage pregnancies, sexually transmitted diseases, and abortions.

Such a time as this is a time of economic injustice and inequality. Nowadays even if you go to college, get a good job, and stay loyal to the firm, your company can be taken over and your pension fund cleaned out, leaving you with nothing. We have homeless and hungry people populating the streets and underground of one of the world's most prosperous and wealthy nations. Such a time as this is a time of drought in terms of national political leaders. Politics is more important than people. Getting reelected is more important than doing the right thing. Such a time as this is a time of crisis in the family with a multitude of problems including rampant divorce, spouse abuse, child abuse, and absentee parents who consider advancement in their career more important than properly raising their children.

Such a time as this is a time of spiritual confusion. Americans have all sorts of views on God and religion. Many follow their own faith path, ignoring the truth that God has given us in the Bible. Look at Branch Davidians, Jim Jones, and others.

- **Where has God called you in such a time as this? How will you use your position?**

We have come to such times as these, and we have in fact come with royal position and dignity. In fact, our royal position is greater than Esther's because we are children of the King of kings and Lord of lords. We have authority from King Jesus himself to bring down God's power in this world and make a difference in the lives of people everywhere. Just as Esther was called to save the Jews, we are called to bring salvation to a multitude of people. We can bring physical relief to their physical needs, but even more significantly, we can bring the gospel to meet their spiritual need for salvation. We can bring them the truth of the Bible and the truth will set them free from their bondage to sin. And what if we do not act? Help and deliverance will come from another place, but we will not be blessed.

How can we affect our world in such a time as this? The same way Esther and Mordecai affected their world in their time. Esther calls for a fast. While not mentioned specifically, fasting is always combined with prayer and seeking God's face. We have the power in prayer to change our world in dramatic fashion. Such changes are being documented in recent books. In places around the world people are taking prayer warfare seriously and praying for their cities and nations. A new kind of evangelism called prayer evangelism is being put into use. Whole cities are experiencing the renewing power of God. Church participation in those cities has doubled, tripled, and quadrupled.

We must admit that in the face of all the situations we face in our world, we must pray the prayer of Jeshoshaphat. We are powerless against this multitude, but our eyes are on God. We can't solve the violence problem, but we can be peacemakers through prayer. We can't make everybody sexually pure, but we can prayerfully make a stand for morality, decency, purity, and chastity and teach these to our children. We can't feed every starving person or house all the homeless, but through prayer and doing our part in our own cities and towns, we can make a difference. We can't make every family happy, but through prayer we can make our families stronger and, one by one, improve the overall quality of families in our city.

Through prayer and fasting, Esther was admitted into the presence of the king and was able to thwart Haman's plot. Deliverance came because she fulfilled her purpose and, we must add, she was willing to give her life in this cause. "If I perish, I perish" (Esther 4:16). We need to remind ourselves that we will die someday, anyway. There comes a time when we need to lay down our lives and follow the call of Jesus into the battle for the world. Some may in fact give their physical lives. Difficult as physical sacrifice is, for many it is even more difficult to sacrifice our lives of ease, comfort, luxury, career, and so on. Jesus says those who follow him must take up their cross and follow him (Mark 8:34). He never promised that our lives would be easy.

It is appropriate to consider that everyone who is born has a purpose and a meaning for the time for when he was born. We have been born to influence the world for God in such times as these. Rather than retreating and considering ourselves helpless victims, let's take the offensive through prayer. God is with us. God will answer us. God wants to change the world through our prayers. If we don't, God will bring help from another quarter, but what will happen to us? Who knows? Perhaps we have been brought to our current residence, in our royal position as children of the King, for such a time as this.

For Further Reflection

Consider the importance of prayer and fasting in this story of Esther. Can you name others in the Bible who combined fasting with prayer and received some amazing answers?

Consider how the story of Esther is a story of Christ and the Church.

Chapter 23

A Peek Behind The Curtain

Job 1 and 2

Until you come to the book of Job, the Bible does not say much about suffering, especially the suffering of the righteous. Yet if we look at the lives of the Old Testament saints, we see that many of them suffered. Abraham's suffering can be seen in the death of Sarah and his many tests of faith. Isaac suffers from blindness in his old age. Jacob suffers grief over the loss of Rachel and Joseph. He also suffers the pain of his dislocated hip. Joseph suffers the indignity and torture of slavery in Egypt. Moses suffers forty years in exile and forty years in the wilderness and never sees the promised land. David suffers exile under Saul, and after he becomes king, he suffers the loss of his sons. We could go on, but it is enough to see that suffering comes to righteous, God-fearing people.

Up until Job, the prevailing theology in Jewish religion came from Deuteronomy. The theme of Deuteronomy is that if you keep the covenant, God will bless you. If you disobey, God will curse you. The motivation to do good is evident. It also made it convenient to identify sinners and sin. If you suffered, you must have sinned somewhere. It was time to confess and repent. If others were suffering, they must have sinned; they need to confess and repent. By comparison, if someone became healthy, wealthy, and wise, it must mean that God really loved them and they were keeping the covenant.

- **Name some examples of how this Deuteronomic theology still influences the Church today.**

Now this theology worked to an acceptable degree for a while, but as time progresses, the inconsistencies become more pronounced.

Some evil people prospered. Some righteous people suffered. Does that mean that Deuteronomy isn't true? Does that mean it doesn't matter whether or not I do God's will? Does it really matter whether I am obedient to the covenant?

Job was written in order to help understand the inconsistencies of the suffering of the righteous and the prosperity of the wicked. Job was righteous (Job 1:1). He did everything correctly. He raised his children to fear God. He treated his slaves with kindness and dignity. He offered sacrifices continually as an expression of confession, repentance, faith, and worship (Job 1:5). In accordance with the Deuteronomic promise, God blessed him. He was healthy, wealthy, and wise. He was a governing leader in the city. He would have lived happily ever after had it not been for Satan, the adversary.

Job had no idea of the conversation going on in heaven between God and Satan. The idea of a personal adversary against humankind is a development in later Jewish religion, after the exile to Babylon. Jewish and Christian faith never wavers. God is good. God is not the author of evil. God does not will bad things to happen to His children. Yet the righteous do suffer, sometimes grievously. The new revelation of Job is that there is an enemy of God, and God's people, who brings about suffering.

Satan means "adversary." In Job and the other late Jewish Scriptures, Zechariah and 1 Chronicles, Satan is portrayed more as an adversary of God and the accuser of human beings. He challenges the motives and intentions of human beings. Not until Jesus and the New Testament is Satan clearly portrayed as the author of all evil and suffering. God shines the spotlight on Job as someone who really knows, loves, and fears God. Satan makes the challenge, "Why not? You've given him everything he ever wanted. Take away all his stuff and his family and you will see that he really doesn't love you. He just loves the things you give him." Here is the moment of revelation. God doesn't bring the suffering on Job. Rather, God gives permission to Satan to test Job by removing his stuff. Satan does exactly that. In one day, Job loses his sons and daughters, his cattle, his fields, and his servants (Job 1:13ff). Even so, Job doesn't give up his trust in God.

- **Have you ever lost everything? How did you react? How would you react if you lost everything?**

Job 2 brings another day in heaven, and another conversation between God and Satan. God challenges the devil, "See, Job didn't crack. I told you he was a good man." Satan retorts, "Really now, everybody knows a human will endure the loss of things. What they really prize is life and health. Take away his health and he will curse you to your face." God takes up the challenge, "All right, Satan. You may take away his health, but you may not take his life." Satan does exactly that and with a vengeance. Job not only gets sick, but he gets sick with a disease that makes the skin break out in open sores. In this, Job not only is in pain, but he can no longer worship God because he has become unclean. Satan deprives Job not only of health, but also access to God in regular worship. Job's wife isn't necessarily trying to be mean by her comments. She encourages him to curse God and die only as a way of shortening his torture. Job says, "Shall we receive only good and not evil from God?" (Job 2:10). Job still doesn't know about the existence of Satan the adversary.

The writer of Job is the first one to pull back the curtain of the heavenly throne room and alert us to the presence of Satan. In all, Satan is mentioned 43 times in 25 verses of the Bible. In the Old Testament, we find him mentioned specifically only in three places. We see him in 1 Chronicles 21 inciting David to number the people. We see him here in Job. We see him in Zechariah 3 accusing Joshua, the high priest. In the New Testament, we see Satan as the enemy of God and God's people (Revelation 12). He causes all kinds of suffering and pain. He is generally viewed as the spiritual power of evil who orchestrates the death of Jesus on the cross (John 14:30). In Revelation, we find that he is the serpent in the Garden of Eden who tempted humankind away from God in the beginning (Revelation 12).

From this pulling back of the curtain, we learn certain things about Satan. First, Satan is our enemy and God's enemy. While he comes across as only an adversary here in Job, the total revelation of the Bible is that Satan is against God and God's people. Satan is the tempter, who tries to lead us away from God. What is really sad and tragic is how often he succeeds. He succeeded against Israel and they suffered tremendously. He wars against the Church and his victories are as visible as God's victories. Satan desires only pain, despair, defeat, and suffering for us.

- **Where is Satan trying to tempt you in your life?**

Second, Satan is limited in his power. He is not God's equal in any way. He is not omnipresent, omniscient, or omnipotent. We see in Job that Satan is limited in his attacks to what God will permit. In fact, because Jesus lives inside us, James can say, "Resist the devil and he will flee from you" (James 4:7). Satan is like the bully on the block. Usually if you just stand up to him, he runs away.

Third, Satan will be brought to justice and punished. The lake of fire was created specifically for the devil and his angels (Matthew 25:41). God will punish him for his rebellion and temptations. Even with this knowledge, we still have to ask ourselves, "Why does God even allow Satan to do all this? What is the point? Why do good people still suffer?" Job asks why, but his question is never directly answered.

I believe the point is in Satan's accusations. If the system were guaranteed that people who follow God will be healthy, wealthy, and wise, and people who persist in sin would suffer, which would most of us choose? That kind of faith really isn't faith because you don't need trust. You need trust when you are righteous and yet you suffer. It is at those times you have to dig deep to believe in God's love, God's goodness, God's justice, God's righteousness, God's kindness, God's power, God's healing, God's forgiveness, and God's deliverance.

Satan's accusations force us to self-reflection on that very pointed question, "Why do I serve God? Why do I believe in Jesus? Why do I come to church? Why do I serve on the board or sing in the choir or whatever? Do I really do these things out of a sense of love and gratitude for what God has done for me through Jesus Christ? Or am I doing these things to show off and have people pay attention to me? Or do I do these things so God will give me even more material things?" Peter says that suffering is the testing of our faith that removes the dross so that our faith will be pure (1 Peter 1:6, 7).

That is what happened to Job. He found his faith was even deeper than he knew. "Though he may kill me, I will yet trust in him" (Job 13:15). "I know that my Redeemer lives and that I will see him apart from my flesh" (Job 19:25-27). Job found that his faith was not only for this life, but also for the life to come. God wants us to know that the full value of our faith is not only for this life, but also as a hope in the life to come. God wanted the best for Job. God wants the best for us. God wants us to trust Him totally, so that He may bless us totally.

The question of suffering, especially the suffering of the righteous and innocent, has been a difficult one for Christians throughout the ages. How can a good God allow bad things to happen? The revelation of the Bible shows that when the curtain is pulled back, there is an interdependent and intertwining series of causes and consequences. But the Bible also affirms that God is in control. God is good. And God will have the ultimate victory. Until then, we are called to strengthen our faith in Jesus, so that we will stand firm not only in the good times, but in the rough times as well. We are called to trust, like Job, that though things may be going in a direction we do not like, God is in control, and we will keep our faith in Him.

For Further Reflection

What is your theology of suffering? Why does God allow it?

Why do you serve God? Do you expect to receive only good?

Discuss some of the times God led you to a deeper faith through trial and tribulation.

Chapter 24

The Forgiveness And Restoration Of Job

Job 42

If we want an excellent example of how *not* to comfort someone who is suffering, we have Job's friends, Eliphaz, Bildad, and Zophar. They come to Job to comfort him in his suffering, but they are the origin of the phrase, "With friends like you, who needs enemies?"

Job's friends are entrenched in the Deuteronomic theology we introduced in the previous chapter. Deuteronomic theology says if you do good you will be blessed. If you sin, God will punish you. Job's friends would like to relieve Job of his suffering. Their logic goes like this: If you sin, you will suffer. Job is suffering. Therefore, Job has sinned. Confession and repentance of sin bring forgiveness of sin. Forgiveness of sin relieves suffering. Therefore, if Job will confess and repent, his suffering will be relieved. All we have to do is convince Job that he has sinned and get him to confess and repent.

- **What is your view on the connection between sin, suffering, and God's discipline?**

Eliphaz confirms Deuteronomic theology by the visions and dreams he has at night (Job 4:12-21). In essence he is saying the spirit world confirms that all human beings are sinful and therefore are subject to suffering at one time or another. This sounds similar to current new age thinking. Just find your spiritual guide and let him lead you into truth. The way this spirit being is described, the source is likely demonic not divine. Jesus said many false Christs and Messiahs would come to try to lead us away from him (Matthew 24:24). We must be on our guard and receive our truth from God, not other spirits. In the same way, I want to urge caution with this new fascination with angels. I believe in angels. I believe they are God's servants here to help us and protect us, but they do not desire worship from us. They don't want to be the center of attention. They want God to be the center of attention.

- **What other "New Age revelations" vie for our consideration? What does the Bible say about them?**

Eliphaz toes the party line, "Blessed is the man God corrects, so do not despise the discipline of the Almighty" (Job 5:17 NIV). So, Job, your suffering proves that you have sinned, and God is disciplining you. God loves you. So confess and repent.

Bildad confirms Deuteronomic theology by the traditions of the ancestors (Job 8:8-10). The tradition passed down from generation to generation is that the righteous will prosper and the evil ones will suffer. In many ways tradition is good. We have learned many things from our past experiences, as individuals and as a society. But blindly clinging to old traditions when the reality demands new thinking is akin to idolatry. Traditions can become fetters which hinder growth and change because we are afraid to leave the familiar. Sometimes you have to break with traditions and do things completely new and different.

Bildad toes the party line, "If you will look to God and plead with the Almighty ... he will rouse himself on your behalf and restore you to your rightful place" (Job 8:5, 6 NIV). Tradition also says that God honors confession and repentance. God will hold your hand if you just confess your sin.

Zophar confirms Deuteronomic theology by wisdom and logic (Job 11:1-6). The wisdom of the mind says that we can find out everything about God with our mind. Here we have the rationalistic approach to religion. God is as we conceive Him and believe Him to be. We observe the world around us and we can logically infer certain things about God and His character. The problem is that the human mind is corrupted by sin. God says, "My ways are higher than your ways, and my thoughts are higher than your thoughts" (Isaiah 55:9 NIV). Human beings will never be smart enough to figure out God.

Zophar toes the party line, "Oh, how I wish that God would speak ... and disclose to you the secrets of wisdom" (Job 11:5, 6 NIV). Wisdom says that God shows His love of the righteous and His hatred towards sinners. Wisdom says confess and repent and God will bring an end to your suffering.

Now in between the speeches of his friends, Job consistently denies any guilt, sin, or wrongdoing. In fact, the more his friends press him to confess and repent, the more Job insists on his righteousness. I have to figure that Job spent a lot of time thinking about his suffering and what sin he must have committed. Remember, up until this event, Job agreed with every theological point his friends have made so far. But now that Job finds himself suffering, with no known sin to cause it, he is questioning the Deuteronomic approach to theology. Job has to get past the *quid pro quo* approach to a relationship with God and learn to trust no matter what. Job doesn't understand it all, but he knows two things — he hasn't sinned, and he is suffering.

- **If you could be one of Job's comforters, what would you say to him?**

As the dialogue progresses, Job's relationship with his friends becomes quite strained. They are frustrated with Job's refusal to listen to them and confess his sin. After all, he is suffering so he must have sinned. That is the only logical explanation. On the other hand, Job is frustrated by their lack of compassion and their lack of trust in his upright character.

Finally the dialogue ends. God speaks to Job from the whirlwind, or storm. The important thing about this isn't that God is angry, or upbraids Job for his attitudes. The important thing for Job is that God is speaking to him at all. Job's attitude all along is that God has abandoned him in his suffering. God has sent his arrows and has not communicated any reason for doing so. The first thing Job did when his suffering began was to do a self-evaluation to see if any sins were present that would have caused this.

After deep introspection, Job is convinced that there is no sin in his life that merits this level of suffering and abandonment.

So when God speaks to Job, Job rejoices that God is present. Let Him say good, let Him say bad, at least God is talking to me. So often we assume that when we are in the midst of trials, tribulations, and suffering, God isn't speaking. God is mad. God is upset. In many ways, we have not progressed beyond the Deuteronomic theology of old. "Sometimes God has to put us on our back so we are finally looking up." "God must be trying to tell me something."

The lesson of Job is that God doesn't abandon us in our suffering. If anything, He draws closer. It may be difficult to hear God in the midst of our pain, but God is speaking to us. God does not abandon us in our suffering, no matter what we may feel.

After speaking with Job, God speaks to Eliphaz.

> *After the Lord had said these things to Job, he said to Eliphaz the Temanite, "I am angry with you and your two friends, because you have not spoken of me what is right, as my servant Job has. So now take seven bulls and seven rams and go to my servant Job and sacrifice a burnt offering for yourselves. My servant Job will pray for you, and I will accept his prayer and not deal with you according to your folly. You have not spoken of me what is right, as my servant Job has." So Eliphaz the Temanite, Bildad the Shuhite and Zophar the Naamathite did what the Lord told them; and the Lord accepted Job's prayer.* — Job 42:7-9 NIV

They have not spoken rightly about God. Throw out your visions; they are not the truth. Don't believe every tradition of the ancestors. Learn something new. Don't rely on human wisdom and logic. Trust in the Lord with all your heart and lean not unto your own understanding. They are commanded to bring offerings as atonement for their folly, but Job is to pray for his friends.

This is instructive. No one could have been poorer friends than these three were to Job in the midst of his suffering. He felt hurt, angry, upset. He considered never talking with these three guys again, but now God is telling him to pray for his friends. In that

God tells the friends to offer sacrifices, God shows that He is desiring a relationship with these friends. He loves them too. He doesn't want them to keep their sin. He provided a way for the sin to be taken away.

In that God tells Job to pray for them, God shows that He is concerned about their relationship with each other. God doesn't want them to lose their friendship with each other. Forgiveness and reconciliation with those who hurt us, upset us, and make us angry is just as important as forgiveness and reconciliation with God. Notice also that after Job is reconciled with his friends, God begins restoring all his fortunes. "After Job had prayed for his friends, the LORD made him prosperous again and gave him twice as much as he had before" (Job 42:10 NIV).

We are human. We are friends. Unfortunately, we sometimes act like Job's friends rather than like Jesus' friends. Unintentionally, with the best of motives, we hurt each other, we upset each other, we make each other angry. When there is a disruption like this we need to see the Job prescription. Pray for each other. Be willing to pray for each other that we may be healed.

Our relationships with each other as brothers and sisters in Christ are just as important to God as our relationship with Jesus. The two go hand in hand. As we work together to keep our relationships strong, we will find our fortunes being restored and growing. Because even if we don't have material things, we will always have each other.

For Further Reflection

What "traditions of the elders" does your church or denomination cling to? How do they compare to the biblical teaching?

Make a prayer list of people you need to forgive, and commit yourself to pray for them this week. Also, keep a list of the good things that happen to you over the next month.

What does this passage suggest about how we show our Christian care for other members?

Chapter 25

Ezra And Nehemiah: Coming Home From Exile

Ezra and Nehemiah were contemporaries who led the exiles back to Judah to rebuild the city and the temple. Ezra was a scribe of the law who helped the exiles to understand the covenant of Moses and to interpret God's will for the times. Ezra was sent by Artaxerxes to bring back certain gold vessels and ornaments for the rebuilt temple.

Ezra finds a disturbing situation when he arrives in Jerusalem. Many of the Jews had intermarried with other peoples of the area. Such intermarriage was in disobedience to the Mosaic law. In Ezra 9 we have one of the most profound examples of corporate confessions to be found in the Bible. (The others are Moses in Exodus 34 and Daniel in Daniel 9.) Ezra confesses on behalf of those who have intermarried, as if he were guilty himself.

- **What are the sins our of our people that we need to confess as if we were guilty?**

Identifying with the sins of others is not something we often emphasize in the Church today. We have that rugged individualist approach that says, "My sins are my problem and your sins are your problem." To some degree that is true, but we must not overlook the corporate consequences of our sin. Our sin is a problem for all of us. When Achan sinned, the whole Israelite community suffered the consequences (Joshua 7). Jimmy Swaggart and Jim Bakker are responsible for their sins, but their sins have adversely affected the whole Church. Paul says in 1 Corinthians 12:26, "If one part of the body suffers, the whole body suffers, if one part rejoices, the whole body rejoices."

We must also remember that the reason Jesus atones for our sin is that he identified with us as sinners. "He who knew no sin became sin for us" (2 Corinthians 5:21). Jesus was not guilty of any sin himself. Nonetheless, he went to the cross for us, identifying with us as sinners, so that he could cleanse us by his death on the cross.

Nehemiah arrived in Jerusalem thirteen years after Ezra, with a vision of rebuilding the city wall. This was no small task and it was complicated by several factors. For one thing, there were outside enemies who were opposed to this construction project. They wanted to keep the Jews and Jerusalem weak and timid. Building the wall would give the Jews protection and unity.

Another factor, and perhaps more insidious, was the apathy of the people themselves. Some of the wealthy people thought themselves too good for heavy work. They felt the lower classes should do the manual labor. Others worked only on the section of the wall close to their home and didn't consider their neighbor's need for protection.

Nehemiah shows himself to be a firm leader as he confronts these problems. The best example of his leadership is his willingness to make personal sacrifices. In Nehemiah 5:14, he says that he did not take the normal allotment of food or taxes that the previous governors laid on the people. The people had strained under the tax burden of previous administrations which lowered morale. Nehemiah set the example by living on only what he needed and not in opulent luxury at the expense of the working people.

All of us who would be leaders must be those who lead first by example. Because the Church is a volunteer organization, we must show people how to live and work together. The Church cannot be a place where the leader says, "Do as I say, not as I do." Rather, the Church is the place where leaders must "practice what we preach." When people see us living out the principles of Christian teaching in our lives, they are more motivated to follow that example for themselves.

Under the leadership of Ezra who led by prayer and teaching of the word, and Nehemiah, who led by example, the returning exiles rebuilt the walls of Jerusalem and a new temple. They became a nation of Israel again in the midst of troubled times. We live in troubled times as well. God calls all Christians to a level of leadership in this world. People like Ezra and Nehemiah provide us fine examples of how we can practice what we preach.

For Further Reflection

What sacrifice are you willing to make as you lead by example?

Discuss intermarriage in light of the New Testament.

Chapter 26

Just How Bad Is Sin, Anyway?

Psalm 51

Perhaps the most noticeable thing about the Psalms is that they are extremely honest with God. The Psalms are songs that various people wrote, in various situations, in various moods. Some were in pain. Some were happy. Some were written for the worship setting. Others were written as a private song to God. Some are to teach, some are to praise, some are a cry to God for help.

The various writers were honest with God about their feelings and what they wanted to happen. Heal me. Answer me. Deliver me. Let my enemies perish. Save me. From the Psalms we learn that it is okay to be ourselves before God. Some people think that we always have to be in a good mood when we pray, or that we can't say anything angry to God about the way He runs things. The Psalmists don't seem to have these problems. If they are angry with God, they say so. "Why do you let the evil ones flourish while the righteous perish?" In their anger, they never question God's integrity, but they wonder about His methods. In the end, they always come back to confessing the greatness of God, in spite of their circumstances. Many of the Psalms were written by King David. Again, he was honest with God. He wrote in many different circumstances.

- **If you were to be honest with God in the spirit of the Psalmists, what would you say to him?**

The circumstances of Psalm 51 and are worth detailing. The inscription about the Psalm states that it was written after the prophet Nathan had confronted David about his sin with Bathsheba. This is the most notorious act of David and is recorded in 2 Samuel 11-12. From his rooftop he observed a beautiful woman, Bathsheba, as she took her bath. Lust filled his heart. Even though Bathsheba was married to one of David's soldiers, Uriah, David sent for and seduced Bathsheba into an evening of adultery. Bathsheba became pregnant. To cover his crime, David ordered Uriah put at the front of the battle, where he was killed in action. David then married Bathsheba and they had the baby. Everything looked appropriate on the outside to the casual observer. David thought he had gotten away with this crime without any political damage. No one knew a thing. No one, that is, except God ... and Bathsheba ... oh yeah, and David, of course.

- **Speculate as to how David rationalized his actions to God. How does God respond to these excuses?**

As we read this Psalm, we can see that even though David got away with it on the outside, on the inside, his conscience bothered him greatly. In Psalm 51:3 David says, "For I know my transgressions, and my sin is always before me" (NIV). To those who do not know God, or care about God, sin does not bother them. In Psalm 53:1, David says, "Fools say in their hearts, 'There is no God'" (NRSV). But for those of us who love God and believe in God, when we sin, our consciences bother us. We know we have done wrong. Our sin is ever before us. The theological word for this is conviction. It is an act of the Holy Spirit in our lives. In John 16:8, Jesus says the Spirit will convict the world of sin, judgment, and righteousness. When we feel guilty, when our consciences bother us, that is the Holy Spirit telling us that we have sinned and we need to be forgiven.

As his conscience bothers him, David begins to feel separated from God. He knows that this sin is causing a break in his relationship with God. This break is acknowledged in Psalm 51:4. "Against you, you only, have I sinned and done what is evil in your sight, so that you are proved right when you speak and justified when you judge." I'm sure David tried to rationalize and justify himself for quite some time: I couldn't help myself, she was irresistible as I watched her taking a bath. She felt the same way. She could have said no. The baby proves that this must have been God's will for us to be together. It wasn't really me who killed Uriah, he died in battle. I was nowhere near the place.

- **Name a time when your conscience bothered you. What did you do about it?**

No matter what line he used, he knew the truth, and God knew the truth. Because of his sin, he has lost the joy of his salvation. "Do not cast me from your presence or take your Holy Spirit from me. Restore to me the joy of your salvation and grant me a willing spirit, to sustain me" (Psalm 51:11-12 NIV). He felt far away from God. Sin cannot feel God's presence. That line about judgment also shows that David knew the consequences of sin. He knew he deserved to die. Sin is serious and the punishment is death.

- **How do you feel when you know you have sinned?**

The reason our world is in such a mess is because of human sin. We talk about evil in two forms, natural and human. Natural evil includes disasters and accidents which kill people. We believe that because God is in control such things shouldn't happen. But the truth is that the world has been thoroughly corrupted by human sin. In Romans 8:20, 21, Paul says that all creation is subjected to futility by sin. All of creation is eagerly awaiting the day of redemption when things will be as they should be. The reason for the futility is that through sin, we handed control of the world over to Satan. Death surrounds us because of sin. Sin is woven into the fabric of this world and the death that comes with it is woven in as well.

The evil that comes through human sin is the greater problem in the world. Human sin causes all the heartaches and heartbreaks we suffer in this world. Sin causes oppression, injustice, unrighteousness, which then creates poverty, violence, terrorism, and torture. Sin causes all kinds of ugliness like sexual abuse, divorce, racism, greed, envy, covetousness. Truly the list of human evil is long and disgusting. Make no mistake about it, we are responsible for the sin around us. God has not and does not let us off the hook. Sometimes in the goodness of God, forgiveness is accompanied by the softening of the consequences, but most times we must still live with the consequences of our actions.

If we really want to see how ugly, disgusting, repulsive, and evil sin is, all we need to do is look at Jesus on the cross. Jesus on the cross is God's ultimate statement of how horrible sin is in His sight. Sinful human beings, acting on sinful compulsions, took the innocent, harmless Jesus and nailed him to the cross out of their greed, pride, and anger. Jesus also bore our sin on the cross. Sin brings death. The miracle of salvation is that the death we deserved to die, Jesus died for us in our place.

So the good news for David in the Psalm is that forgiveness of sin is available from God. Even David's horrible sins of murder and adultery, not to mention the gross abuse of his royal powers in order to commit these crimes, could be forgiven and in fact were forgiven. How? Through confession, contrition, and repentance. David confessed his sin. He told God the truth of his actions and agreed with God that they were wrong. "Have mercy on me, O God, according to your unfailing love; according to your great compassion blot out my transgressions. Wash away all my iniquity and cleanse me from my sin. Surely I was sinful at birth, sinful from the time my mother conceived me. Surely you desire truth in the inner parts" (Psalm 51:1-2, 5-6 NIV).

Second, David showed genuine sorrow for his sin. "You do not delight in sacrifice, or I would bring it; you do not take pleasure in burnt offerings. The sacrifices of God are a broken spirit; a broken and contrite heart, O God, you will not despise" (Psalm 51:16-17 NIV). David knew that his formal acts of sacrifice were worthless without the heart of truth and sincerity to accompany them. David came to God knowing that God had every right to put him to death, but asking God to forgive.

Third, David asked for forgiveness. "Cleanse me with hyssop, and I will be clean; wash me, and I will be whiter than snow. Let me hear joy and gladness; let the bones you have crushed rejoice. Hide your face from my sins and blot out all my iniquity. Create in me a pure heart, O God, and renew a steadfast spirit within me" (Psalm 51:7-20 NIV). David knew that God was the only one who could forgive him this sin.

Fourth, David repented. He showed his willingness to walk in paths of righteousness. "Then I will teach transgressors your ways, and sinners will turn back to you. Save me from blood guilt, O God, the God who saves me, and my tongue will sing of your righteousness. O Lord, open my lips, and my mouth will declare your praise" (Psalm 51:13-15 NIV). The good news for David, and for us, is that God does forgive our sins. He forgives when we confess, show true sorrow, ask forgiveness, and repent.

We need to underscore that even though David was forgiven, and although he did not die for this sin, he still suffered the consequences. The baby conceived from this act died. David's family life was thrown in turmoil and he lost two other sons. Because sin has such devastating effects, we must avoid sin, rather than think we can get away with sin.

There are some who think they have gotten away with their sin. There are missing children who have never been found. There are unsolved mysteries and murders and assassinations. They may have been covered up in this human world, but God knows the truth. Moses says, "Be sure that your sin will find you out" (Numbers 32:23 NIV). Nobody will escape from the judgment of God. Repent now and be forgiven. That is the good news.

For Further Reflection

Make a "confession list" of all your recent sins. Use this list in a serious time of prayer and confession with God. Go through all of David's steps of confession, sorrow, and repentance. At the end of your time with God, tear up the list and claim God's forgiveness.

Name some of the times your sin had a "ripple effect" and hurt others.

Suppose you had the opportunity to talk David out of his decision. What would you say?

Chapter 27

May I Help You?

Psalm 121

Perhaps there is not a sweeter question to hear when you are in the midst of a problem or troubling situation than, "Can I help?" People with a helping spirit about them can do more to communicate the love of Christ to a person than a thousand sermons. That is because helping puts actions with words. God uses people with a helping spirit to lend His help in the time of need.

This Psalmist was in the midst of some kind of unspecified problem. He needed help. Sometimes there is nothing we can really do to help a person. Words fall short. Actions on our part cannot change the course of reality. I feel this most acutely with people who are dying and know their time is short. What can you really say that is going to change that situation? Unless God grants the healing miracle, there is nothing we can really do either. I have a feeling this was how the Psalmist felt. "I lift up my eyes to the hills — where does my help come from?" (Psalm 121:1 NIV). There is no person who can really help with the Psalmist's problem. He looks to the hills. Where will his help come from? Sometimes we feel just like this. No one can help me now. There is no way out. There is no one who can solve this situation. It is nice to have friends who comfort, well-wishers who try to cheer us up. But in terms of real help, human efforts will not make any serious difference.

- **Talk about some times in your life you felt helpless. Include some times when you felt no one could help you, and when you felt you couldn't help another person.**

There is only one place left to turn. "My help comes from the Lord, the Maker of heaven and earth" (Psalm 121:2 NIV). No matter what the problem or situation, the Lord has the power to make a difference. That is why the Psalmist reminds himself that the Lord is the Maker of heaven and earth. He made them, therefore He has control over them. Whatever situation we find ourselves in, it is an earthly situation. God is the maker of the earth. Therefore, God has power over this earthly circumstance. In effect, the Psalmist is saying, "There is nothing that will happen today that God and I can't handle."

Not only is God the Maker of heaven and earth, but by implication, God also made me. The Psalmist is remembering that he or she is an important part of God's creation. God made me, and God has a plan for my life. That plan is for good, not for evil. It is a plan for salvation and wholeness, not loss. Because I am a child of God, whatever comes my way is God's problem as well as my problem. Because God is in control of my life, I can affirm with Paul that God will provide all my needs through His riches in glory in Christ Jesus.

The Psalmist has other ways of describing God's providence and protection. "He will not let your foot slip — He who watches over you will not slumber; indeed, He who watches over Israel will neither slumber nor sleep" (Psalm 121:3-4 NIV). God is a God who gets no breaks and takes no breaks. You won't find God asleep at the switch in your hour of need. Sleep is the time when things happen and we don't know about them. We cannot control them. Sleep is the time we are most vulnerable, but while we sleep God is always awake. Not only does God watch over individuals, but He has the power to watch over whole nations, in this case Israel. He will not let your foot slip. He will guide us in our steps all the days of our lives.

The Lord's protection is always present so that no harm will come to us. "The Lord watches over you — the Lord is your shade at your right hand; the sun will not harm you by day, nor the moon by night. The Lord will keep you from all harm — he will watch over your life; the Lord will watch over your coming and going both now and forevermore" (Psalm 121:5-8 NIV).

No harm will come to us. How many times have you been protected from something potententially disastrous? We can think of countless times. You left the iron on and the house didn't burn down. You missed the car ahead of you just as they pulled an unexpected turn. You get that intuitive impression to check on your child just as she is about to harm herself. These things happen all the time. The Lord watches over us.

- **Name some of the times you escaped harm or danger.**

Many times and in many ways, we take God's providence for granted. God's providence is seen in the everyday, common things He gives us for the living of our lives. We have air to breathe. We have water to drink. We have clothes to wear. We have houses to live in. Beyond all that, God has provided for various luxuries and conveniences that make our lives a lot easier.

Jesus described the goodness of God in terms of His providing for everyone's needs without discrimination. "Love your enemies and bless those who persecute you that you may be children of your Father in heaven. He causes His sun to rise on the evil and the good, and sends rain on the righteous and the unrighteous" (Matthew 5:45 NIV). Every day the sun shines on every person. It doesn't shine only on the good people. It shines on everybody. God provides the basics of life even to people who don't love Him, don't like Him, don't believe in Him, don't obey Him. While the evil take these things for granted, we as God's children should be continually thankful for God's providing our every need, especially the basics.

Jesus' lesson in providence shows that God provides for all creation; therefore we can trust God to provide for us: "Look at the birds of the air; they do not sow or reap or store away in barns, and yet your heavenly Father feeds them. Are you not much more valuable than they?" (Matthew 6:26 NIV). Jesus says, don't worry about the necessities of life, God knows you need them. Concentrate on the kingdom of God and all these things will be added to you.

The sun will not harm you by day, nor the moon by night. The sun will not smite you by day. We all have seen days when the sun can be brutal. It blinds our eyes. The heat is oppressive. In the desert experience of the Psalmist, having shade as a protection from the sun was truly providential, sent by God. The moon by night. I have never been smitten by the moon. Perhaps the Psalmist is harking back to the fact that God never sleeps. In essence we are under God's watchful care day and night.

"The Lord will keep you from all harm — He will watch over your life" (Psalm 121:7 NIV). Evil is all around us. We have talked at length about Satan and his schemes to do us harm. We pray in our Lord's prayer, "Lead us not into temptation and deliver us from evil, or the evil one." The Psalmist knew about evil.

"The Lord will watch over your coming and going both now and forevermore" (Psalm 121:8 NIV). Here is where the Psalmist lets us know that God's protection and providence does not necessarily mean only in this world. Certainly the Psalmist knew of good people who suffered harm in one way or another. This is not blanket protection. We still need to remember the lesson from Job. But in the going out and coming in forevermore, we hear the Psalmist telling us that there is life beyond this life where God's protection is perfect and we will have nothing to fear. Jesus also tells us not to worry even about life and death. "Are not two sparrows sold for a penny? Yet not one of them will fall to the ground apart from the will of your Father" (Matthew 10:29 NIV). If God concerns himself with the sparrows, God will focus even more attention on us.

So in the basics of life, and in those rock-and-hard-place situations of life, our help comes from the Lord, the Maker of heaven and earth. We can trust God to provide all our needs. We can trust God to protect us from evil, even through death. We should be continually aware and continually grateful for everything that God has provided for us. The Lord will keep your going out and your coming in from this time forth and forevermore.

For Further Reflection

How can you and your church be a help to those who are helpless?

Make a list of all the things God has provided for you. Use this list in your next prayer time to say thanks.

Chapter 28

God Knows Me, Do I Know God?

Psalm 139

One thing that distinguishes human beings from the rest of the animal world is self-awareness. Self-awareness is that mental faculty that tells us we are somebody, we have a past, a present, and a future. It includes the ability to reflect on our thoughts and actions and make changes. It includes our ability to think and reason and question our existence. Because we are self-aware, we are also aware of other human beings, who are self-aware. Our self-awareness gives us the capacity to be in relationship with others to varying degrees. Self-awareness makes us conscious of those things we have in common and our differences. I am aware that I am a man; there are other selves who are women. I am white-skinned. Others are black-skinned, or olive-skinned. As I write this, I am 42 years old. Others are older, younger, or the same.

As we reflect on ourselves in comparison to the stars at night, or when someone close to us dies, we also become aware that we are mortal, earthly, and temporary. Here begin the reflections of our religious consciousness. Is there a being greater than ourselves? What happens to the self when this physical body ceases to function? Many who have done such reflections have come up with various religious systems and beliefs to answer these questions. As Buddha reflected on the suffering in the world, he decided there was no supreme being per se, and that our spirits are absorbed into a great spiritual pool, Nirvana. As Mohammed reflected on these questions, he decided that Allah was the supreme being and our spirits go to be with him. We could take up the rest of the book with what others have developed but all of these have a serious flaw. How do we know which reflects truth and reality?

Since we are self-aware, a supreme being must also be self-aware. In order for us to know God truly, God will have to reveal Himself in some way, show Himself in some way, so that we may know what He is truly like. God is more than human conjecture. We do not like it when people pigeonhole us according to their stereotypes. Why should we then think that God likes it when we describe Him, instead of letting Him describe Himself. The Bible is the record of various human beings who met God and wrote down their experiences with God. As we read the Bible, we begin to see what God is like.

- **Discuss some of the human conceptions of God. How do they contradict what God has revealed about himself in the Bible?**

One person who knew God intimately was King David. Psalm 139 tells us much about what God is like in terms of His knowledge of us. While we may be self-aware, God knows us better than we know ourselves. "O Lord, you have searched me and you know me. You know when I sit and when I rise; you perceive my thoughts from afar. You discern my going out and my lying down; you are familiar with all my ways. Before a word is on my tongue you know it completely, O Lord" (Psalm 139:1-4 NIV). As David describes God's knowledge of us, we see that it is perfect and complete. God knows who I am. This is more than just knowing my name, address, and phone number. God knows who I am. In these opening verses, God knows my words, my thoughts, and my actions. God knows us inside and outside.

Beyond this, God knows the motives and intentions that lie behind my thoughts, words, and actions. This is why making excuses, rationalizing, and other escapist techniques we try on God don't work. They may work with other humans, but not with God. He knows why you give what you give, why you attend church when you do, why you serve where you serve. God knows. Other humans must rely on your words and actions because they can't read thoughts; but God knows everything. That is why we must strive for complete honesty and integrity in everything we do. We are not doing things for other human beings alone. God knows. As

Christians, we have the power of God's Spirit so that we can have a harmony of motives, intentions, thoughts, and actions. David found God's intimate knowledge comforting, but I wonder if it is comforting for us? The only way we can be comfortable with God is when we act with integrity so that our consciences are clean and pure. When we have guilty consciences, God knows that as well.

God also knows where I am, every day, every hour, every minute, every second.

> *You hem me in — behind and before; you have laid your hand upon me. Such knowledge is too wonderful for me, too lofty for me to attain. Where can I go from your Spirit? Where can I flee from your presence? If I go up to the heavens, you are there; if I make my bed in the depths, you are there. If I rise on the wings of the dawn, if I settle on the far side of the sea, even there your hand will guide me, your right hand will hold me fast. If I say, "Surely the darkness will hide me and the light become night around me," even the darkness will not be dark to you; the night will shine like the day, for darkness is as light to you.*
> — Psalm 139:5-12 NIV

There is no escape from God's presence. Jesus promised his disciples that he would be with them always. We confess that God's Spirit lives inside us. Implication — where I am, God is. God sees everything we do, good or bad. If I go to the adult movie theater, I take God with me. If I get drunk and beat my spouse, I take God with me. If I cheat on my taxes or pad my expenses, I take God with me. It is a reminder that we are witnesses for Jesus. The crucial question is, are we good witnesses or bad witnesses?

God knows where we are. This is a comfort in times of trial and tribulation. If I am laid up in the hospital bed, God is with me. If I am in depression or sadness, God is with me. If I am anxious over some problem or person, God is with me. Knowing that God is always with us should encourage us to practice the presence of God by ongoing prayer with God. He is always with us to listen to our requests, our thanks, and our praise. Prayer is always a local call and never long distance because God is always with us.

God knows who I am. God knows where I am. Third, God knows what I am.

> *For you created my inmost being; you knit me together in my mother's womb. I praise you because I am fearfully and wonderfully made; your works are wonderful, I know that full well. My frame was not hidden from you when I was made in the secret place. When I was woven together in the depths of the earth, your eyes saw my unformed body. All the days ordained for me were written in your book before one of them came to be. How precious to me are your thoughts, O God! How vast is the sum of them! Were I to count them, they would outnumber the grains of sand. When I awake, I am still with you.* — Psalm 139:13-18 NIV

God was there when we were blastocysts, embryos, and fetuses. This passage is strong support that human life begins at the moment of conception. God knows us in the womb. Every abortion, then, is the taking of the life of someone God knows intimately. In the womb, God watches as each part is developed and put together. Not only was God creating the physical body, but He created our inmost being, our self, which eventually becomes self-aware.

God knows what we are. We are the handiwork of His creation. We are human beings, the crown of creation. He also knows we are sinners, in need of forgiveness. God thinks about us all the time. David says His thoughts are without number. How often do we think about God? Paul says in Philippians 4:8, whatever is good, pure, lovely, beautiful, and true, that is what we should fix our thoughts on. Paul says in Romans 12:2 to be transformed by the renewing of our minds. Our thought processes should be fixed on God. That is the first place the battle for sin is fought. If we can win the battle in the mind, then our battles in other areas will diminish.

God has numbered our days. I would not read into this a hard and fast doctrine of predestination. I see this affirming our confession that God has a plan for our lives. The days God wrote down constitute His perfect will for our lives, but God has also created us with freedom to choose. We can choose not to follow the script God has written. It is then that we get ourselves in trouble.

- **What times in your life did you follow God's script? What times in your life did you try to rewrite the script to your own preference? What happened?**

God knows what we can become with His power. They are written in the book. We can become victorious Christians who secure the victory of Christ not only in our own lives but in the lives of many others in our city. We can become the people of God, exercising the power of God through prayer to bring down the will of God on earth. We can become the ambassadors of Christ, who through prayer and proclamation and joyous Christian living make a real difference in this world for Christ. God has numbered our days. This is not meant to be fatalistic but liberating. God has a wonderful plan for our lives. Are we willing to trust God and live according to His will so that our script can be fulfilled?

God knows who we are, where we are, and what we are. God knows us intimately. That should encourage us to enter into relationship with God so that we know Him intimately. God invites us into that relationship through Jesus Christ, the Son of God who died on the cross. God knows us. We can know God through a lifestyle that includes a consistent time with God in Bible reading and prayer.

God knows where we are. That should encourage us to be in the places God wants us to be. We need to be with other Christians in worship and service. We need to be with those in need of comfort and encouragement. We need to be with those who need to hear about Jesus and find a relationship with him.

God knows what we are. We need to confess to God that we are sinners, that we have not perfectly followed the script that He ordained for us in the womb. We need to confess that we are forgiven through Jesus Christ. We no longer need to listen to sin, temptation, or the devil. We need to confess that we are the victorious people of God, bought by the blood of the Lamb. We need to confess that we are ambassadors for Christ, God's representatives on earth. It is up to us to spread the love of Christ in word and deed.

God knows us. It is our joy to know God and tell others about Jesus so that they may know God too. Psalm 139 begins with a confession that God already knows us, has searched us, and knows our thoughts. It ends with an invitation to God to continue that process: "Search me and know me and try my thoughts. Lead me in the way everlasting" (Psalm 139:23-24 NIV). As we invite God to know us better, we are inviting ourselves to know God better. In that intimate knowledge of God is eternal life.

For Further Reflection

How do you answer those basic religious questions: Who am I? Why are we here? What is our purpose in life? What happens after death?

Imagine that your "numbered days" ended tomorrow. What would you do differently?

The Psalmist's line about being formed in the womb has been used in the abortion debate. How do you see this Scripture impacting the issue of abortion?

Chapter 29

Wisdom For Everyday Living

Proverbs

As we come to the book of Proverbs we enter into a genre of literature known as the wisdom literature. In these books the virtue and practice of wisdom is exalted and explained. Proverbs 1:7 says that the fear of the Lord is the beginning of wisdom. Only as we trust in God will we have true wisdom. "Trust in the LORD with all your heart and lean not on your own understanding; in all your ways acknowledge Him, and He will make your paths straight. Do not be wise in your own eyes; fear the LORD and shun evil. This will bring health to your body and nourishment to your bones" (Proverbs 3:5-8 NIV).

- **How would you compare wisdom as defined by the Bible with "common sense?"**

The first ten chapters of the book are in discourse form. The major topic is the importance of getting wisdom. The sub-topics include listening to your parents and avoiding adultery. Starting with chapter 10, we have a succession of sayings known as proverbs. They really aren't in any order and are rather repetitive. Yet this repetitive style is intended to help drill in the practical applications of wisdom.

Hebrew wisdom cannot be defined as merely what is intelligent or smart. Hebrew wisdom has to do with putting your smarts into action and living righteously, according to God's will. Teaching is not only to edify the mind. Teaching that has real value is teaching with practical applications so that you can easily put the lessons into action in your life. I want to take as many proverbs and their lessons as we have space in this chapter and think for a minute about their practical applications in today's society.

One major concern of Proverbs is the necessity of parents teaching their children to be wise and the necessity of children to learn wisdom from their parents. One familiar proverb is, "Those who spare the rod hate their children, but those who love them are diligent to discipline them" (Proverbs 13:24 NIV). Similar proverbs are 19:18 and 22:15. I wonder how these proverbs play in a society where the issue of child abuse receives so much media attention. Let's not focus too literally on the rod and forget the point of the proverb. This proverb is talking about the necessity of disciplining children. Discipline does not exclusively refer to punishment for misbehavior. It means that their young lives need structure, order, rules, limits, and boundaries. If these rules are broken or if the limits are crossed then there are negative consequences. Periodically, we hear arguments about how to discipline children. Should they be spanked? Should you try to reason with them? If we stifle their negative behavior will we inhibit their innate creativity? I don't want to get too mired in this swamp, but I will tell you that I believe what the Bible teaches more than I believe what current psychology teaches. In my experience, children who are raised with a balanced upbringing including discipline, freedom, love, and clear explanation of the boundaries of right and wrong become the upstanding adults in society. Children who are raised without discipline consistently come across to me as rude, selfish, and ill-mannered. Proverbs 13:24 is not a biblical license to beat children senseless. The practical application for parents is to establish an environment of discipline so that children will grow up with character.

- **What is your view on child discipline? What is too harsh or abusive discipline?**

The complementary admonition to the children is that they should listen to their parents. "A wise child heeds their father's instructions, but a mocker does not listen to a rebuke" (Proverbs 13:1 NIV). Similar admonitions occur in Proverbs 15:20 and 23:22-25. All of these talk about wise children listening to their parents.

Now I know, parents are square, unhip, clueless, uncool, out of touch, out to lunch, orbiting another planet, not in tune, have no idea, can't relate, dweebs, nerds, and whatever. But the message of the Bible is that your parents are always wiser than what you will give them credit for. Wise children listen to their parents. Why? Because however out of tune or out of touch they may appear to be, they have been where you are already. While they may not want to remember what it was like to be a kid, or a preteen, or a teenager, or a young adult, they do remember. They remember all their mistakes, all the ways they got in trouble, all the stupid things they did that nearly got them killed and in a lot of trouble. The fourth commandment is "Honor your mother and father." You could learn a lot, just by listening to Mom and Dad.

- **What mistakes have you made in your life that you want your child/children to avoid?**

- **Name a time when you experienced your parents as wiser than you thought or gave them credit for.**

Another area for practical living from the Proverbs relates to the current trend for new religions. The writer of Proverbs was familiar with the human propensity to devise our own ways to heaven. "There is a way that seems right to a person, but its end is the way of death" (Proverbs 14:12 NIV). New religions and spiritual ways are cropping up all the time. This is nothing new. The current fad in our country is the mix of humanism and eastern spirituality that manifests itself in what is called the New Age Movement. New Age is really a hodgepodge of various religious teachings and ideas. Some fundamentals include: a) We have the potential to be our own gods. b) Human beings can make the world better. c) If we just get in touch with our spiritual guides, we can live better lives. d) Reincarnation is a reality that we have lived lives in the past. e) Truth is in how you perceive reality. There is no absolute or objective truth.

Many people today want to live in the way that seems right to them. Follow the Ten Commandments. Just do good deeds. Live by the Sermon on the Mount. Love other people. Do unto others as we would have them do unto us. Do no harm. Those who have the most toys win. Do unto others, then split. Thou shalt not hassle. Live and let live. I'm okay and you're okay. Some of these are good, but if we are living by our own ideas, the end is death. In contrast to the way that seems right to us, Jesus says in John 14:6, "I am the way, the truth and the life, no one comes to the Father except by me." If we want to avoid death, we must walk with Jesus, who is the way, the truth, and the life. There is no alternative, there is no second option. We must also avoid the temptation to mix Jesus with other religious or spiritual ideas. It is not Jesus *and*, it is Jesus *alone*. Only Jesus' death on the cross atones for sin. Only faith in Jesus can give eternal life and forgiveness of sins. This goes back to Proverbs 3:5: "Trust in the Lord with all your heart and do not lean on your own understanding." Whatever new way or religion comes to us next, we must measure it by the Word of God. It may seem right, but if it conflicts with the Bible, the end is death. Avoid it.

Several proverbs deal with practical applications as we live our lives in relationship with each other. One problem is anger; sometimes, in the heat of anger we say things we wish later we would not have said. "One who is slow to anger is better than the mighty, and one whose temper is controlled than one who captures a city" (Proverbs 16:32 NIV). Some parallels are 19:11 and 25:28. Wise people control their anger and do not let their anger control them. Anger is a natural, normal, and helpful emotion. Anger tells us there is danger or hurt that we need to respond to. Used wisely, anger can help us grow in our relationships. Used unwisely, anger destroys relationships.

- **When was the last time you got really angry? What happened?**

Another application for wise living is forgiveness. "One who forgives an affront fosters friendship, but one who dwells on disputes will alienate a friend" (Proverbs 17:9 NIV). Forgiveness is as essential to human relationships as oil is to an engine. Both lubricate so that all parts flow freely and unhindered. Jesus obviously thought forgiveness of one another was a critical ingredient in living our lives.

A third area has to do with our work, career, professional relationship, and the economic ties of that relationship. The proverbs have a lot to say about laziness and how that can lead to poverty. "Laziness brings on deep sleep; and an idle person will suffer hunger" (Proverbs 19:15 NIV). My favorite is Proverbs 22:13: "The lazy person says, 'There is a lion outside! I shall be killed in the streets!' " (NIV). As I read the Bible, God has a very low tolerance level for laziness. In 2 Thessalonians 3:10, Paul says, "If anyone will not work, let him not eat" (NIV). When we come to our jobs, we are not working for the boss, or the firm, or the company. We are working for God Himself. We should imagine all our paychecks cosigned by God. The Bible tells us to work as unto the Lord.

The proverbs speak to all ages in all generations. They are here to give us some practical applications for living the Christian life.

For Further Reflection

Given what the Bible says about work, how would this speak to our system of welfare?

How did your parents raise you? Were they strict, loose? What is the most valuable thing they contributed to your life? What was their most dismal failure or fault?

How does Hollywood mix in various religious beliefs for public viewing?

Chapter 30

Is All In Vain?

Ecclesiastes

When you read Ecclesiastes, it is hard to believe that it belongs in the Bible. The tone is despair almost to the point of hopelessness. The Preacher's constant refrain is, "Vanity, vanity, everything is useless and pointless." The word "meaningless" (NIV) or "vanity" (NRSV) is used 25 times in the book.

- How would you answer the Preacher's statement? Is all vanity and meaningless?

- Where do you find hope and meaning?

Ecclesiastes is traditionally ascribed to Solomon, who was at a point in his life where he reflected on all his wisdom and knowledge and was trying to discern the meaning of life. Evidently he didn't find much. Several times, he concludes that there is nothing better in life than to do your job, eat, drink, and be content with what you have. Yet in other places, he says that the whole duty of a person is to follow the commands of God. In chapter 3 he writes, "To everything there is a season." This became the foundation for the song by the Byrds in the 1960s.

What does the book have to teach us? I find significant parallels between the Preacher's experiences and philosophy and our world today. "There is nothing new under the sun. Everything that is happening happened before." We live in a world of intense sensory stimulation. We have radio, stereos, televisions, movies, shows, concerts, computers, and a host of print media. We are able to try just about anything, in reality, or increasingly, in virtual reality. We travel from experience to experience looking for a new high, a new sensation, a new rush. We try bungee jumping, skydiving, and other things that are risky in search of that higher rush.

The Preacher did all this before. He tried everything to see if he could find the meaning of life. He explored sex, food, alcohol. Then he went to the opposite extreme of deprivation and fasting. In all of this, his conclusion was that everything was meaningless under the sun. The best we can do is fear God and keep his commands.

Many people today are searching for meaning through all the things I mentioned above and more such as new age meditation, other religions, drugs, alcohol, sex, and so on. The Preacher's words tell us that they won't find meaning in any of those things. Meaning and purpose in life must come from something deeper and more significant.

Yet the Preacher's conclusion in Ecclesiastes 12:13 is really only the beginning. To fear God and keep His commandments doesn't sound like the abundant life of spiritual power that Jesus promises and delivers. The best we can do is surrender our lives to Jesus and let him be Lord of our lives. At that point, life has meaning and purpose. We become servants of the living God. Jesus gives us a mission to accomplish: to spread the good news of salvation through Jesus to everyone we meet. When we come to Jesus in faith and submission, everything is transformed. The meaningless becomes meaningful. The purposeless becomes purposeful.

That transformation carries over into our sensory experiences. Each new day is filled with God's goodness, providence, and direction. Our material things are no longer toys to be used selfishly but gifts from God to be used as tools in our ministry and mission. We don't have to search for that ultimate rush, because the ultimate rush is knowing God face to face in a living relationship with Jesus Christ.

The message of the Bible as a whole is that there is help for all the people who think life is meaningless and vanity. We can find wholeness by putting our faith in Jesus Christ and following him.

For Further Reflection

What things in the Preacher's list have you tried? What is your opinion of them now?

Chapter 31

This Is Not Logical, Captain!

Isaiah 44 and 46

We modern, sophisticated, cultured, educated, civilized Western Americans truly understand the absurdity of worshiping idols. We would never think of worshiping a statue, idol, totem pole, or picture. Even though we have several pictures and paintings of what someone thinks Jesus looked like, you won't find us bowing down before a picture as if the picture had power to answer our prayers. We emphasize the cross of Christ. Most churches have crosses or crucifixes in the sanctuary, but we do not pray to the cross as if it had some kind of magical power. We confess that we believe that the Bible is the Word of God. Many churches put a Bible on the altar table, but we don't bow down before this table and pray to the Bible.

We realize that these things are just that — things. They are lifeless, inanimate objects with no power. Now we respect what these things stand for. Pictures of Jesus remind us of Jesus and various events in his life. We would never rip up or destroy a picture of Jesus because we would not want to show disrespect. The cross reminds us of the death of Jesus. Burning a cross would show disrespect. We would never tear up a Bible out of respect for God's written word. Nonetheless, they are things. They have no power in and of themselves.

- **How do these various objects make you feel when you see them?**

That is why it is difficult for us to imagine how people in ancient times couldn't figure that out for themselves. Isaiah addresses the issue of idolatry in chapter 44. Here are the iron smith and the carpenter, using the tools and materials of their trade to make an idol or image. Isaiah uses significant amounts of sarcasm in this passage. Isaiah's observes that those who make idols burn half of the tree to keep warm and worship the other half of the tree in the form of an idol. I hear Mr. Spock saying, "That is highly illogical, Captain!" Isaiah agrees. "They know nothing, they understand nothing" (Isaiah 44:18 NIV). In the ancient world, there was widespread animism, worship of spirits who were believed to inhabit things such as trees, rocks, and mountains. There was also idol worship where each idol represents a power. That is why Paul states in 1 Corinthians 10:20 that those who worship idols worship demons. Demonic powers are behind the images.

- **What would you say or do to convince an idol worshiper that the idol has no power?**

Isaiah continues his sarcasm in chapter 46. These idols are false gods that cannot even deliver themselves. They can't transport themselves. If the oxcart in which they have been placed hits a speed bump, they cannot steady themselves. If someone cries to them, they cannot answer.

In contrast to the sarcasm we find wonderfully descriptive prose emphasizing the majesty and holiness of the Lord God Almighty.

> *This is what the Lord says — Israel's King and Redeemer, the Lord Almighty: I am the first and I am the last; apart from me there is no God. Who then is like me? Let him proclaim it. Let him declare and lay out before me what has happened since I established my ancient people, and what is yet to come — yes, let him foretell what will come. Do not tremble, do not be afraid. Did I not proclaim this and foretell it long ago? You are my witnesses. Is there any God besides me? No, there is no other Rock; I know not one.*
> — Isaiah 44:6-8 NIV

If we try to compare God to idols, there is no comparison. The wood is burned in the fire; our God *is* a consuming fire. Humans create idols; God creates human beings. Idols cannot answer; God talks to us all the time. Idols cannot move themselves; God is everywhere. Idols are things of this world; God is the Supreme Being who brings us into the next world.

God is the only God. God created everything. God therefore owns everything. God is the only God to pray to, to talk to, and to worship. God is the only God who can save us and forgive us from our sins. God has a plan for this world and our lives and nothing is going to frustrate that plan or make it fail. "I say: My purpose will stand, and I will do all that I please" (Isaiah 46:10 NIV). We know all this. We are sophisticated Americans. We know that there is no God besides God. Right?

Many in our country, city, and state have been led astray by Satan. Even though you won't find a statue in their house, idols abound in this land of ours. Technically defined, an idol is any *thing* that takes God's rightful place in our lives. Jesus says we can know people by the fruit they exhibit. It really isn't all that difficult. Some people live for self. Self has become an idol because they care about themselves more than they care about God or anybody else. They live for their own pleasure and gain. Some people live for an addiction of some sort. We have a wide variety to choose from. Some people are addicted to essentially good things, but because they overuse them, they become idols. In this category, we could list food and sex. Other addictions include drugs and alcohol. Some people live for material gain either in money or possessions. Some people live for popularity, publicity, or fame. Some people live for power, influence. In all of these, these things have become their reason for living. They may come to church, but not because God is first in their lives. God is a convenience. He is necessary to get to heaven, but let me live my life the way I want to live it.

- **Be honest. What idols are competing for first place in your life?**

The biggest problem is that we don't see that all of these idolatries are just as illogical as bowing down to the statue. Drugs can't move. Drugs can't hear. Drugs can't save. Power with people is not influence with God. Popularity in this world does not guarantee popularity with God. Jesus is still the only God. Beside him there is no other. If Jesus isn't first in your life, you are robbing him of his rightful place in your life. That is idolatry. There is no negotiation, there is no compromise. Jesus must be first. Period. If Jesus isn't Lord of all, then he isn't Lord at all. Jesus can hear us. Jesus can deliver us. Jesus can save us. Jesus deserves to be Lord of all our lives.

The lesson of the craftsmen in Isaiah 44 holds a valuable lesson for us in learning how Jesus must be Lord of all. The craftsmen are guilty of poor stewardship in their lives. Everything they had went to idols. First, they worked overtime on making the idol (Isaiah 44:12). If Jesus is to be Lord of all, he must first be Lord of our time. Time is one of the great equalizers of human beings. No one has more time than another person. We all get 24 hours in each day, seven days in each week, and so on. Our only limit on time is the span of life we have, how long we will live. Since all of us will eventually die, that makes time our most precious possession. We must give all our time to Jesus so that it will be used wisely. Many people live to regret the time they wasted. Time to say, "I love you." Time spent with the parents or the children. Time they spent fashioning an idol rather than doing God's will.

We average 112 waking hours each week. Jesus says that we will be judged on how we stewardship our time here on this earth. Do we use our time serving God, serving people, trying to make this world a better place in the name of Jesus? Or do we spend our time on ourselves, selfishly uncaring what happens to anybody else? Is tithing only for our money or should that apply to our time as well? If we all gave eleven hours to the church each week, how would our attendance, participation, and service be affected? Jesus must be Lord of our time. We must spend our time as he tells us to.

Second, the craftsman spent his talent making the idol (Isaiah 44:13-16). All of us have gifts and talents from the Lord that we use all the time. Most people are blessed that they can use their talents in their careers and employment. It makes the job fun. But if we become workaholics, using work to avoid our other relationships and responsibilities, then we have made idols with our talents and gifts. God calls us to use our gifts and talents within the life of the church to build up the church and help it grow. If you are not using your gifts and talents in the church, then you hinder us from being all we can be and doing all we can do. Jesus must be Lord of our talents and gifts. They must be used as he directs us.

Third, the craftsman used his resources to make this idol (Isaiah 44:14). As Americans, we have been blessed with an abundance of wealth, money, and material possessions. Yet we never seem to be satisfied. There is always more to have, more to want. The practice of tithing is the best cure for this. By giving ten percent from the beginning, we are saying that God comes first in our lives, and here is the proof. When you tithe, you will have to make sacrifices. It isn't that you won't ever get that new thing you want, but you will have to wait for it. By that sacrifice we are making a statement that God comes first. This passage also tells us that stewardship is not just the ten percent God commands. It also has to do with the other ninety percent. If we take the other ninety percent and make an idol from it, then our ten percent tithe will not say anything significant about our faith or priority in God. God owns everything. Everything we have God gave us, and we really don't possess them. We have a temporary lease on these things, that expires when we die. If Jesus is Lord of all, then he must be Lord of our finances. Faithful giving through the ten percent tithe is the best way to show that Jesus is Lord of our finances.

There is only one God. His name is Jesus. Every other thing we would make the center of our lives is an idol. Jesus deserves to be Lord of our lives. Lord of our time. Lord of our talents. Lord of our wealth. We, of course, are sophisticated Americans. We know this. Don't we?

For Further Reflection

How does Isaiah 44:6-8 impact our world of religious pluralism? Are all religions paths to the same God?

Discuss your stewardship of the things God has given you: time, talents, material wealth, and money.

Chapter 32

Higher Thoughts And Higher Ways

Isaiah 55-58

The third section of Isaiah, beginning at Isaiah 55, is a section of hope and restoration. It begins with God's invitation to all those who are thirsty. You may come and drink for free. To all those who are hungry, you may come and eat bread without price. There is the invitation to get to know God personally. He will make with us an everlasting covenant, as He did with David. We are invited to return to the Lord, for God will abundantly pardon. Let the wicked forsake their ways and begin to seek after God.

But then come the questions, "What does God want from us? How are we to seek God? How are we to please God?" Those who worship idols begin with their own ideas of what pleases God. It is no different today. People still want to follow God on their terms rather than on God's terms. If we really desire to follow God, we must follow on God's terms, and God does not necessarily want us to do things the way we think. God's ways are not our ways. God's thoughts are not our thoughts (Isaiah 55:8, 9). Fortunately for us, God tells us what pleases Him and what He is looking for. The Israelites thought they knew what God wanted, but, according to Isaiah, they have only the shell and not the contents.

They ask their first question in chapter 58, "Why do we fast and you don't see it?" (Isaiah 58:3). We need to say from the outset, fasting is a valuable spiritual devotion. When done with proper motives and proper actions, fasting adds power to our prayers. Fasting is denying ourselves some pleasure in order to focus our thoughts on God. Most often, fasting involves denial of food, but we can also fast from sleep, sex, television, or other activities that are morally neutral. So, the Israelites were denying themselves the food and calling that a fast, but their prayers were not answered. What's up, God? What's the deal here? God tells them that they may be fasting on the outside, but that is not all there is to fasting.

- **Have you ever fasted to focus on prayer? What happened?**

In verse 3, God says they oppress their workers and seek after their own interests. With our current labor laws, oppression of workers in the United States has decreased significantly. Yet even though we don't have the outright oppression of workers, it still exists. We hear of immigrants and refugees to this country being put to work in sweat shops. American companies have moved manufacturing operations overseas to take advantage of lower wages and fewer labor restrictions in those countries. Just because it is legal doesn't make it righteous. Even as we look at the current practices of American business, we see down-sizing. Down-sizing results in people having to take on more work without an increase in pay or benefits. Work is a sacred activity in God's sight. Therefore, to oppress workers is to do a serious injustice to those engaged in serving God.

Another form of worker oppression we have become aware of is sexual harassment. Sexual harassment occurs when people in power use their power against those who do not have power for sexual favors or activity. It can be outright and blatant: If you want a raise, here is what you have to do. It can be subtle as an unwanted touch. The message is clear. Fasting, if it is accompanied by oppression of workers, will not result in answered prayers.

- **What other current business practices might be called oppressive?**

Another reason that God wouldn't notice is that the people are seeking their own self-interest. This is such a contradiction to the whole spirit of fasting. Fasting is done to seek God's interests. Fasting is done to secure God's will. Fasting is designed to draw attention away from ourselves and towards God. We should always seek

God's interests, but especially when we are in fasting. They quarrel and fight. Their fighting is violent. Fighting comes from hate and intolerance. Quarreling comes from a refusal to listen and negotiate. If we are at enmity with another person, we cannot be friends with God even if we fast.

God then gives the list of His higher thoughts and ways about what constitutes true fasting. True fasting begins with self-denial that leads us into closer communication with God (Isaiah 58:9). Having heard God and met God, it transforms our actions with the rest of humanity. True fasting, according to Isaiah 58:6, 7, leads us to seek justice and stop oppression. It means sharing our food and resources with the poor, the homeless, and the naked. True fasting means spending time with your family. If we truly meet God when we are fasting, we become better people, more concerned for the people around us.

God says that then our light will shine forth in the darkness (Isaiah 58:8). This is a critical point. Jesus tells us to let our light shine. Our light shines when we show forth God's character through good deeds. People know we belong to Jesus when we do the things Jesus would do. Would Jesus seek justice? Would Jesus free the oppressed? Would Jesus show concern for the needy? Of course he would. If we want people to see Jesus in us, we must show Jesus to them by acts of love and kindness. When we act like this, we are thinking according to God's higher thoughts and acting according to God's higher ways.

The Israelites were also guilty in another area — failing to keep the Sabbath. Oh, they had the day marked on their calendars. They went to the temple and made their offerings. They had the outer form but they lacked the inner meaning. Again, in Isaiah 58:13, God says that they were pursuing their own interests on the Sabbath. Is there a message for modern America in this verse? Technically, the Sabbath is Saturday, and it should be a day of spiritual renewal, rest, relaxation, and recreation. If you are unable to get Saturday off, the spirit of this law is that people should take one day each week and focus on God.

- **What is your "day off"? How do you spend that day?**

For Christians, the day for worship is Sunday, or the Lord's Day. We celebrate Sunday as the Lord's Day because Jesus rose on the first day of the week. Until recently, Sunday has been a day consecrated to church and spiritual activities. The "blue laws" were intended to preserve Sundays for this purpose. With their disappearance, a whole myriad of activities is available on Sunday. We really need to examine our attitudes and actions about Sunday, the Lord's Day. How important is this day to us as a day set aside to the Lord? Certainly, we face our temptations. The malls have sales. The pleasant weather beckons us to the beach, the lake, the mountains, the golf course, or whatever. Sports teams play on Sunday. We certainly want to get there before the crowd builds up. If the weather is not so nice, then it is a great day to sleep in, get projects done around the house, or read the Sunday paper.

- **How do you spend your Sundays?**

For some, Sunday is a drag. Do I haveta go to Sunday school? Do I haveta go to church? The answer is no, you don't haveta. Church is a volunteer organization. You only do what you want to do. Commitment to the Lord on Sunday begins with a commitment to the Lord. If we really care about serving God's interests instead of our own, then Sunday will become a priority for being at church and serving at church. God tells us to call the Sabbath a delight and to keep the holy day honorable. We honor the holy day by honoring God first. We are not to go our own ways or pursue our own interests. Even on a normal Sunday you have from about 1:00 p.m. free to yourself. Many churches still have evening services. However, we need to ask ourselves if reserving only Sunday morning to God is enough. God commands that the whole day be holy unto Him. We can call into question many of the Sunday activities of modern society, sports, leisure, and so forth. Of course, God should be first every day of the week, but putting God first on Sunday, consistently, week in and week out is another way to let our light shine. When we make Sunday school, worship, and special church activities our priorities for Sunday, people know we mean business for God. To the degree that we dilute that day with our own interests, we are saying to those around us, Sunday is my day, too. God got His part, now I get my part. Maybe God gets His part if I feel like it. If we honor God's day for God, the Bible promises that we will ride upon the heights of the earth. In Isaiah 56:4-8, He makes other promises of blessing to those who keep the Sabbath.

Jesus calls us to let our light shine among people that they will glorify God for the good works they see in us. Our light will shine if we combine the outer activities with the inner truth. Meaningful religion must be an inside and outside activity. When we fast on the outside, we must meet God on the inside and do His will. When we come to church, it should be to honor the day for God. When we do these things, we are acting according God's ways and thinking God's thoughts.

For Further Reflection

Discuss some of the popular conceptions of God today. For example, some believe God doesn't send anyone to hell. What others can you think of?

Some churches have started to have worship services on other days and nights of the week. What do you think about this?

Suggest some changes American business could make to be more in line with scriptural teaching.

Chapter 33

Do Not Pray?

Jeremiah 7:16; 11:14; 15:1

I have a lot of sympathy for the prophet Jeremiah. He had one tough ministry. Jeremiah was prophet for the forty years before the exile to Babylon. Those forty years were years of decadence and decline in Israel. There was political decline as the kings of Judah were deported by various conquerors. They were replaced with kings who had no leadership ability. There was social decline as segments of the population were deported to Babylon. There was moral decline. Idol worship was rampant. Injustice abounded. There was spiritual decline. The Israelites had religion on the outside, but no spiritual power on the inside.

Into this setting, God called Jeremiah to preach to a people who had no desire to listen. They were intent on living the way they wanted to live. The Israelites at this time felt they were divinely protected from any invasion because they had the temple of the living God in their midst. Jeremiah tried every way to convince them that having the temple of God meant nothing if they did not live according to God's will, laws, and decrees.

- **Discuss some times you had to talk to people who had no desire to hear what you had to say.**

As you read through Jeremiah, until chapter 30, you find the messages from God getting increasingly more angry and threatening. You would think that with all these threats, people would listen, but the leaders of the time scoffed at Jeremiah and threatened his life. The people followed the example of their leaders and didn't listen to the prophet's message.

Jeremiah had a difficult ministry preaching to people who didn't want his message. His life was threatened several times. Two times, he was brought to trial. He was imprisoned. Only because God intervened did Jeremiah live to see the fall of Jerusalem. Jeremiah is often called the weeping prophet. That is because the book of Lamentations which follows is credited to Jeremiah. Even without Lamentations, Jeremiah had every reason to cry. He lived to see the nation of Israel totally defeated, humiliated, and exiled. He lived to see the temple of the living God burned to the ground. Reading through this book, I would title it, "When God Gets Angry." Angry is probably too mild a term. Let's say, "When God Gets Totally, Completely, Irreversibly Enraged."

Lots of nasty things happen when God gets this angry. I remember a television show from the 1980s, *The Hulk*, with Bill Bixby. The opening scenes included one where he said, "Don't make me angry. You wouldn't like me when I'm angry." The Hulk is tame compared to an angry God. The important thing to learn here is that God can and does get angry. We so often emphasize the love and the grace and the forgiveness of God that we forget that God is also a God of wrath. Paul says in Romans 1:18 that the wrath of God is continually revealed from heaven against all unrighteousness. Sin makes God angry. While we rejoice that we are forgiven because of Jesus' death on the cross, we must remember that Jesus went to the cross in the first place to take our punishment because God was angry with us.

If we look around at paintings of Jesus, we see a depiction of a humble, meek, quiet kind of man. It is hard to picture that man as angry. Yet when we read about the driving of the merchants from the temple, or the letters to the churches in Revelation 2 and 3, we see a Jesus who gets plenty angry.

Why was God so mad at the Israelites? Because they said they loved Him, but lived their lives entirely against His will. Sin makes God angry. People who know God, who have heard God's laws and decrees, should know better. Israel had the law. The people knew what God wanted, but they did not obey. In the midst of their disobedience, they still expected God to love them and protect them. They were clueless.

- **Discuss some beliefs and practices in the Church today that you think make God angry.**

The lesson for us is that our walk must match our talk. It is not enough to say, "Jesus, I love you," or "Jesus, save me." Our lives must demonstrate our belief in our statements. If our lifestyles do not match what Jesus teaches us in the Bible, then we are no better than Israel in the time of Jeremiah. Jesus says in Matthew 7:21, "Not everyone who says to me, 'Lord, Lord,' will enter the Kingdom of heaven. But the only the one who *does* the will of my Father who is in heaven" (NRSV). Our doing must match our speaking. This was the primary problem of Israel. The people said they loved God, but they were not doing God's will. That makes God very angry.

What about America? Some people call us a Christian nation. I guess that implies we know what God wants. How are we doing? God condemns Israel for its violence, murder, and crime. Can anyone doubt that we in the United States have a problem with violence and murder and crime? The history of this nation has a foundation in violence as we slaughtered the Native Americans and took possession of their land. That violence continued as each new group of immigrants was oppressed on the bottom rung of the social ladder. There has been racial violence. We have millions of abortions each year in this country. Can such murder of unborn innocents go unnoticed by God? We have violence in the schools and violence in the media. Are we less deserving of judgment than Israel?

God condemned Israel for its political corruption. One look at our political system reveals widespread corruption. In several major and minor cities, politicians are being indicted and convicted for corruption. The corruption spreads to state governments. This corruption reaches to the House and Senate. With Watergate, Whitewater, the Lewinsky scandal, and the campaign financing scandal, it has even reached the President and Vice-President of the United States. Are we less deserving of judgment than Israel?

God condemned Israel for its moral depravity. While freedom of the press has been a blessing in some ways, it has also led to the proliferation of pornography, including the most depraved kind of pornography such as child pornography and snuff films. We have an epidemic of child abuse. Are we so much better than Israel that we don't deserve judgment?

God condemned Israel for its spiritual depravity. How are the churches in America doing, really? While I have hope for the future, the Church has contributed to the above problems over the years. Churches get ingrown. Churches have had KKK members as their deacons. Churches have not spoken out with a unified voice because we all have different views on some issues like abortion, homosexuality, gambling, and a host of other issues. According to recent surveys of American religious beliefs and practices: nine percent of the population read their Bible daily, 44 percent attend church four times per month, 28 percent don't attend at all. Fifty-two percent think that it doesn't matter what religion you follow because all are alike. Forty-five percent agree that we have a responsibility to tell others our religious convictions. Sixty-one percent believe that if you live a good life you can earn a place in heaven. Thirty-six percent believe that Jesus must have made some mistakes. Sixty-four percent have made a personal commitment to Christ. Eighty-five percent believe Jesus was crucified, dead, resurrected, and is spiritually alive today. With so much confusion in the church, is it any wonder why there is confusion outside the church? (George Barna, *The Barna Report*, 1994: Ventura, CA; Regal Books, 1993, pp. 165-305).

We have to ask, "Why did Israel go into exile but America is still here?" If we look closely at Jeremiah, I see one critical component. Jeremiah was commanded *not* to pray for his people. Not once, not twice, but three times. When Jesus said we are the salt of the earth, one of the ways we act as salt is through our ongoing intercession for our city, our state, our nation, and our world. Our prayers for our leaders, and for our nation, hold back the hand of God's judgment on this nation.

At this time, I am not aware that God has commanded the Church to stop praying. Our prayers will have their maximum effect if we live according to God's will. I am sure that there were many Israelites praying to God, but because they did not live according to God's will, their prayers were not listened to. It seems that Jeremiah is the only one God would listen to because he was righteous, and yet God commands him not to pray. God says flatly that he won't listen. Once the prayer protection is removed, judgment is sure to come. The condition of Israel was so bad that there was no way prayer could help. God says that even if Moses and Samuel were praying, it wouldn't be enough to keep the judgment away (Jeremiah 15:1).

We must be people of constant, consistent prayer. As long as we are faithful in our praying, there is hope for God's blessing. God will bless our city, our state, our nation, and our world. Obviously, there is one major condition to this. We must do God's will. Doing God's will begins with us. Truly, the only people we can control are ourselves. As we live holy lives before the Lord, that too acts as salt for the world. We also give other people an example to follow. Just as Jeremiah experienced, not everybody is going to listen to our message and obey. But God has called us to the mission of telling others about Jesus Christ and the forgiveness of sins available in Christ. God has called us to the ministry of intercessory prayer for the world around us. Until God commands us to stop, we must make prayer a priority in our lives. If we don't pray, we have only to look at what happened to Israel, and realize that America deserves the same kind of judgment. That judgment will come, unless we model God's will, unless we pray.

For Further Reflection

How would you answer God if He told you *not* to pray for a certain situation that you were very concerned about?

What signs of God's anger or wrath do you see in today's world?

What changes will you make in your prayer life, or in the prayer life of your church, based on this Scripture?

Chapter 34

Between The Lines: The Prophets

The major Old Testament prophets — Isaiah, Jeremiah, Ezekiel and Daniel — had a unique ministry to Israel before, during, and after the exile to Babylon. The exile came because of Israel's faithlessness by worshiping idols. The exile is viewed as a watershed event in the history of Jewish religion. It was in exile that the Pharisees and Saducees had their beginnings. There was a cleansing of the Israelite religion and a return to faithfulness to the Mosaic Law. Prophets were recognized as prophets because their words had come true. Because the temple in Jerusalem had been destroyed, synagogues became the center for Jewish worship.

The prophets consistently emphasized the importance of prayer. Isaiah tells the story of Hezekiah's prayer when Sennecherib threatened Jerusalem. That night, an angel destroyed the Assyrian army. Jerusalem was spared. Jeremiah shows the importance of prayer for a city by showing what happens when we don't pray. Daniel was a man of prayer. His prayer life led him to the lion's den, and out again. Ezekiel also understood the importance of prayer. In Ezekiel 22, God catalogs the list of Israel's sins. In Ezekiel 22:30, God says, "I looked for a man among them who would build up the wall and stand before me in the gap on behalf of the land so I would not have to destroy it, but I found none" (NIV). God is always searching for at least one person to stand in the gap. This is an awe-inspiring picture of the intercessor before God and how much influence the intercessor can carry.

Moses stood in the gap on several occasions. He pleaded for Israel. God heard Moses and did not wipe them out entirely (Exodus 32:11-14). Samuel stood in the gap during his ministry. Even though Israel asked for a king, God was gracious because of

Samuel's intercession (1 Samuel 8). Elijah and Elisha stood in the gap in their ministry. All of these prophets were intercessors as well as preachers, teachers, and healers. They prayed to God on behalf of Israel. God heard their prayers and Israel was spared, saved, and in some cases, renewed, and revived.

God is continually searching for intercessors, pray-ers, people who will come before God and stand in the gap. These are people who don't whitewash the sin of the land. They don't pretend there aren't problems. Rather, they come honestly before God confessing the sins and the problems. They come showing repentance asking for forgiveness and renewal. They come asking God for grace instead of judgment, mercy instead of punishment. Notice Daniel's prayer in Daniel 9. He confesses the sin of the nation, and then is bold enough to ask God for forgiveness and return to the promised land. Daniel stood in the gap.

God calls all His children to stand in the gap to some degree. We are all called to pray for one another that we may be healed (James 5:16). We are called to humble ourselves and pray and seek God's face (2 Chronicles 7:14). We are called to lift up supplications, prayers, intercessions, and thanksgivings for everyone, for kings and all who are in high positions (1 Timothy 2:1-2). While there are some who are truly gifted as intercessors, all believers in Christ are commissioned to be interceding for their world, their nation, their people, and the Church of Jesus Christ.

I invite you to come stand in the gap, to be a prayer partner with others who have a burden, to pray for your city and your church. As God searches for people to stand in the gap, I encourage you to echo Isaiah's response, "Here I am, send me!"

For Further Reflection

Read Deuteronomy 18:15-22. What are the other ways of validating a prophet from the Lord?

What connection do you see between being a prophet and being a person of prayer?

Chapter 35

How To Treat Your Bible

Jeremiah 36

The year is 1844. The place is Saint Catherine's Monastery, at the foot of a mountain in the Sinai peninsula, which is traditionally known as Mount Sinai. The man is Konstantin von Tischendorf, a Christian scholar from Russia. He is a visitor to the monastery and notices a large basket full of old parchments. The librarian tells him that these heaps of moldy paper are all over the place and they use them to start fires. As Tischendorf inspects one of the parchments he recognizes the pages of an ancient Greek Bible. He is so excited that the monks perceive they have something valuable and they let him take only forty pages.

- **How would you have convinced the monks to stop burning the paper without giving away your excitement over them?**

In 1853 he arranges a return visit. He hopes to obtain the rest of the sheets, but now only a scrap remains. This scrap had been used as scratch paper. On a third visit in 1859, he is having refreshments with one of the monks, and in conversation the monk casually mentions that he has read the Septuagint, the Greek Old Testament. He takes down a bulky volume wrapped in red cloth and lays it before Tischendorf. To his surprise, it is the same fragments from fifteen years before and other portions of Scripture. "Full of joy, which this time I had the self-command to conceal from the steward and the rest of the community, I asked, as if in a careless way, for permission to take the manuscript into my sleeping chamber to look it over more at leisure. There I could give way to the transport of joy which I felt. I knew that I held in my hand the most precious biblical treasure in existence" (T. S. Kepler, "Sinaiticus," *The Interpreter's Dictionary of the Bible*, Vol. 4, [Nashville: Abingdon, 1962], p. 378). Tischendorf eventually received permission to take the manuscript, which is now in the British Museum.

What was Tischendorf so excited about? A fourth century (300-399) Greek codex (book) manuscript of the Bible containing the entire New Testament and practically all the Old Testament before Ezra 9:9 and other later portions.

The Word of God is like that, isn't it? Some people read it and feel wondrous joy and transport, like Tischendorf. Others read it and want to destroy it, like King Jehoiakim whom we read about in Jeremiah 36:20-26. Don't you get a shiver down your spine as you read the passage about the king slicing up the scroll and throwing it in the fire? Even though most of the king's servants didn't outwardly protest for fear of the king, I wonder if on the inside they were thinking, "That's gutsy." "I wouldn't want to fight God like that." "Are you crazy?" "Stand back so I won't get hit by lightning." "This guy is cold." Three men did urge the king to stop, but I wish they would have said something more. It seems as if they really cared what Jeremiah said because they brought it to the king.

- **What would you have said or done if you were these men?**

Every time I read this, I can't believe anyone could be so impudent, proud, rude, crass, and callous as to burn the words of God a little bit at a time. Yet throughout history, the Bible has had its enemies, critics, and persecutors. In 303 A.D. the Roman emperor Diocletion gave an edict that all Christian Scriptures should be destroyed. He evidently didn't succeed. In 1778 the French philosopher Voltaire predicted that within 100 years Christianity would be swept into history and pass away from the scene. Fifty years later, the Geneva Bible Society used his printing press to produce stacks of Bibles. Many have criticized the Bible and tried to convince us that it isn't relevant, isn't the Word of God, isn't useful. But the Bible still remains at the top of the all-time bestseller list. Jehoikim's actions are not unique, but they do raise questions about how we got our Bible, and what we do with our Bible.

The Old Testament began with oral traditions. Since this was the major method of transmitting history, books and writing were not common. It took a long time to produce a single scroll. Little by little Jewish leaders began writing down the various stories, laws, poems, and prophecies. Typically, the writings of prophets were not accepted at first; witness the scroll of Jeremiah in this passage. But as the prophecies were fulfilled, the Jews recognized that God had spoken through His prophets. Their prophet's messages were valuable not only for the generation contemporary to the prophet but also for generations to come. The Hebrew Bible was translated into Greek by about 100 B.C. By the time of Jesus, several Hebrew and Aramaic scrolls were in existence.

Until 1947, the oldest Hebrew text we had was the Massoretic Text dating from about 900 A.D. The Hebrew Bible was copied by scribes throughout the centuries. The Hebrew canon was officially formed at the council of Jamnia in 90 A.D. Unofficially, this same canon had been in use since about 400 B.C. That means that between the finalizing of the canon and the Massoretic Text, there were about 1300 years of copying time. How do we know there weren't any mistakes made in all those years of copying? The discovery of the Dead Sea Scrolls in 1947 helps answer this question. The scrolls give us Old Testament texts dating to 125 B.C., nearly 1000 years older than the Massoretic Text. The two texts agree 95 percent of the time and the differences are mostly cosmetic.

The New Testament also began as oral tradition, but within a generation the first books were written. As early as 60 A.D., Paul's letters were known as a collection and were circulated among the churches. At first the sayings of Jesus were passed on from the apostles to their disciples. They took written form as the Gospels between 50-100 A.D. The earliest complete text we have of the New Testament dates to about 200 A.D. Some fragments date even earlier to about 125 A.D., less than 100 years after the death of Jesus. There are about 5,000 Greek manuscripts with various amounts of the New Testament. While there are variations among the manuscripts, most are spelling or grammar variations and do not significantly affect interpretation, theology, or Christian doctrine. The Hebrew Scriptures were closed in 90 A.D. by the Council of Jamnia. The New Testament Scriptures were endorsed by the Council of Hippo in 393 A.D.

- **How many Bibles are in your home? How often are they read?**

If we are to respect and revere the Bible as the written Word of God, we must have confidence that what we are reading is what the authors wrote. Beyond that step of faith is to trust that what the authors wrote is what God inspired them to write. My own statement of faith is that I believe the Bible to be the inspired, God-breathed Word of God. It is useful for teaching, correction, rebuke, and training in righteousness (1 Timothy 3:16).

But before we pat ourselves on the back and commend each other for our faith in the Bible as the Word of God, we need to examine our actions more closely. We say the Bible is the Word of God, but do we act like it is the Word of God? Are we any better than Jehoiakim if we take out our interpretation razors, hack the Bible to pieces, and throw it away in the fires of higher criticism and scientific rationalism? Most Christians are guilty of selective obedience. Granted, it's necessary to exercise discernment as we read, but we must be extremely careful about what parts of the Bible we choose to explain away and not obey. On the other hand, we must be careful not to overemphasize a particular doctrine or teaching that is not critical to Christian faith.

Once we open the door to wrong use of the Bible, even a tiny crack, a whole Pandora's box of heresy and false teaching can sweep in as well. What have we made all-important? What have we hacked off? There is still controversy over issues like women in the pulpit (1 Timothy 2); women wearing hats (1 Corinthians 10); anointing the sick with oil (James 5); handling snakes and drinking poison (Mark 16); baptizing dead people, or proxy baptism for dead people (1 Corinthians 15); foot washing (John 13); speaking in tongues (1 Corinthians 12).

There are numerous major points concerning morality and doctrine. Sexuality, especially homosexuality, is an area where people are trying to alter or dilute or reinterpret the moral standards God has given. The reality of Satan, demons, spiritual warfare, and hell are being questioned. The reality of miracles, including the virgin birth and resurrection of Jesus, are being denied by those considered to be learned scholars. Some deny the sinless perfection of Christ. Some deny the reality of sin and the necessity of repentance. All of these things are taught by the Bible. Which doctrines have we taken the penknife to?

Believers are called to study the Bible as the Word of God. Reading the entire Bible through annually is a way of fulfilling that call. If we don't read our Bible, if we don't come to Sunday school to study and understand the Bible, if we don't obey the Bible, we are no better than Jehoiakim. We can shudder and gasp in horror at how much disrespect he shows for the Word of God, but we have to ask ourselves if our actions are that much better. Begin today reading your Bible through. Choose a Sunday school class or Bible study group to increase your learning. Feel free to ask questions. The Bible is the written word of God. Let's revere it with joy and not hack it to pieces.

For Further Reflection

Discuss some doctrines from the Bible that your denomination or church have developed from the Bible. In the list of controversial doctrines above, where does your church stand?

What do you believe about the Bible? Which parts do you emphasize? Which ones do you avoid?

Chapter 36

A Tale Of Three Cities

Ezekiel 3, 9, 10 and Acts 19

It was the best of times, it was the worst of times.

For the city of Jerusalem in 587 B.C., it was the worst of times. We see in Ezekiel just how depraved the Israelites had become. In a vision recorded in Ezekiel 8, God shows Ezekiel idols and images within the temple of God. People were bowing down to the idols and worshiping. The elders of Israel, thinking they were not seen, were in the temple worshiping vile images. The women were worshiping Tammuz, a Sumerian fertility god. They were worshiping the sun god of Egypt.

It was the worst of times. God says to Ezekiel in 9:10, "As for me, my eye will not spare, nor will I have pity, but I will bring down their deeds upon their heads" (NRSV). There was no longer any recourse or hope. Judgment was on the way. Just as we saw judgment coming when God told Jeremiah to stop praying for Jerusalem, here in Ezekiel we see another image that shows the inevitability of the coming judgment. In Ezekiel 10-11, Ezekiel watches as the glory of the Lord, which had dwelt in the temple above the ark, came up out of the temple and departed Jerusalem. God's presence could no longer stand the stench of unrepented sins. God's glory departs through the east gate, to the Mount of Olives and on to heaven. It isn't too long after this vision that Jerusalem was conquered and the people were taken into exile. It was the worst of times. Why did this happen?

- **If you had seen the glory of the Lord depart from Jerusalem, what would you have done next?**

Time and again the Bible insists that the Israelites went into exile because of their unfaithfulness to the covenant God had given them. They were not supposed to worship idols. They were not supposed to rob widows or orphans or take advantage of the poor. But they did all these things with impunity. God warned Israel that if the people did not keep their part of the covenant, they would not be allowed to stay in the promised land. God abandoned them to their sins, and they reaped what they sowed. It was the worst of times in Jerusalem in 587 B.C. The people turned away from God, and God turned away from the people. Judgment and suffering were the only options left.

Acts 19 describes the best of times in the city of Ephesus around 53 A.D. Ephesus was a city ripe for the gospel. The ground had been prepared by Apollos sometime before. Even though Apollos had not preached the whole gospel, what he preached made the people hungry for more. Enter Paul, who gave them the rest of the story about Jesus Christ. The people believed, repented, and the Holy Spirit filled them. The Bible says that God did extraordinary miracles through Paul which served to confirm the preaching about Jesus (Acts 19:11).

The Bible also describes the battle with the evil spirits in Ephesus. Ephesus was a city engrossed with evil. The people worshiped Diana or Artemis. Ephesus was the center for Artemis worship, trafficked through a huge temple built for her. We also know that before the coming of the gospel, the people practiced magic arts and talked with demons. The miracles Paul did confirmed that Jesus was more powerful than Satan. But only those who know Jesus have Jesus' power. Acts 19:13-16 records the story of the sons of Sceva as they tried their own formula for exorcism in Jesus' name and it backfired. That incident proved to the people that Jesus, as preached by Paul, was the most powerful. Revival broke out throughout the city. People brought their magic books and burned them as a symbol of their belief and repentance.

- **What do you believe about exorcism and spiritual warfare?**

The Word of the Lord grew mightily and prevailed. It was the best of times. People were being saved. Lives were being transformed.

Families were together. The power of evil retreated into the darkness. Light prevailed. The Church grew. Love abounded. Crime decreased. It was the best of times. Jesus was Lord over Ephesus.

- **Is it the best of times or the worst of times in your city or town?**

It is the best of times and the worst of times in present day America. In ways it is the worst of times. Our government at all levels has become corrupt, greedy, and full of lust and covet. Leadership has degenerated into partisan bickering with the citizens becoming the biggest losers. There is dissension and strife among various leaders over the place of social services to the poor and needy. We have homeless people roaming the streets while abandoned buildings rot in the noonday sun and other houses are being torn down as eyesores. And, yes, we have machine guns in the streets, drugs, gangs, murder in the schools, poverty, and teenage pregnancy.

In ways, it is the best of times. New companies are starting, renewing some factories and giving hope for future jobs. Downtowns are physically renewed and only await some courageous businesses to come in and make a go of it. We have churches, brothers and sisters in Christ of all persuasions who truly care about this country and are praying to God to bless this nation and working with each other to make that prayer a reality.

But if we really want the best of times, we need revival from the Lord on a grand scale comparable to Ephesus in Acts. If survey numbers hold true, around 43 percent of people in the United States attend church regularly. Based on a population of 250 million, that means somewhere around 150 million people in this country have no church home, or no relationship with Jesus. While perhaps we are not into magic, Satan has used all kinds of deceptions to help people drift away from God, Jesus, and the Church. Our first order of business is to pray for God's power to come on this city in a mighty way. We need miracles as Paul had to confirm the message of the gospel. We need unity among the Christians that Jesus is Lord and only Jesus can save.

- **What else do you think we need for revival in America?**

In Ezekiel 3, God appointed Ezekiel a watchman over Israel. He was personally responsible to see that God's messages were delivered. If he did not, he was responsible for their lives. We are responsible for our cities and towns. God has appointed us as watchmen and watchwomen. That duty includes fervent prayer for the salvation of people in your city. That duty includes bold witness about God's salvation through Jesus Christ. That duty includes unwavering faithfulness to the vision and mission of the Church. We must abandon our addiction to the idyllic American life and ask ourselves, "What does God want us to do?" We are not here to seek our own pleasure and luxury. We are here to accomplish a mission for God. That mission will mean a sacrifice of time and money and resources and ability. We are the watchmen. We could have truly the best of times if we will take our responsibility seriously. Pray, witness, and be faithful.

For Further Reflection

What sin in America do you see that might cause God's glory to depart?

What can your church do to bring revival in your city or town?

Chapter 37

God Has A Plan

Daniel 7

Daniel lived during troubled times for Israel. Around 600 B.C., he was exiled to Babylon at an early age. Because of his abilities and talents, which he used for God, he became an important official in the Babylonian government. Daniel was also a prophet who had the ability to interpret dreams from God. He saved the wise men of Babylon by interpreting Nebuchadnezzar's dream. In chapter 7, Daniel himself receives a dream, and a wild dream it is.

- **How seriously do you take your dreams? Do you believe God can speak through your dreams?**

This is the kind of dream that makes you wonder what Daniel ate before he went to bed. Daniel sees a vision of four beasts: a lion with eagle's wings, transformed into a human-like creature, a bear, a leopard, and a dreadful, indescribable beast. No more garlic with ice cream before bed. As the angel interprets this vision in Daniel 7:17, we understand that these beasts represent four empires of the ancient world. These empires are further described in the vision in Daniel 8. I don't want to speculate as to their present identities. I don't think the import of the passage rests with the identification of these beasts with specific nations, past, present, or future.

We should make some general observations about what these beasts represent within the passage. First, they represent human kingdoms. Specifically, because they arise out of the sea, they represent Gentile nation empires. Second, the stirring of the sea shows the restless nature of humankind without God (Isaiah 57:20). The nations always are restless. Because they need something, anything, to do, they decide to try militarism. These beasts represent violent, militaristic, oppressive, military nations. The bear has teeth to devour. The leopard has dominion given to it. The fourth beast is extremely cruel and violent. Third, each of these beasts is here today and gone tomorrow. One empire rises, then falls as another rises and then falls. Human empires, kingdoms, and nations are temporary. Borders are always changing, wars change whole countries. Life is hard when an oppressive regime is in power, but every regime or empire is temporary. Think about all the fallen empires: Egypt, Assyria, Babylon, Greece, Rome, the Barbarians, Genghis Khan, the Ottoman Turks, the British empire, the Moors, Nazi Germany, the Japanese empire, communist Russia and its satellites, just to name a few. They come, they oppress, they fall.

Human beings from various corners of the world have tried to rule the world through various methods. Some rule through fear and oppression; we call them dictatorships. Some rule through military power and presence. Some rule through economic power and oppression. We have tried monarchy, oligarchy, anarchy, socialism, communism, idealism, rationalism, democracy, republics, commonwealths, states, militarism, colonialism. All of these forms of government have one huge problem. Sinful human beings are in charge. While some systems have their advantages, all have weak points as well. Their common weak point is that none address the inherent sinful human nature that besets us. Even the best of these systems can be twisted and perverted so that the rich get richer, the poor get poorer, the powerful get more power, the weak become weaker, and so on.

- **Discuss the strengths and weaknesses of the American Government in light of the Bible.**

Will there ever be a government on earth that can maintain order so that human beings will be truly free and prosperous? In Daniel's vision the answer to that question is found in the coming of God's kingdom. Daniel 7:9 says the kingdom was established, "as I watched." Those three words are so important: as I watched.

The kingdom of God does not come like human kingdoms. It does not come by human will and energy. It does not come with human power and military might. It does not come by human intellect, wisdom, or political philosophy. It does not come by revolution or ballot box.

The kingdom of God comes as Daniel watches and as we watch. The coming of the kingdom leaves us on the sidelines as God takes total control of the situation. Thrones are set in place, and the Ancient of Days takes his throne. Notice the parallels of the description of the Ancient of Days here and of Jesus in Revelation 1. They both have clothing white as snow, denoting purity of character and being. They both have hair like wool, denoting wisdom and omniscience. They both have thrones of fiery wheels and streams of fire from their presence, symbolizing the penetrating nature of God's judgment and righteousness.

Judgment is passed on all the nations, and especially the nations and emperors who were arrogant. God will judge our leaders, presidents, kings, prime ministers, senators, dictators. Some will lose their dominion but be allowed to live, but those who have arrogantly defied God will be punished. Why should we be praying for our political leaders? Because we are the watch people. We must pray for them to do God's will so that when their judgment comes, it will go well with them.

We need to pray that the United States doesn't become one of those arrogant nations. It didn't happen overnight to Germany in the 1930s. They woke up one day in the 1940s and they had become arrogant, slaughtering millions of God's chosen people, the Jews. It won't happen overnight in America, but we show some signs of arrogance:
- abortion on demand;
- the elimination of prayer in schools as well as in our own personal lives;
- a criminal justice system more concerned with the wrongdoer than justice for the victim;
- white supremacists, racists, and hate mongers who are rewarded by the government; and

- weakening churches, turned inward, worried more about their own pleasure than reaching the world for Christ and making it a better place.

Human governments fail, but the kingdom of God will be established as we watch.

Then comes a human being to the Ancient of Days. He comes with clouds of heaven. That is how the coming of Jesus is described. He is given dominion and glory and kingship, that all peoples, nations, and languages should serve him. His dominion will never pass away. Here is Jesus, being proclaimed and appointed King of the world by the Father, the Ancient of Days. Human kingdoms are temporary, but the reign of Jesus shall never end. The angel says to Daniel in 7:18, "The holy ones of the Most High shall receive the kingdom and possess the kingdom forever" (NRSV). The wonderful thing about King Jesus is that he has no need or desire to hoard his power. He shares his power with his saints, his holy ones. That's us.

There are times when we need God's perspective. Everything on this earth is temporary. Nothing is permanent, even if it is written in stone. The O.J. trial finally ended. Saddam Hussein will eventually die or lose power. *Titanic* finally left the movie theaters. The things around us are as temporary as the beasts in Daniel's dreams. Much as we try to set up our own little fiefdoms, thinking they will last, sooner or later we learn that nothing is permanent. We raise our families in a constantly changing environment. Our jobs flow with the cycles of the business we have chosen to work in. Our physical bodies age, and with each new stage of life we have something different to deal with. The God perspective of time reminds us that all these things are temporary. Nothing is the same as it was, and next year it will all be different again. There is only one kingdom that will last forever — the kingdom of God and our Lord Jesus Christ.

The theme of this book is "God has a plan for you." God has a plan for this world. It was formed in Eden, it will be fulfilled in the new Jerusalem. God has always had a plan. That plan is what we need to commit our lives to. If we commit ourselves to the things of this world, we commit ourselves to the temporary. If we spend our energy trying to build our own little empire, we must eventually see that empire fall and become a memory. Our plans are doomed to temporariness, but God's plan will last forever. To be a participant in the kingdom of God is to be a participant in something much greater than ourselves, something that we will be participating in long after this life is over. To participate in God's kingdom is to commit ourselves to Jesus Christ, and his Church, the expression of the kingdom in this world.

Nothing lasts forever except God's kingdom. We must continually challenge ourselves to commitment to the kingdom. Each day we wake up we must confront ourselves, "What does God want me to do today?" Every decision we make, the important and the unimportant, deserves the question, "What is God's will for me in this matter?" Every action or word from our being needs to be tested against the standard, "Will this advance God's kingdom, or hide it from view?" To be a participant in God's kingdom is to begin now, rather than waiting for some future day. Jesus says, "The kingdom of God is within you" (Luke 17:21 NIV).

God has a plan. You are a part of that plan in that Jesus died for you. But how big a part do you really want to be? Are you willing to commit yourself totally to the kingdom, to be a part of something much larger than yourself, which will last forever and ever?

For Further Reflection

Compare Daniel and Joseph in their abilities and events in their lives.

What changes do you foresee in your life? How will your faith help you in those times of change?

Speculate on the governing system Jesus will use. For example: Jesus says that some will be governors over ten cities, some over two.

Chapter 38

Ezekiel: A Lesson In Personal Responsibility

We live in times when many want to be relieved of their personal responsibility for their actions and blame someone else. We blame previous abuse, delayed stress, living in poverty, being on drugs. All of these things make us do the bad things we do. A closer reading of Ezekiel 18 provides God's view. The Israelites at that time had a proverb, "The parents eat sour grapes and the children's teeth are set on edge" (Ezekiel 18:2 NRSV). It reflected the law of Exodus 20:15 that the sins of the parents would be visited upon the children. Ezekiel's generation used this proverb to blame their parents for the exile and all their troubles. "If only our parents had been faithful to the Lord, we wouldn't be in trouble." They were also using it as an excuse for sin. "I can sin, and not worry about the consequences because it will be passed on to my child."

- **How do you feel when somebody tries to excuse his evil actions by blaming someone else?**

In Ezekiel 18, God lays down the law concerning personal responsibility for one's own actions. No longer will we be able to blame our parents' behavior for our troubles. No longer will we be able to escape the consequences of our actions by thinking we can pass them on to our children. God says, "Know that all lives are mine; the life of the parent as well as the life of the child is mine: it is only the person who sins that shall die" (Ezekiel 18:4 NRSV).

God then illustrates through three generations. The father is righteous and he lives. The son does not follow his father's righteous example, and dies. The grandson does not follow his father's unrighteous example, and therefore lives. But there is more warning. If the righteous person turns away from righteousness toward sin, Ezekiel 18:24 says, "None of the righteous deeds that they have done shall be remembered; for the treachery of which they are guilty and the sin they have committed, they shall die" (NRSV). We must continue to live righteous lifestyles. We cannot think that our lives are in some kind of balance, that as long as the good deeds outweigh the bad we are safe. God looks at our behavior at the present.

But there is also hope. If the wicked person repents and seeks the Lord, and begins to live a righteous life, then Ezekiel 18:22 says, "None of the transgressions that they have committed shall be remembered against them; for the righteousness that they have done they shall live" (NRSV). God looks at the present. If we are living for God, then we will be saved. If we are living outside of God's will, there is danger.

God asks and answers an important question, "Have I any pleasure in the death of the wicked, says the Lord God, and not rather that they should turn from their ways and live?" (Ezekiel 18:23 NRSV). The answer is found in Ezekiel 18:32, "For I have no pleasure in the death of anyone, declares the Sovereign Lord. Repent and live!" (NIV).

Perhaps that is the question for us. "Do we have any pleasure in the death of the wicked?" Would we really desire that they turn from their ways and live? That question eventually led God to come Himself to this planet as Jesus Christ. He died on the cross to save us from our sins. He came to show us how to live as God's righteous people. He came to show us how to live, and live more abundantly. God cared enough for the wicked to come and die on the cross. How much are we willing to do so that the wicked will turn and live?

This question forms part of the foundation for our mission as Christians. That is why we support missionaries around the world telling people about Jesus. We want the wicked to turn from their wicked ways and live. That is why our mission to our own cities is so critical. We desire that people should turn from their wicked ways and live. That is what we want, isn't it?

God says that He takes no pleasure in the death of anyone. We need to remind ourselves that those who die in their sins die spiritually as well as physically. Jesus called the place of torment Gehenna and insisted that it was worth cutting off an arm or a foot if necessary in order to avoid going there. I don't think we will need to do anything that radical to reach people but it will take some sacrifice and effort. Do we care about reaching the lost? God cared enough to send Jesus. Jesus cares enough to send us. We are personally responsible for accomplishing the mission Jesus has given us. In accomplishing that mission, we help the lost to turn and live.

For Further Reflection

How do you feel about the wicked? Are you willing to go to the drug dealers or prisoners and tell them about Jesus?

Whom are you called to warn?

Discuss the differences and similarities between individual responsibility and corporate responsibility.

Chapter 39

Dreams And Visions: Reflections On My Fortieth Birthday

Joel 2:28-29

Author's note — Sunday, October 1, 1995, a communion Sunday, was my fortieth birthday. I enjoyed this opportunity to bring my personal testimony at forty.

> *And afterward, I will pour out my Spirit on all people. Your sons and daughters will prophesy, your old men will dream dreams, your young men will see visions. Even on my servants, both men and women, I will pour out my Spirit in those days.* — Joel 2:28, 29 NIV

What I really want to begin with today is to say with Jesus, "Today, this Scripture has been fulfilled in your hearing." I am willing to state that God has poured out his Spirit on me. He did this not because I am anything special or great. I don't deserve it. I didn't earn it, bribe it, or steal it. No, God did it out of His love and grace. I believed God's promise, and He kept His promise.

I begin this testimony on my fortieth birthday with the confession that all that I am and all that I have is from God. Jesus alone deserves all the glory and honor. Whatever mistakes or sins I have committed are my fault. The times when I didn't listen to what God was telling me are my responsibility. Nonetheless, God has done an awesome work of grace in my life. As I reflect on my life, God has kept His promise to pour out His Spirit on His sons and daughters. I am one who prophesies. I am one who dreams. I am one who sees visions.

My journey with Jesus began on August 21, 1976, when I committed my life to Him in an Assembly of God church in Cape May,

New Jersey. From the beginning, I have been in love with Jesus. He cleansed me of my drug habit. He saw me through the difficult year after my father's death in May of 1977. On December 26, 1978, God called me to the ministry, to go to seminary. Being in a Southern Baptist church at the time made that financially possible. God has empowered me not only to receive my M.Div., but also my Ph.D. I have seen God's action in my life. I believe that the God of the Bible is real and alive. I believe that Jesus Christ is God who came in human form. He lived among us. He died on the cross for our sins. He was raised from the dead. I believe in the Holy Spirit as the Spirit of the living God who lives inside us, empowering us for holy living and Christian service. I believe it now to the point where it is no longer belief, or faith, it is knowledge. I know God is real. I know Jesus is alive and living in me. I know that Jesus has forgiven me of my sins, and has given me eternal life. I know it.

I believe the Bible is the written Word of God. While I come to the Bible with the scholarly knowledge I was given in seminary, I am not willing to accept the doubt and confusion that comes with scholarly conjectures about the Bible. I believe the Bible is an accurate faith record of God's actions in human history through the people of Israel, through the life of Jesus Christ, and through the writings of the apostles. My experience in having read the Bible through nineteen times, now coming to the twentieth time, is that it is not the proof texts, it is not the stories which are of the utmost value, but the fact that God is revealed through the text and story. It is much like a 3D picture. You have to keep staring and eventually the image of God comes blasting through the pages. I believe the Bible is the first and foremost book we should use to evaluate our human existence, thought, goals, and actions. For me the Bible is the authority for human living. If our living doesn't measure up with the Bible, then it is deficient and needs improvement.

I believe in the power of prayer. I believe in the power of prayer because every day I live with answered prayer in my life. Barbara is an answer to prayer. I know prayer works. Megan is an answer to prayer. I know prayer works. Kristen is an answer to prayer. I know prayer works. My job is an answer to prayer. I know prayer works.

I believe in the Church as the foremost expression of God's kingdom in this world. I believe the Church is loved by God more than any other institution in this world. I can say that because Jesus died for the Church. He gave himself up for her. I can say that because the Church is an institution that will last into eternity. Every other institution is part of the kingdoms of this world, and eventually, they will pass away. While the Church is expressed in many forms and ways, I believe the traditional gathering of the saints for worship, praise, education, ministry, proclamation, and fellowship is the characteristic expression of the Church. I say that because that is how Church developed in the New Testament. While parachurch organizations are doing a good work for God, I believe that the accomplishment of the mission will ultimately have to be fulfilled by local congregations preaching, witnessing, and serving in their own cities and communities.

God has called me to pastoral ministry within the local church at this time. My job description as I define it comes from Ephesians 4:12: "to equip the saints for the work of the ministry." It comes from the various commissions of Jesus that we are sent by Jesus to preach the gospel, make disciples, and be witnesses for Jesus. Part of my gifts as a pastor, and as one on whom God has poured his Spirit, is to dream dreams and see visions. I see every church as having the potential to transform the community for Jesus. I believe that because every church has the power of God at its fingertips. Every church has the Holy Spirit. Every church has been called to mission.

Yet we see many churches that do not have power, do not evidence the Spirit, that are not concerned with their mission. Why? The critical difference between an on-fire church or Christian and every other church or Christian is commitment. Lack of commitment, distracted commitment, halfhearted commitment, watered-down commitment, divided commitment has diluted the power of the church and thereby diluted its ability to transform its community. The pastor can see the vision. The pastor can dream the dream. The pastor can be committed to making them happen. But if he or she is the only one, the vision and the dream will never become a reality.

What makes any organization or person great? They are great when they are committed to their goal, vision, or mission. Every church could be great in the kingdom of God. Winning this country to Jesus Christ is not only possible but attainable, because nothing is impossible with God. Are you committed to the mission of Jesus Christ enough to make that happen? What things are you committed to that will not last for eternity? What things are you committed to that Jesus didn't die for? I am not the only one here upon whom God has poured out His Spirit. Speak to the wind. Ask for eyes to see the vision and minds to dream the dream. See the opportunity before you to make a lasting transformation in this city through the power that God has set before us. We are the Church of Jesus Christ. Our mission, on Jesus' personal authority, is to win this world for him. We have the power of Jesus, especially in prayer. We have the message of Jesus that he died for us on the cross, rose again from the dead, is coming again to reign in glory, and that he will pour out his Spirit on all who trust in him.

As I reflect at forty, I see the dream and vision of what the Church can become, and what we can do in this country. It is attainable. But it will take commitment. Total commitment. Do you want to be part of something that will last beyond human history into the heavenly hall of fame? Or will you content yourselves with the *status quo*? Speak to the Spirit. Dream the dream. See the vision. Commit yourself.

For Further Reflection

What is your testimony? What does Jesus mean in your life?

Chapter 40

Concern For The Great City

Jonah 4:11

Jonah has often been called the reluctant missionary, or the prophet who became a missionary in spite of himself. Out of all the minor prophets, we are most familiar with Jonah because of the great fish that swallowed him. The book of Jonah is unique in that it isn't oracles and prophecies like most prophetic books, but rather a story of Jonah and his experience. Jonah is mentioned in 2 Kings 14:25, during the reign of Jeroboam II (786 to 746 B.C.). Jonah is also important in Jesus' preaching in the New Testament. Jonah's stay in the fish for three days is seen by Jesus as a foreshadow of Jesus' being buried in the earth for three days (Matthew 12:39-41).

In chapter 1, God calls Jonah and tells him to go to Nineveh and cry against it for its wickedness. Nineveh was the capital of the Assyrian empire. Samaria was conquered by Assyria in 722 B.C. We don't know if Jonah's call was before or after the conquest. In any case, Assyria was an empire to be reckoned with. It was feared throughout the region. Jonah's mission is to preach to a city that he would rather see destroyed. Its people are wicked, evil, unrighteous. Beyond that, they are political and military enemies of Israel. If God were to destroy them, that would eliminate a serious threat to the health and welfare of Israel. In hopes of seeing that happen, Jonah decides he would rather go on vacation and opts for the cruise to Tarshish in southern Spain. The Bible says he was trying to flee from the Lord's presence. Good luck.

- **If you had the opportunity to convince Jonah to be true to his mission, what would you say?**

As you read through Jonah, you will notice that everything is prepared by God or done by God. The Lord hurled the storm on the sea (Jonah 1:4). The Lord prepared the fish to swallow Jonah (Jonah 1:17). The Lord prepared the vine to shade Jonah (Jonah 4:6). The Lord sent the worm to destroy the vine (Jonah 4:7).

The Lord stirs up a great storm, and here is the first instance of our reluctant missionary. He witnesses to the sailors about God's character — who his God is and what his God is like. Jonah tells them their only option is to throw him overboard. They do this and the sea becomes calm. The sailors worship the Lord. The reluctant missionary wins the converts on the boat.

- **Has there been a time in your life when you found yourself witnessing when you didn't intend to? What happened?**

Now here is a fish story if ever you were to hear one. While many want to doubt the literal meaning of this, I find myself asking, "Isn't God able to do all these things?" Sure, it sounds impossible, but with God, nothing is impossible (Luke 1:37 NIV). The point of the fish is that when we don't do what God tells us to do, He has ways of convincing us that His way is the best. It's as if God were saying, "Okay, Jonah, where would you rather be, inside this fish, or at Nineveh preaching my message? Let me know when you make up your mind." Disobedience is a very dangerous tactic with God. Jonah sees the light, repents, and promises to serve God. The fish delivers Jonah onto dry land. I can only imagine how he must have looked and smelled.

The commission comes again. Go to Nineveh. So the reluctant missionary goes. I wouldn't call Jonah's message exactly detailed. "Yet forty days and Nineveh will be destroyed" (Jonah 3:4). That's it. No in-depth media interviews. No film at eleven. "Yet forty days." I'll bet our missionaries today would like to experience the phenomenal kind of success that Jonah enjoys here. The whole city repents. Even the king puts on sackcloth and fasts in repentance. The king orders even the animals to participate in the fast for repentance. A whole city converted to God with just a few days of street preaching.

- **What would you do if your whole town or city repented?**

Now we have told the story in broad strokes to get to this point and slow down a bit. In Jonah 3:10, when God sees their repentance and humility, He decides to give them another chance. Now Jonah is really upset with God. Have you ever been upset with God? Times when you really wanted your prayer answered but God didn't do it? Join the club. One of the charter members is Jonah. Notice that even as he is upset, Jonah does not charge God with evil, nor question God's authority. In fact, Jonah is upset because God has acted exactly according to His character. Jonah is upset because God spared the city. Jonah feels he can't go back to Israel because he has acted as a traitor to Israel by having Nineveh spared through his preaching. He wishes to die. We may also read in here some bigotry and hatred towards these evil Assyrians. They deserve to die. If God is going to let these guys live, then let me die.

Jonah waits outside the city to see if God will destroy it. On day one, a bush grows up to protect Jonah from the heat. But on day two, the bush is destroyed and Jonah is angry enough to die again. God's question in Jonah 4:4 is the whole crux of the book — "Have you any right to be angry?" (NIV). Jonah was totally concerned about a plant, but didn't see the people in front of him. This is the question for us. What have we centered our lives on? Do we see the people in front of us? American society has gotten to the point where we live in our own little worlds, with little concern for the people around us. If one of our toys gets broken or stolen, we become angry. Like Jonah, we have become self-centered, reluctant missionaries. When we witness, it is almost by accident, in spite of ourselves.

The heart of God and therefore the heart of missions is concern for people who don't know their right hand from their left. Do we believe in the inherent lostness of humankind? The Bible says that all have sinned and have fallen short of the glory of God. The Bible says that those who die in their sins will rise to eternal punishment. Maybe the reason we want to discount the story of the great fish is so that we can discount some other parts of the Bible we don't want to be real, like the reality of hell. Jonah knew the

Ninevites were lost. That was fine by him. As far as he was concerned, they deserved to go to hell. How about us? Do we believe in hell? Is it okay by us if people go there? Do you want your parents to go there? Do you want your children to go there? Do you want your family or friends to go there?

Our mission is to tell people about Jesus Christ so that they can make their own decision to repent or not. If we don't tell them, we have run away from our call and we are no better than Jonah. We are to pray for the lost that they will hear the message. We are to go to the lost so that we can tell them the message of God's salvation. Do we care enough about people to make a significant effort to reach them? It is important for us to focus here at home. How do our prejudices and bigotries interfere with our mission efforts? Do we care about the African-Americans that they hear the gospel and repent? Do we care about the Latino-Hispanic population that they hear the gospel and repent? Do we care about the tens of thousands of unchurched Anglo-Americans that they hear the gospel and repent? Do we care about the gangs, the drug dealers, the prostitutes, the unwed mothers, the people on welfare that they hear the gospel and repent? Do we care about the idle rich, the materialistic, the selfish that they hear the gospel and repent, or like Jonah, are we content to sit on the outskirts of the city and wait for their destruction?

God asks the compelling question in Jonah 4:11: "Should I not be concerned about Nineveh, that great city, in which there are more than 120,000 persons who do not know their right hand from their left, and also many animals?" (NRSV). God is concerned for the city. Cities are where people concentrate in population. With the concentration of people comes a concentration of sin. Judgment piles up. Cities need faithful preachers and witnesses for God. God wants to have mercy and spare cities from judgment. He spared Nineveh here. He spared Jerusalem several times.

God has always been concerned for cities. Sodom and Gomorrah. Jerusalem. Babylon. Rome. We live in cities that God is concerned about. Are we concerned about our city? When we hear our call to be witnesses, there might be some temptation to flee on the next cruise ship. But God is concerned with this city.

He has called us as His witnesses, reluctant and otherwise, to bring His message to our neighbors. Rather than risk being swallowed up by a fish, let's be obedient to God's call and preach the message. Let's pray for our cities that from that preaching we will have Jonah's kind of success. When a city comes to Jesus, it makes life better for everybody. Let's listen to God's call and obey. Shouldn't you be concerned for your city, and its great number of people who need to know Jesus Christ as their Lord and Savior?

For Further Reflection

How would you feel about preaching to your enemies? How would you feel if they converted?

What does this passage say about the power of repentance to avert God's judgment?

What does this passage say about God's compassion for the lost and unsaved?

Chapter 41

Malachi And Matthew: Elijah Comes Back

The last and the first, Malachi and Matthew. Malachi is the last book of the Old Testament. He was a prophet living around 500 to 450 B.C. His primary concern was faithfulness to the Lord's covenant. For Malachi, there was only one way to serve the Lord — wholeheartedly. Malachi calls for faithfulness from the priests. They are called to be faithful ministers who faithfully perform the rituals and services of the Lord and teach the people how to be faithful to God's covenant. They were to instruct the people on the right ways of worshiping the Lord. But they were offering inferior sacrifices and not doing their job. God calls them to account.

God calls the people to account for their high divorce rate. We live in a time where divorces are as common as marriage. While I believe there ought to be grace and mercy to those who have been divorced, we need to remind ourselves that divorce is not God's will. In Malachi 2:16, God says, "I hate divorce." The words of Jesus are just as clear in the New Testament that divorce is not God's will. Divorce is not the unforgivable sin, but it is sin nonetheless. Those who divorce need to confess this sin before God in order to find forgiveness.

- **What are your beliefs about divorce and remarriage?**

In Malachi 3:10, God calls the people to account for their failure to tithe. Funny how we like the commands against murder, stealing, adultery, lying, idolatry, and so on. But when we get to tithing we say, "Oh, that's the Old Testament. We don't have to listen to that because we are New Testament Christians." For the early Christians, the Old Testament was their Scripture. Tithing is just as valid today as it was in Malachi's time, in Jesus' time, in Paul's time. Tithing is God's standard for faithful giving. If we insist on giving less than a tithe to the work of the Church, we had better be thoroughly prepared to explain our actions to God on Judgment Day.

Then Malachi gives the promise of things to come. In Malachi 3:1, God promises a messenger before the Lord. Then the Lord will come. But who can stand it? If you think Malachi's message was pointed, wait until the Lord himself comes and speaks. In Malachi 4:5, God promises that Elijah will come before the great day of the Lord. Notice Elijah's mission: to turn the hearts of the parents to the children and the children to the parents, so that God will not strike the land with a curse.

Listen to God's concern for our families. God wants parents and children whose hearts are turned towards each other. We live in such perilous times for children. We have abused children, neglected children, latchkey children, single-parent children, runaway children. Parents these days have become distracted by career, leisure, addictions, and irresponsibility. For some, children are an adornment to their lives. For others, children serve to keep the grandparents happy. For others, children are an unwelcome intrusion. They are the result of a night of passion, but with no forethought to the consequences. The Bible says that children are a gift from the Lord (Psalm 127:3). They are to be treasured and nurtured and appreciated. The main reason God hates divorce is because God desires that godly children will be reared in godly homes where both husband and wife are partners in rearing the children. We run to and fro, hither and yon, taking our children to a multitude of different activities, sports, clubs, and so on. In the process, church receives less priority. Then we wonder why they don't come to church when they grow up. Is this how we are to raise godly children for the Lord?

- **What methods do you use to promote your family unity? How does your church help?**

We live in perilous times for parents. Children in therapy are remembering abuse that never happened and bringing their parents to court with false accusations. Government and humanistic psychology, in their zeal to stem abuse, have made it difficult to administer appropriate discipline without parents feeling guilty or mean. Children are killing their parents, disobeying their parents, ignoring their parents, especially in their older years, as they are relegated to nursing homes where they don't have to deal with them.

Families are important to God because that is where godly living is first learned and lived out. One component of our ministry as a church is to strengthen and encourage families, both the traditional nuclear families and the nontraditional, single-parent families. In all family settings, our goal is that the hearts of children and parents will be turned toward each other and godly living will be practiced.

Elijah is coming. That is Malachi's message. There will be a messenger who prepares the way for the Lord. With that promise, the Old Testament ends.

In terms of our Bible, the next 400 or so years are called the silent years. There are no official books during these years. In the Catholic canon, these are the years covered by the Apocrypha. The Apocrypha is a group of books that Catholics and Orthodox recognize but which Protestants do not recognize. Although they contain interesting stories, there is no doctrine or point of theology that is critical to our thinking revealed in these books. During these 400 years, the land of Israel passes from the Greeks to the Ptolemies and eventually into the Roman empire. The Essenes, a puritanical cult, begin their life in the Qumran community on the shores of the Dead Sea. The Pharisees and Sadducees rise to the top or religious leadership in Jerusalem. The local synagogue becomes the religious gathering place in the villages of Israel.

In the time of the Pax Romana, a relatively stable time in world history, God begins to move again, through His people Israel. The Gospel of Matthew begins with the birth of a baby who is destined to become the king of the Jews. We can see that Jesus is obviously the Lord who was foreseen in Malachi 4:1. Luke fills in the details about the birth of John the Baptist to Elizabeth and Zechariah. They are told that John is the messenger who comes preparing the way of the Lord just as foretold by Malachi. Jesus confirms this in his evaluation of John (Luke 7:27)

John the Baptist deserves more attention than he usually receives, but I think John would rather not be in the spotlight. He says in John 3:30, "He (Jesus) must increase, I must decrease." Yet Jesus treats John as the significant prophet who connects the times of the Old Covenant and the New Covenant. John the Baptist is the connector between the prophets of the Old Testament and Jesus, the Son of God. He joins the two ages.

God has a plan. John announces the end of the Old and the beginning of the New. That is why Jesus tells John to baptize him in spite of John's protests. "Let us do so to fulfill all righteousness" (Matthew 3:15). Here, righteousness has to do with fulfilling God's plan. The baptism was a way for John to point out Jesus to the people. It was a way for Jesus to identify with us as humans and show his complete dedication to God's plan as it was detailed in the Old Testament.

Jesus says much about John in his ministry. Jesus says that of all born of women, none was greater than John (Matthew 11:11). This is a statement about his role as the last of the Old Testament prophets. He was greater than Moses, Samuel, Elijah, Isaiah, Jeremiah, Ezekiel, and Daniel. How can Jesus say that? Because John's mission was to prepare the way of the Lord. John's mission was to point out Jesus, the Messiah, to Israel. No one had a greater mission than that. John was the one who culminates all the Old Testament prophecy of the Messiah by being the one to point to the Messiah in the flesh, Jesus Christ.

Jesus also says that even the least in the kingdom of God is greater than John. This is a statement about John's role within the New Covenant. John's mission was short and limited — to point out the Messiah to Israel. Those who come into the kingdom by believing in Jesus have the opportunity to witness to the world about Jesus, the Messiah. John pointed to the New as it is beginning. We point to the New by exemplifying the power and grace of Jesus in our lives in the present time. Coming down from the mount of Transfiguration, Jesus says that John was indeed the "Elijah" promised by Malachi, but most people didn't recognize him (Matthew

17:11-12). They were looking for the old Elijah himself, rather than one who had the power and presence of Elijah. We have to admit, John's preaching went straight to the point. He didn't beat around the bush: "But when he saw many of the Pharisees and Sadducees coming to where he was baptizing, he said to them: 'You brood of vipers! Who warned you to flee from the coming wrath?'" (Matthew 3:7 NIV). He confronted Herod about his adultery: for John had been saying to him: "It is not lawful for you to have her" (Matthew 14:4). Notice that John and Malachi both spoke against divorce and for the preservation of the family. In their failure to understand the importance of John the Baptist, the people missed "Elijah," and by that, many missed Jesus the Messiah as well.

- **Is John's blunt kind of "in your face" preaching needed in today's world? How would people you know react to it?**

We have crossed the threshold from the Old into the New. John the Baptist is the prophetic bridge. As great as he was, any one of us can be greater if we fulfill our mission to point out Jesus to the world. We can be greater if we minister to the world to keep families strong. We can be greater if we show how Jesus has saved us by living for him each day.

For Further Reflection

What other comparisons can you make between John the Baptist and Elijah?

In what ways can we point others to Jesus as the Messiah?

Chapter 42

The Rich Man And The Poor Widow

Mark 10 and 12

In the movie version of the Richie Rich comic, Richie Rich has everything he wants, except friends to pal around with. We often think that the rich and famous must be happy because they have so much money. They can get anything they want, whenever they want. They have big houses filled with all kinds of beautiful things. Yet the tabloids and celebrity news continually show that many people, even though they are rich, are not happy. They divorce more often. They die earlier. They are depressed and reclusive. Rich people have a need that only God can fill. Because of the way our society glorifies and promotes wealth, they think they can buy whatever they need. Only too late do they learn the truth of the Beatles song, "Can't Buy Me Love."

- **How much money would you have to have before you considered yourself rich?**

In today's text, we have "Richie Rich" approaching Jesus and asking Jesus how he can fill this void, this emptiness he is feeling: "As Jesus started on his way, a man ran up to him and fell on his knees before him. 'Good teacher,' he asked, 'what must I do to inherit eternal life?' " (Mark 10:17 NIV). Do you hear the real question of this rich man? Do you hear what he doesn't have in spite of all his wealth? He is searching for a relationship with God. Jesus begins by telling him to obey the Law.

> "Why do you call me good?" Jesus answered. "No one is good — except God alone. You know the commandments: 'Do not murder, do not commit adultery, do not steal, do not give false testimony, do not defraud, honor your father and mother.' "
> — Mark 10:18-19 NIV

We often overlook the importance of keeping the commandments as part of our covenant with God. God has not repealed the Ten Commandments. Here, Jesus validates the commandments as a legitimate expression of our relationship with God. Jesus says in John 14:23, "Those who love me will keep my commandments." The rich man affirms the rightness and goodness of the commandments. " 'Teacher,' he declared, 'all these I have kept since I was a boy' " (Mark 10:20 NIV). This man is described in the other Gospels as a rich young ruler. He may have been a Pharisee or Sadducee or Scribe. In any event, he knew the Law and the importance of keeping the Law. I love what comes next:

> Jesus looked at him and loved him. "One thing you lack," he said. "Go, sell everything you have and give to the poor, and you will have treasure in heaven. Then come, follow me." At this the man's face fell. He went away sad, because he had great wealth.
> — Mark 10:21-22 NIV

- **If Jesus had asked this of you, would you be able to sell all you had, give it to the poor and follow Jesus?**

Jesus loved him. A relationship with Jesus was beginning. He was obedient to the commands. Yet Jesus says, "One thing you lack." How can Jesus say such a thing? "One thing you lack." The guy was rich, what could he possibly lack? He could buy it if he didn't already have it. Jesus can say this because what the young ruler lacks is the relationship with God he was so desperately seeking.

Did you notice which commands Jesus cited and how quickly the rich man agreed that he was following them? Did you notice which commands Jesus did not cite? Jesus gave the last half of the decalogue, all of which deal with relationships with our fellow human beings. Jesus did not cite the first three commands: Only one God, no idols or images, and don't use the Lord's name frivolously or blasphemously. These commands have to do with our relationship with God. God must be first in our lives. There must not be any other gods before him. We must not worship idols or images. The quality of our relationship with God will affect the quality of our relationships with our fellow human beings.

I'm sure this young ruler thought he had obeyed the first commands as well as the last set of commands, but Jesus brought this young man's idol to the front of his face. Was God first in this man's life? No, money and things were first. Did this man have an idol? Yes. Money and things were more important to this man than knowing God. One thing you lack. The young man went away sad, unwilling to give up his possessions in order to have a clean and pure relationship with God. If we really want a living and pure relationship with God, nothing can stand in the way of that relationship. According to Jesus in this passage, riches, wealth, and possessions can easily become idols that keep Jesus off the throne of our lives. The tough question for us is, if Jesus said to us what he said to this young man, would we sell everything? To the degree that we hang on to our riches, that is how much we need to grow. The paradox is that by selling everything, this young ruler would gain the one thing that he lacked.

- **What is hindering your relationship with God?**

At the opposite end of the socio-economic scale, we sit with Jesus at the temple as the people are bringing their offerings. Mark records it this way:

> *Jesus sat down opposite the place where the offerings were put and watched the crowd putting their money into the temple treasury. Many rich people threw in large amounts. But a poor widow came and put in two very small copper coins, worth only a fraction of a penny.*

> *Calling his disciples to him, Jesus said, "I tell you the truth, this poor widow has put more into the treasury than all the others. They all gave out of their wealth; but she, out of her poverty, put in everything — all she had to live on."* — Mark 12:41-44 NIV

The widow represents in all ways a direct contrast and opposite to the rich young ruler. He was rich, she was poor. He was a powerful ruler, she had no power and was at the mercy of all. He was young, she was old. He had no relationship with God, and would not trust enough to give up his wealth. She trusted enough to give up what little wealth she had. Did she give all she had because she had a relationship with God? The Scripture doesn't specify but it is difficult to think otherwise. When faith is deep and mature, we know we can't outgive God. When faith is deep and mature, we know that if we make a sacrificial gift, God will provide for all our needs. When God is truly first in our lives, we see money for what it really is and recognize that it doesn't have any power to provide true happiness or eternal life. Only God can give us those things. While the widow didn't give the largest amount to the treasury, Jesus exalts her because in proportion to how she had been blessed, the widow gave everything. The rich man had everything but lost it when he wouldn't follow Jesus. The widow had nothing, but gained everything when she gave it back to God.

So the first questions we need to ask ourselves in relation to our stewardship do not deal with how much or how often. No, the questions are more basic and more difficult. Is God first in your life? If Jesus came and told you to sell everything you own and give it to the poor, would you? Could you? How much do you trust God to provide for your needs and your desires if you were to give at a sacrificial level like the widow? And if God chose to provide only your needs, but not your desires, would you give at a sacrificial level? Is your goal to get rich, or is your goal to follow God? Is your goal to have fun, or follow God? Is your goal to get for yourself, or share with God and others?

Jesus shows us in the Gospel that the most valuable asset we could have is our relationship with God. Our relationship with God is worth selling everything we have. Our relationship with God will lead us to give sacrificially to the work of the Church, so that God's work can be accomplished without obstacle or hindrance. When Jesus evaluates our relationship with God in terms of our giving, will he say "One thing you lack," or "That person gave more than all the others"?

For Further Reflection

Who or what is first in your life?

Compare Abraham or Job, whom God made wealthy, and the warning in 1 Timothy 6:10, "Love of money is the root of all evil." Is God against wealth?

Read 1 Timothy 6:17. What should be our attitude towards wealth?

How can faithful giving and tithing help us have the right attitude toward wealth?

Chapter 43

Jesus: The Fulfillment Of The Old Testament

The coming of Jesus to earth is the zenith of God's plan for redemption from sin. As you have been reading through the Old Testament, you may have thought at times, "What does this have to do with anything I can relate to?" But the point of all the books of the Old Testament was to foretell the coming of Jesus, the Son of God, the Messiah, who would take away the sin of the world. Consider:

- In Genesis Jesus is the one who would crush the serpent's head, he is the way that all nations would be blessed, he is the ram caught in the thicket to redeem Isaac and all peoples.

- In Exodus Jesus is the Passover lamb.

- In Leviticus Jesus is our atonement sacrifice, our peace sacrifice, and our fellowship sacrifice.

- In Numbers Jesus is the serpent lifted up in the wilderness.

- In Deuteronomy Jesus is the Prophet who is to come.

- In Joshua Jesus is the Captain of the Lord's army, and the one who leads us into the promised land.

- In Judges Jesus is the Angel of the Lord.

- In Ruth Jesus is our kinsman redeemer.

- In 1 and 2 Samuel Jesus is the promised son of David, heir to the throne.

- In 1 and 2 Kings Jesus is the wisdom of Solomon and the power of Elijah and Elisha.

- In 1 and 2 Chronicles Jesus is the one who will establish the true temple with true worship.

- In Ezra Jesus is the true teacher of the Law.

- In Nehemiah Jesus is the faithful governor who will rebuild Jerusalem.

- In Esther Jesus is the one who extends the scepter to the Church, to come into his presence.

- In Job Jesus is the Redeemer who lives, who will stand upon the earth.

- In Psalms Jesus is the Lord who sits at the right hand of God, the one betrayed and the one pierced.

- In Proverbs Jesus is the Wisdom of God, more precious than gold.

- In Ecclesiastes Jesus is the one who comes preaching good news instead of vanity.

- In Song of Songs Jesus is the lover, the bridegroom who marries the Church.

- In Isaiah Jesus is the Suffering Servant who is wounded for our transgressions, the child born to the virgin, whose name is Wonderful, Counselor, the Mighty God, the Everlasting Father, the Prince of Peace, the One who is anointed by the Spirit of the Lord.

- In Jeremiah Jesus is the one who will bring the new covenant.

- In Ezekiel Jesus is the Son of Man, who is the responsible watchman of the people.

- In Daniel Jesus is the one who approaches the Ancient of Days.

- In Hosea Jesus is the son called out of Egypt.

- In Joel Jesus is the one who pours out the Spirit on his sons and daughters.

- In Amos Jesus is the one who brings the Day of the Lord.

- In Jonah Jesus is in the heart of the earth for three days just as Jonah was in the belly of the fish for three days.

- In Micah Jesus is the one who will usher in the millennial age of peace, the king born in Bethlehem.

- In Zechariah Jesus is the shepherd who will be struck, whose life is worth thirty pieces of silver, and the king of Jerusalem coming humbly on a colt.

- In Malachi Jesus is the Lord who will come suddenly to his temple.

As you read the accounts of Jesus in the Gospels, keep your eyes open to note when Jesus fulfills all these prophecies and types. Many times the Gospel writers identify the passage for us. That Jesus fulfilled all these prophecies is the proof that Jesus is the Messiah. Jesus is the promised one who takes away the sin of the world.

For Further Reflection

The above list is but a sampling. Where else did you see Jesus in the Old Testament?

Chapter 44

One Small Offering

John 6:1-12

My daughter Megan came home with a math problem in the form of a proposition for her parents. She would agree to do the dishes for thirty days. She would begin at one penny for the first day. On each succeeding day she would work for double the previous day. So on day two it would be two cents, day three, four cents and so on. Sounds like I might be out ten or twenty dollars by the end of the month, right? Fortunately, I had heard this problem before so I did not agree to the terms. While the initial payments are small, on day number 27, I would owe Megan for that day alone $671,088.64 for doing the dishes. By day thirty, she would be pastor of the church. Small things, when multiplied, eventually grow to huge proportions.

Jesus had been teaching the crowd in a lonely place for quite some time. There was not much food around, and the nearest town wasn't very near. There were no McDonald's and no Dominos pizza deliveries. The people were getting hungry, and Jesus was concerned about their physical needs. "When Jesus looked up and saw a great crowd coming toward him, he said to Philip, 'Where shall we buy bread for these people to eat?' " (John 6:5).

- **If you had been here with Jesus and the crowd, what solution(s) would you propose?**

We need to be reminded that God is concerned about our physical needs. He knows we need food, clothing, and shelter. He knows we need a job, friends, and community. God is aware of our physical needs and wants to help us meet those needs. The number of men is 5,000. That would probably translate to a crowd of 10,000 or more. Philip is obviously aware of the situation. "Philip answered him, 'Eight months' wages would not buy enough bread for each one to have a bite!' " (John 6:7 NIV). If we consider a McDonald's value meal at $3.75, it would take nearly $40,000 to feed this crowd.

- **Was there a time in your life when the need was so overwhelming you weren't sure how that need was going to be met? What happened?**

The next idea comes from Andrew. He scouts around to see who may have food and if it could be shared. Only one person came prepared. "Another of his disciples, Andrew, Simon Peter's brother, spoke up, 'Here is a boy with five small barley loaves and two small fish, but how far will they go among so many?' " (John 6:8-9 NIV). Who would like to carve these five loaves into 10,000 equal portions? Our deacons are good at carving the bread, but I think this would challenge even the best of them. Then the miracle.

> *Jesus said, "Have the people sit down." There was plenty of grass in that place, and the men sat down, about five thousand of them. Jesus then took the loaves, gave thanks, and distributed to those who were seated as much as they wanted. He did the same with the fish. When they had all had enough to eat, he said to his disciples, "Gather the pieces that are left over. Let nothing be wasted." So they gathered them and filled twelve baskets with the pieces of the five barley loaves left over by those who had eaten.* — John 6:10-13 NIV

How did he do that? Where did it come from? The Bible is really short on description here. We just don't have the mechanics of this miracle described for us. It just happens. Not only did everybody get a bite, all of them ate until they were stuffed. Not only was everybody completely fed, twelve baskets of leftovers were collected to see Jesus and the disciples through the week. All this from five measly barley loaves and two little fish. What is that to a crowd of 10,000? Dinner, not only for tonight, but for the week.

There is a penetrating application here, namely that small things can accomplish great things when given to Jesus. I wonder what this boy thought when Jesus and Andrew asked him for his lunch. "Yeah, right. Do your math. If everybody else didn't think to bring their lunch, that's their problem." On the other hand, maybe he really wanted to help but felt like Andrew. "Here is my lunch, but I don't think that will really solve the problem." Others see the boy volunteering his lunch. He overheard the disciples talking with Jesus, came over and said to Andrew, "If it will help, I will share my lunch with everybody."

- **If you had been the boy with the lunch, what would you be thinking about giving it to Jesus, and its ability to solve the situation?**

I like this last picture. It is the picture of faithful stewardship. What God has given to us was never meant to be hoarded. God expects us to share. When we share, God is able to multiply our resources so that together, they accomplish far more than what one of us alone could accomplish. Utility bills represent some of the biggest costs of having a church building. Would any one of us want to be the responsible party for this bill, all by ourselves? Though no one individual could take on the whole amount, when all of us work and give together we are able to meet this bill as well as many others. God takes our individual gifts and multiplies them to meet needs beyond ourselves.

Many churches are also blest with money that has been passed on through wills and bequests. The example of these benefactors reminds us that sharing is not just for while we are alive. Good stewardship of your resources would certainly dictate that every adult have an up-to-date last will and testament. Your will is also an excellent place to remember your church with one final bequest. Whether small or large, you will know that we take our stewardship of these funds seriously and the money will be used for the good of the church, the spread of the gospel, and the advancement of the kingdom of God. We see that little gifts, when given to Jesus, can be multiplied to meet needs far beyond our individual capabilities.

- **Do you have a will? Have you remembered your church in your will?**

When we meet around the communion table, we are reminded how Jesus can meet our needs as he multiplies our resources. The bread reminds us of Jesus' body, and also how he met the physical needs of this crowd in John 6. John 6 continues with Jesus describing himself as the bread of life. In the Lord's Supper, we partake of the bread of life, and the cup of the new covenant together. When we meet with Jesus around the table, we should thank him for multiplying our shared resources. Ask Jesus how you might share a little more next year, that your church's resources will grow stronger as well.

For Further Reflection

How can your church encourage the "small givers" that their contributions are being used by God as well as the larger donors?

Where are the places where you can increase your sharing with others and the church?

Chapter 45

Stewardship In The Early Church

Acts 4 and 5

Robert Fulghum's popular book, *All I Ever Needed, I Learned in Kindergarten*, has become a pop classic. One thing we all learned in kindergarten, or in preschool, is to share with others. It is one of the most important lessons children learn. We were told that if we wanted to have friends and get along with others, we had to share our toys. We had to take turns playing with the toy that everybody wanted to play with.

Sometimes I think the official parent uniform should be either a zebra shirt with a whistle or a judge's robe with a gavel. We are constantly having to intervene to make sure things get shared. If we learned our kindergarten lesson well, we also learned that when we share, everybody gets to have fun. Everybody has a good time. But if we hoard a toy to ourselves, we may have the toy, but we wound up with no friends to play with.

- **What favorite toy do you remember in your childhood? Did you share it with others?**

The early church had a practice of sharing with each other that has seldom been duplicated. A few groups today practice a form of communal living; but for the most part, we have embraced the principle of private property. What's mine is mine, what's yours is yours. We have to concede that this example of sharing in the early Church is not mandated to the entire body, nor held up as the only model for church living. But the principle behind the model is valid and has its roots in the teaching of Jesus. The principle is that of sharing.

Jesus spoke often about the foolishness of trying to hoard everything for yourself. The most potent example is the parable of the rich fool in Luke 12:16-21. Here the man decided to keep everything for himself. Yet that night, God said, "Your time is up. Now who will get all these things you have hoarded for yourself?" Jesus said that those who seek to keep their lives would lose them, but those who lose their lives for his sake would find them. Jesus said, "A person's life is not to be measured by the abundance of their material possessions" (Luke 12:15). Jesus said, "Lend to those who ask of you and don't worry about being paid back" (Luke 6:35). He said to that rich young ruler who was materially wealthy, "One thing you lack."

- **What is your most prized possession now? Could you give it up or share it?**

Jesus made a habit of sharing. He shared his godly power to work miracles in the lives of people. He shared his teaching from God. He shared salvation by dying for us on the cross. The early Church evidently went the second mile in putting Jesus' teaching into action. They shared everything as if they no longer owned it:

> *All the believers were one in heart and mind. No one claimed that any of his possessions was his own, but they shared everything they had. With great power the apostles continued to testify to the resurrection of the Lord Jesus, and much grace was upon them all. There were no needy persons among them. For from time to time those who owned lands or houses sold them, brought the money from the sales and put it at the apostles' feet, and it was distributed to anyone as he had need.* — Acts 4:32-35 NIV

The first benefit from this practice is that it strengthened the bonds of love among the members. They cared about each other enough to meet each other's needs. A second benefit was that there were no needy people. That doesn't mean all of them drove Mercedes chariots with ten horsepower. It means that everyone's needs were met. A third benefit was that this witness of love was visible to those outside the Church. The early believers gained a good reputation in Jerusalem because they didn't just talk about the love of Jesus, they lived it out in their day-to-day lives. A fourth benefit is that their stewardship is a witness to the importance of knowing God and the transience of worldly wealth. They showed that they had learned their kindergarten lesson of sharing what they had with others.

The stewardship of the early Church raises the questions, Do we really own our possessions? Why has God given us so much stuff? Is it really to hoard for ourselves? Or is it to share with others so that none of us will be needy? How well have we learned the lesson of kindergarten, to share with others?

One of the effects of the sharing in the early Church was that the spirit of giving began to spread, almost to the point of becoming a contest about who could give the most. Our first contestant is Barnabas: "Joseph, a Levite from Cyprus, whom the apostles called Barnabas (which means Son of Encouragement), sold a field he owned and brought the money and put it at the apostles' feet" (Acts 4:36-37 NIV). He sold a field. We don't know how big it was, but we do know that then as now, land was valuable. For him to sell a field represented a big sacrifice. Not only did he sell a valuable asset, he brought the entire amount of money to the church offering plate. Not just a ten percent tithe, not a twenty percent double tithe, not half, but the entire amount. How many of us would like to step into this contest with Barnabas? The spirit of sharing and giving can be contagious and infectious. I would guess Barnabas was seeing how much good the other gifts were doing and he wanted to be part of the good deed brigade.

Our next contestants are Ananias and Sapphira: "Now a man named Ananias, together with his wife Sapphira, also sold a piece of property. With his wife's full knowledge he kept back part of the money for himself, but brought the rest and put it at the apostles' feet" (Acts 5:1-2 NIV). Ananias and Sapphira wanted to be part of the good deed brigade. They wanted to show — or show off — that they could give too. They wanted their fellow believers to think they had contributed the entire value of the sale, but they wanted to keep some for themselves as well. Now here we may have to speculate a bit. What were Ann and Saph thinking? Maybe they had an unexpected expense. Maybe they wanted to take that vacation they always wanted. Maybe they had more than enough to beat Barnabas' gift and they would keep the rest for themselves. It isn't that they didn't give, or gave too little. They misrepresented their gift to the Church. They lied. And they suffered grave consequences (literally).

> *Then Peter said, "Ananias, how is it that Satan has so filled your heart that you have lied to the Holy Spirit and have kept for yourself some of the money you received for the land? Didn't it belong to you before it was sold? And after it was sold, wasn't the money at your disposal? What made you think of doing such a thing? You have not lied to men but to God." When Ananias heard this, he fell down and died. And great fear seized all who heard what had happened. Then the young men came forward, wrapped up his body, and carried him out and buried him. About three hours later his wife came in, not knowing what had happened. Peter asked her, "Tell me, is this the price you and Ananias got for the land?" "Yes," she said, "that is the price." Peter said to her, "How could you agree to test the Spirit of the Lord? Look! The feet of the men who buried your husband are at the door, and they will carry you out also." At that moment she fell down at his feet and died. Then the young men came in and, finding her dead, carried her out and buried her beside her husband.*
>
> — Acts 5:3-10 NIV

- **How would you react if something like this happened in your church today?**

The most important lesson from Ananias and Sapphira is the concept that we have the freedom to give or not give as much as we choose. "It was yours as a field, it was yours as money to do with as you desired." What angered God was that they came lying about what their gift represented. You also have the freedom to give or not to give. While I will say there is the expectation that Christians will faithfully give, there is no force, no coercion, no duress that we will use to compel you to give. The Bible says that God loves a cheerful giver. The only way we can give cheerfully is when we give of our own free will with no force or compulsion.

What you have, is what God has granted to you. You are free to give or not to give. You are encouraged to be faithful in your giving as a symbol of your faith and gratitude to God and to support the church of which you are a member. When we pledge, we need to be honest with God about what we are giving. If we check that we are going to give ten percent, but then write an amount that doesn't reflect that ten percent, we are lying to God, just as Ananias and Sapphira did. When we write an amount in our pledge card, let's consider the attitude with which we make our decision. Be honest. Is this the amount you want to give? Does this amount represent the best you can give? Are you really making a sacrifice?

- **How do you decide what your church giving will be each year?**

Fortunately, most pastors do not have Peter's gift of discernment. They are not able to discern whether you have made a worthy pledge or whether you are sandbagging. But God is able to discern and He is able to take action based on what He sees. The question raised by the story of Ananias and Sapphira is, "Is this pledge honestly the best I can do, the most I can give, the closest I can come to a tithe? Is this truly what I feel led to give?" Be honest before God about what your pledge represents. Peter would say everything we have is from God. Right now, it is your money. God has given it into your stewardship. You have the freedom to give as much or as little as you decide in the Lord. All God asks is your honest appraisal of what that gift represents.

For Further Reflection

If we practiced mutual sharing as they did in the early church, what would you sell to support the common ministry?

Do you think most giving is done cheerfully or grudgingly?

How can we improve our attitudes towards giving?

Chapter 46
God Has A Plan: Jew And Gentile

Romans 11

As I write this chapter exploring the role of Jew and Gentile in God's plan, I cannot claim to have the complete and comprehensive answer. But the issue is of profound interest and importance. The basic question is what is God's plan concerning the Jews? With this question comes a whole host of sub-questions. Why did God choose the Jews? Why are the Jews victimized with such disdain and hatred? Are the Jews saved? Why don't they believe in Jesus?

There are several reasons for my interest in this subject. First, as a Christian, one who has inherited salvation through a Jew named Jesus Christ, I am interested in his people. Second, I have Jewish blood in my heritage. My grandfather on my father's side was an orthodox Jew who gave up his heritage when he married a Gentile woman. Third, I wrestle often with the Holocaust under Hitler and wonder how that could possibly fit into God's plan for the Jews.

All of us as Christians should be interested in this subject because of our spiritual heritage which comes from the Jews, and our future is bound up with the Jews. That is the message of Romans 11.

> *Again I ask: Did they [the Jews] stumble so as to fall beyond recovery? Not at all! Rather, because of their transgression, salvation has come to the Gentiles to make Israel envious. But if their transgression means riches for the world, and their loss means riches for the Gentiles, how much greater riches will their fullness bring! I am talking to you Gentiles. Inasmuch as I am the apostle to the Gentiles, I make much of my ministry*

> *in the hope that I may somehow arouse my own people to envy and save some of them. For if their rejection is the reconciliation of the world, what will their acceptance be but life from the dead? If the part of the dough offered as firstfruits is holy, then the whole batch is holy; if the root is holy, so are the branches.*
> — Romans 11:11-16 NIV

Our faith heritage comes from the Jews. Israel is God's chosen people to bring salvation to the world, and that means us. God said to Abraham, "Through you, I will bless all the nations." He renewed that promise to Isaac and Jacob. He continually renewed that promise throughout the time of the Old Testament. Jesus was born to Joseph and Mary, who were Jewish. The apostles were Jewish. If it weren't for the faithful Jews who cooperated with God's plan, we would not be here today.

- **What preconceptions or questions do you have about the Jewish people or religion?**

We are also here because of the unfaithful Jews, as this passage implies. Because of their refusal to believe in Jesus as their Messiah, God has authorized the good news of salvation to be preached among the Gentiles. That's us. Their loss meant our riches. Their rejection meant our acceptance. Furthermore, our future is bound up with the nation of Israel:

> *I do not want you to be ignorant of this mystery, brothers, so that you may not be conceited: Israel has experienced a hardening in part until the full number of the Gentiles has come in. And so all Israel will be saved, as it is written: "The deliverer will come from Zion; he will turn godlessness away from Jacob. And this is my covenant with them when I take away their sins."*
> — Romans 11:25-27 NIV

Paul states God's plan is for Jews and Gentiles to be saved through Jesus Christ. The day will come, says Paul, when the Jews, as a people, will embrace Jesus as Messiah. Scholars of biblical prophecy recognize that God's clock is running on Israelite time. What happens with the nation of Israel is a sign for us who are looking for the return of Jesus.

Our future in heaven is that Jews and Gentiles will dwell together in peace and harmony, so it is important for us to understand the significance of the Jews in our heritage and our future. The Church throughout its history has been guilty of persecuting the Jews. It happened during the inquisition, the crusades, the holocaust, and in other periods. This persecution of the Jews is not God's will. Keep in mind what Paul says:

> *As far as the gospel is concerned, they are enemies on your account; but as far as election is concerned, they are loved on account of the patriarchs, for God's gifts and His call are irrevocable. Just as you who were at one time disobedient to God have now received mercy as a result of their disobedience, so they too have now become disobedient in order that they too may now receive mercy as a result of God's mercy to you. For God has bound all men over to disobedience so that He may have mercy on them all.* — Romans 11:28-32 NIV

Although our Jewish neighbors reject the gospel, God still loves them on account of the patriarchs, Abraham, Isaac, and Jacob. Would God really have us hate and persecute someone He loves? No way. In this passage, we see God's plan for Jew and Gentile. His plan is to have mercy on all who call upon the name of Jesus. At one time, all of us were disobedient. Which means now, all of us need mercy.

- **The Jews aren't the only ones rejecting Jesus. What do these passages say about God's attitude towards non-Jews who reject Jesus?**

What about the other questions Paul raises? First, has God rejected the Jews? Is the church the new Israel, as some would interpret? Based on Romans 11 and a few other passages, I believe we can confidently say, "No."

> *I ask then: Did God reject his people? By no means! I am an Israelite myself, a descendant of Abraham, from the tribe of Benjamin. God did not reject his people, whom he foreknew. Don't you know what the Scripture says in the passage about Elijah — how he appealed to God against Israel: "Lord, they have killed your prophets and torn down your altars; I am the only one left, and they are trying to kill me." And what was God's answer to him? "I have reserved for myself seven thousand who have not bowed the knee to Baal." So too, at the present time there is a remnant chosen by grace. And if by grace, then it is no longer by works; if it were, grace would no longer be grace.*
> — Romans 11:1-6 NIV

Paul says God's gift and call to the Jews to be the people of God are irrevocable. God said through the prophet Jeremiah:

> *This is what the Lord says, He who appoints the sun to shine by day, who decrees the moon and stars to shine by night, who stirs up the sea so that its waves roar — the Lord Almighty is His name: "Only if these decrees vanish from my sight," declares the Lord, "will the descendants of Israel ever cease to be a nation before me." This is what the Lord says: "Only if the heavens above can be measured and the foundations of the earth below be searched out will I reject all the descendants of Israel because of all they have done," declares the Lord.* — Jeremiah 31:35-37 NIV

The Jews are still God's chosen nation. They are to keep the Law and the Covenant. Where they have fallen short is that they have not recognized Jesus as their Messiah. God's ideal will is that they will recognize Jesus and put their faith in him. There is, in fact, a remnant today. We call them messianic Jews, Jews who believe that Jesus is the Messiah.

Second question: Are the Jews automatically saved because they are chosen of God? The point of Paul in this chapter is that God has made everybody equal in His sight. We are all disobedient and therefore we are all in need of mercy and forgiveness. The only way to receive this mercy is to put our faith in Jesus Christ as Lord and Savior. No one is automatically saved, not Jews, not Gentiles, not anybody. We all need Jesus.

Third question: Why then have the Jews been so persecuted? The answer demands more than just a few lines, because the reasons are complex and change from time to time. At one point, the Jews were called Christ killers, and therefore it was said they deserved death. In several countries, Jews were among the wealthy, and they were persecuted in order to get their money. They have been persecuted out of fear, jealousy, hatred, and in the search of a scapegoat of national problems. Why does God allow this? I don't know. Why did the holocaust happen? I don't know. One thing I do know — those who persecute the Jews are not doing God's will and sooner or later, God's judgment will catch up with them.

Fourth question: What should be the Christian's approach and attitude toward the Jews? I believe they are lost, just like the rest of us, if they don't know Jesus. They need to hear the gospel and believe. Our attitude should be one of gratitude for the heritage they have given us. Our attitude should be one of love, that through the love of God shown by us they will be drawn to Jesus and be saved.

The treatment and attitude of Gentiles towards the Jews bring up the problem of racism in general. One cause of racism is an attitude of superiority, that somehow we are better than another ethnic or national group. Jews were and are persecuted because some have the attitude that Jews are inferior and deserve to be persecuted. Fill in the blank with whatever ethnic-cultural group you like, and you have a cause of racism towards that group. While the Jews are God's chosen people, we must remind ourselves that Jesus died for all people, of all races, cultures, tribes, and language groups. Racism is sin. It has always been sin, and it will always be sin, to persecute, discriminate against, or oppress another person based on his race, creed, color, nationality, culture, or physical appearance. Jesus' golden rule is, "Treat other people as you would like to be treated" (Matthew 7:12). If everybody followed that rule, the world would be a wonderful place.

The bottom line is that the Jews, like us Gentiles, are an integral part of God's plan of salvation. This plan was promised to come through Abraham, Isaac, and Jacob. This plan was fulfilled in the Jew named Jesus Christ of Nazareth. Advent celebrates that God's plan was fulfilled with the birth of a baby boy to devout Jewish parents. We are part of God's glorious plan for the ages. We can thank the Jews that we are a part of that plan.

For Further Reflection

Name some of the times throughout history God has preserved the Jews through intense persecution. What does this say about God's purpose for the Jews?

How does the Holocaust of WWII impact the Church?

Some teach that the Church has replaced Israel. How do these Scriptures relate to such a view?

Chapter 47

The Center Of Christianity

1 Corinthians 15

As we look at the religions of the world, we see that they all deal with a similar construct on human life. Most religions posit some kind of supreme being or God. For some the being is impersonal, for example, Buddhism or Hinduism or Shinto. For other religions, the being is personal as in Judaism, Islam, and Christianity.

Most religions deal with moral behavior and most religions have a similar moral code. All forbid murder, theft, and lying. Most teach respect for parents and elders. Most religions make the state of afterlife contingent on how well you keep the moral code. Most religions have writings or scriptures that act as the guide for the religion. Most have places of worship and worship rituals. Most have religious professionals, clergy or priests. Most religions have an idea of what lies beyond death.

I believe the need to explain life and death is the major power behind religious behavior and the major reason religions came into being. Some religions foresee a place where we go after we die. Others offer the afterlife as only a state of mind. Others would have us absorbed back into the universal oneness.

- **What do you believe about the origins of religions?**

With so many religions to choose from, and with many of them proclaiming to have or teach the truth, to the exclusion of the others, how do we know which one is really right and true and correct? That is a critical question, because some religions teach that they have the truth and no one else does. Islam is certainly an exclusive religion. Christianity is certainly an exclusive religion. Hinduism and Buddhism are more inclusive, but still promote themselves above other religions. How can we know which one is true?

- **What test or tests would you propose to prove the truthfulness of any given religion?**

There is one thing that separates Christianity from the rest of the world's religions. Hinduism has no real founder. It emerged in India in several forms and still has various factions and philosophies. Buddhism was founded by Buddha. Buddha died and his tomb is in India. Islam was founded by Mohammed. Mohammed died and is buried in Mecca. Confucius is dead, Lao Tze is dead, Zarathrustra is dead, Moses is dead, Abraham is dead, and David is dead.

There is only one religion which claims that its founder is alive from the dead. His name is Jesus. The resurrection is the center of Christian faith. Without the resurrection, we have no better hope than any other religion. The resurrection of Jesus makes Christianity different from every other world religion.

- **Can you think of other features of Christianity that distinguish it from other world relgions?**

Paul tells us in 1 Corinthians just how important the resurrection is:

> *For what I received I passed on to you as of first importance: that Christ died for our sins according to the Scriptures, that he was buried, that he was raised on the third day according to the Scriptures, and that he appeared to Peter, and then to the Twelve. After that, he appeared to more than five hundred of the brothers at the same time, most of whom are still living, though some have fallen asleep. Then he appeared to James, then to all the apostles, and last of all he appeared to me also, as to one abnormally born.*
> — 1 Corinthians 15:3-8 NIV

Paul passed on as of first importance the death and resurrection of Jesus Christ. Jesus died for our sins according to the Scriptures. Jesus rose from the dead on the third day according to the Scriptures. This is of first importance. These facts must be believed. They are the heart of salvation. In Romans 10:9, Paul says that if you confess with your lips that Jesus is Lord and believe in your heart that God raised him from the dead, you will be saved. If you do not believe that Jesus died for our sins and rose from the dead, you still have some work to do on your faith. Belief in the death and resurrection of Jesus is of first importance.

What proof do we have that Jesus rose from the dead? What proof could we offer that would be adequate? Paul's proof to the Corinthians was the fact that Jesus was seen alive from the dead by at least 514 people. According to Paul, Jesus appeared to the twelve apostles, then to 500, then to James, then to Paul: 514. Paul says that most of those people were still alive at the time he wrote this letter, which is usually dated in the mid-50s, or about 25 years after Jesus was raised. I believe that seeing Jesus physically alive from the dead gave Paul his motivation, conviction, and enthusiasm to endure all he had to endure.

Paul was convinced of Jesus' resurrection, but evidently there were some in Corinth who did not believe that Jesus was truly raised from the dead. Times don't change much, do they?

> *But if it is preached that Christ has been raised from the dead, how can some of you say that there is no resurrection of the dead? If there is no resurrection of the dead, then not even Christ has been raised. And if Christ has not been raised, our preaching is useless and so is your faith. More than that, we are then found to be false witnesses about God, for we have testified about God that He raised Christ from the dead. But He did not raise him if in fact the dead are not raised. For if the dead are not raised, then Christ has not been raised either. And if Christ has not been raised, your faith is futile; you are still in your sins. Then those also who have fallen asleep in Christ are lost.*
> — 1 Corinthians 15:12-18 NIV

This is the whole crux of our faith — the resurrection. If Jesus has not been raised from the dead, then nobody else has a hope of resurrection either. Our faith is useless, pointless, and meaningless if there is no resurrection from the dead. Or as Paul puts it, "If only for this life we have hope in Christ, we are to be pitied more than all men" (1 Corinthians 15:19 NIV). When we look at our world, we see people who live as though there is no resurrection. They live their lives with no thought of eternal consequences. Paul knew what they were thinking. Life is a beach and then you die. Or in Paul's words:

> *Now if there is no resurrection, what will those do who are baptized for the dead? If the dead are not raised at all, why are people baptized for them? And as for us, why do we endanger ourselves every hour? I die every day — I mean that, brothers — just as surely as I glory over you in Christ Jesus our Lord. If I fought wild beasts in Ephesus for merely human reasons, what have I gained? If the dead are not raised, "Let us eat and drink, for tomorrow we die." Do not be misled: "Bad company corrupts good character." Come back to your senses as you ought, and stop sinning; for there are some who are ignorant of God — I say this to your shame.* — 1 Corinthians 15:29-34 NIV

If the dead are not raised, what are Christians doing in church every Sunday morning? Paul's point is that he would not endure everything he had endured to this point if he wasn't convinced of the resurrection. Paul is not alone. Ask yourself. Why do you come to church any morning you come to church? Why do you serve on boards and committees, teach Sunday school, and sing in the choir? Why? Because deep down, you believe in the resurrection of Jesus. That gives you hope for your own resurrection when you die. Because you know God is the only one who can raise people from the dead. You come, you serve, you give, you worship.

Paul's further point is that since we are convinced that we will rise from the dead, then sin is not an option. We must avoid sin, and live for God totally, completely, and wholeheartedly.

The Corinthians had more questions, the same questions we have:

> *But someone may ask, "How are the dead raised? With what kind of body will they come?" How foolish! What you sow does not come to life unless it dies. When you sow, you do not plant the body that will be, but just a seed, perhaps of wheat or of something else. But God gives it a body as He has determined, and to each kind of seed He gives its own body ... So will it be with the resurrection of the dead. The body that is sown is perishable, it is raised imperishable; it is sown in dishonor, it is raised in glory; it is sown in weakness, it is raised in power; it is sown a natural body, it is raised a spiritual body. If there is a natural body, there is also a spiritual body. So it is written: "The first man Adam became a living being" the last Adam, a life-giving spirit. The spiritual did not come first, but the natural, and after that the spiritual. The first man was of the dust of the earth, the second man from heaven. As was the earthly man, so are those who are of the earth; and as is the man from heaven, so also are those who are of heaven. And just as we have borne the likeness of the earthly man, so shall we bear the likeness of the man from heaven. I declare to you, brothers, that flesh and blood cannot inherit the kingdom of God, nor does the perishable inherit the imperishable.*
> — 1 Corinthians 15:35-50 NIV

- **What speculations do you make about the resurrection body?**

What will our resurrection bodies be like? I don't know. Paul says here that the even though the physical body and the spiritual body are related, just like a seed and the plant that springs from it, the two are completely different. Our spiritual bodies will be totally different from our physical bodies. We can cite the obvious — no aging, no sickness, no death, no deformity, no handicap, no weakness. We can look to Jesus in his resurrection state and gain some more insight. He ate fish. Will we eat food in heaven? I don't know. Maybe only chocolate. He could be touched and handled. There was a physical dimension to Jesus' resurrection body. Yet he could go through walls and disappear. There is certainly a wondrous spiritual dimension to the resurrection body. Jesus could be recognized, yet typically there was some uncertainty when people first encountered the resurrected Jesus.

The hope of the resurrection is more than just a new body. It is also the hope of ongoing identity. I am Rob now, I will be Rob then. I will keep my memories, my experiences, my accomplishments, my personality. The only thing that will change is that my sin will be totally cleansed away. Because Jesus showed continuity of identity in his resurrection, I believe we also will keep our personalities.

- **What aspect of the resurrection gives you the most anticipation and excitement?**

Another question is, when will all this happen? Do we die and go immediately to heaven? Or is there some kind of intermediate state like soul sleep? The Bible can be interpreted both ways, immediate and intermediate. When Jesus says to the thief on the cross, "Today, you will be with me in Paradise," it implies an immediate afterlife experience of resurrection. Paul says in Philippians 1, "I would rather depart and be with Christ." That sounds like it is an immediate resurrection. But reading Paul in 1 Corinthians 15, it could be thought that there is some kind of delay:

> *For as in Adam all die, so in Christ all will be made alive. But each in his own turn: Christ, the firstfruits; then, when he comes, those who belong to him. Then the end will come, when he hands over the kingdom to God the Father after he has destroyed all dominion, authority and power. For he must reign until he has put all his enemies under his feet. The last enemy to be destroyed is death. Listen, I tell you a mystery: We will not all sleep, but we will all be changed ... in a flash, in the twinkling of an eye, at the last trumpet. For the trumpet will sound, the dead will be raised imperishable,*

> *and we will be changed. For the perishable must clothe itself with the imperishable, and the mortal with immortality.* — 1 Corinthians 15:22-26, 51-53 NIV

"Each in his own turn" sounds like there is a delay. The dead will be raised first sounds like they may be in some sort of intermediate state before the return of Christ. The answer is not firm, but I lean towards an immediate resurrection. After all, Jesus is already raised. It is now our turn in God's plan.

This whole chapter was written to encourage the Corinthians and us in our spiritual labors for Jesus. Christ's resurrection gives meaning and purpose to our lives. How we live our lives not only makes a difference in this world, but also in the world to come. Paul encourages the Corinthians, "Therefore, my dear brothers, stand firm. Let nothing move you. Always give yourselves fully to the work of the Lord, because you know that your labor in the Lord is not in vain" (1 Corinthians 15:58 NIV). Why do we know our labor is not in vain? Because we will live to see all the fruits of our labors for Jesus. The resurrection must be at the core of our faith, giving us energy and hope and enthusiasm and confidence as we live our faith in the world. We are going to live forever. That is motivation to live for God wholeheartedly and unreservedly. Praise God for the victory of resurrection which we have in Jesus Christ.

For Further Reflection

Discuss how the world religions treat Jesus and his resurrection.

Describe how your faith would be if you were to see Jesus alive.

Discuss how your work will go this week, remembering that "your labor is not in vain."

Chapter 48

Born Of A Woman

Galatians 4:4

Texts for the Christmas season usually come from the Gospels of Matthew or Luke, or perhaps from the Old Testament messianic prophecies. Preachers find it difficult to preach Christmas from the letters of Paul and the other New Testament writers. They don't talk about Mary, Joseph, Zechariah, Elizabeth, Simeon, the shepherds, the wise men. There is nothing about the virgin birth in the letters of Paul or the others. There is nothing about Bethlehem, Herod, the flight to Egypt, the presentation in the Temple. The closest we come to a Christmas theme is Paul in Galatians 4:4. Here Paul says that when the time was fulfilled, God sent His Son, born of a woman, born under the Law.

- **Why would Paul avoid mentioning Mary by name?**

Born of a woman. Mary's name is not even mentioned. Yet if we look deeper into this small phrase, everything is there. Why would Paul need to go into detail? Everybody knew by this time who Jesus' mother was. She was an active member in the Jerusalem church. I find it interesting that Paul does not accord her the "queen-of-heaven, mother-of-God" status that our Catholic friends have accorded her.

"Born of a woman" tells us a lot about Jesus. It tells us he was human. It tells us that he came into this world like any other person. He didn't magically appear out of nowhere. He didn't transport down from the starship. He was born. There was labor, there was pain, there was mess to clean up.

It also tells us that Jesus was born into a family — mother, father, and children. Jesus grew up in a family environment.

Christmas, along with Thanksgiving, is the time we make an extra effort to be with family. Family gives us strength, comfort, encouragement, roots, connectedness.

- **What traditions and rituals does your family celebrate at Christmas?**

Unfortunately, not everyone has a good experience with his or her family. Not everyone has family remaining. Our mission, as a church, is to provide a family for those who do not have one. To the fatherless, we men can provide a fatherly role model of Christian maturity. To the motherless, the women can provide the motherly nurture of Christian compassion. To the widowed and divorced, we can provide companionship that comes from Christian friendship and fellowship. While we may not have physical family, we can be a spiritual family to those around us. Indeed that is the call of God.

Paul also says that Jesus was born under the Law. The immediate meaning is that Jesus was born a Jew and into the covenant of Abraham, Isaac, and Jacob. Again, there is deeper meaning. Jesus was born into a political situation of Roman Law. Jesus had to deal with government and its encroachment on freedom as well as its liberation from chaos. Jesus became the victim of the Roman Law when he was crucified on the cross.

Jesus was born into a religious situation of Jewish Law. For Jesus, doing God's will meant being faithful to the Law of the Covenant. This did not mean faithfulness to all the traditions that had arisen by this time, but faithfulness to the original Law that God had given to Moses. Jesus was born into a moral expectation that came from the Jewish Law. Born under the Law means that Jesus was born into society, civilization, and culture. There were expectations, roles, values, customs, rituals that Jesus followed. It is Paul's way of saying that Jesus lived a life that any other normal Jewish peasant would live.

- **What are the expectations and roles in your life?**

Jesus was born of a woman, born under the Law, so that he might redeem us who were under the Law and receive adoption as God's children. Because Jesus was born, we can now be born again. When we are born again, we become part of God's family. We call God our Father, or Abba, meaning Daddy. We call one another brothers and sisters in Christ. Now we are no longer slaves, but children of God.

When we come to the communion table, we do so as the family of God, bought by the blood of the Lamb. The bread symbolizes Jesus' body, the body he was born with when he was born of a woman. "This is my body, broken for you." Jesus' body is the body of a perfect sacrifice for our sins. When we partake of the bread, we partake of the sacrifice that Jesus made for our sins. It also symbolizes us as a church body. We partake of the loaf together. We are the children of God, fed by God. We are family, sitting down at the family meal headed by Jesus.

The cup symbolizes the blood of Jesus, poured out for the redemption of our souls. The blood which Jesus shed is the blood which cleanses us from all unrighteousness. It is the blood of the new covenant, inviting us into a new relationship with God. The new covenant releases us from the old covenant of the Law. We are no longer under Law but under grace. We partake the cup together and we bind ourselves together as brothers and sisters in Christ. We commit ourselves to Jesus and to the fulfillment of his vision and mission.

For Further Reflection

How do doing God's will and living according to the law impact our lives? Where are the common points? Where are the conflicts?

Discuss ways your church can emphasize the family atmosphere.

Chapter 49

We're On The Way

Philippians 3:12-16

Being on the way seems to describe the lives of many of God's saints. Abraham was on his way from Haran to the promised land. Jacob was on the way to Paddan-Aram, and then back again to the promised land and then to Egypt. Moses was on the way through the Red Sea and into the wilderness. David was on the way to establishing his kingdom. Israel was on the way to exile, and then on the way back again. Even Jesus' life is one of constant travel as he goes from town to town in Galilee and then sets his face toward Jerusalem.

- **If God were to tell you to move right now, and you were limited in what you could take, what would be the top five things you would take?**

Being on the way is nothing new for God's people. Sometimes, like Jesus, they knew exactly where they were going and what would happen when they got there. Others, like Abraham, set out for a place they knew not. Abraham knew he was there only when he arrived at his destination. We are on the way, but are we like Abraham or like Jesus? Many Christians are on their way, but you wouldn't know it by looking at the fruit of their trees. Like Israel in the wilderness, they wander aimlessly, complaining about every hardship they encounter. They have no goal, no objective, no focus in their lives. Other Christians are very focused and know exactly what they are doing and why they are doing it. What is the difference? I think we can learn from Paul how to be focused in our Christian lives.

This passage in Philippians is one of my favorites. There is much to learn. The immediate context is Paul's description of his life before Jesus. Paul had made a great career as a zealous Pharisee. He knew the Law. He had studied under Gamaliel. He was on his way to the top. Then he met Jesus, and everything changed. He says that everything he valued before meeting Jesus he now considered trash, rubbish, garbage. Now his only goal is to know Jesus Christ in the power of his resurrection, becoming like Christ through suffering and experiencing God's resurrection power. Paul's goal: "I want to know Christ." Paul was on his way to knowing Christ in the full power of his resurrection. What are we on our way to? What is our goal in our Christian life?

How committed was Paul to this goal? In Philippians 3:12, he confesses that he has not already attained this. Imagine that! Paul, the great apostle, admitting that he had not arrived at Christian perfection. One sure way to lose ground is to begin thinking that we have arrived, to think that we are totally mature and have no room for improvement. Paul saw room for improvement in his life. How much more do we have room for improvement in our Christian walk?

- **Make a quick list of five areas in your life that could use improvement.**

"But I press on to make it my own." Such was Paul's commitment and determination. Being a Christian can be tiring, exhausting work. It isn't just what we do when we are at church. Being a Christian is a 24-hours-a-day, seven-days-a-week calling from God. Paul's image in this passage is that of a marathon runner in a race. That is an apt image for our pilgrimage. There is a finish line in heaven. We must press on. There is abundant life here on earth. There is a mission. There is a vision. We must press on. While we can sprint at times, jog at times, and maybe fast walk at times, we must press on. "God gives strength to the weary ... they will soar on wings like eagles, they will run and not grow weary, they will walk and not grow faint" (Isaiah 40:29-31 NIV). Paul could press on because of God's strength. We can press on only in God's strength.

"Beloved, I do not consider that I have made it my own. But this one thing I do: forgetting what lies behind and straining forward to what lies ahead, I press on toward the goal for the prize of the heavenly all of God in Christ Jesus" (Philippians 3:13 NRSV). "This one thing I do." There is the secret. We live in the days of variety, distraction, multiple opportunities for work, leisure, and activity. What is the one thing we do? Many people focus on the earthly, temporal things. One thing I do — career and job. One thing I do — drugs and partying. One thing I do — sex. One thing I do — play and fun. One thing I do — exercise and work out, and sports. One thing I do — money and things. These have become idols for these people and they have forgotten the heavenly prize.

- **What one thing dominates the focus and goal of your life?**

Yet even more dangerous are the forty things I dabble at. A little sports here. A little service club there. A little work here. A little play there. Oops, what do you know? No time left for God or church. In either case, Paul shows us the secret to knowing Christ. It is the one thing he does. God says to Jeremiah, "You will seek me and you will find me when you seek me with all your heart" (Jeremiah 29:13 NIV). All your heart. We cannot afford to be distracted by forty things or focused on the wrong thing if we want to know Jesus Christ. In the parable of the sower in Matthew 13, Jesus says some seed falls among the thorns, which represent the cares of this world. Being distracted by the cares of this world, the word is choked out. One thing I do. That is the secret to knowing Jesus Christ. Once you know him, in the power of his resurrection, all the other distractions of life fall into priority. It isn't that you never do sports, or earn money, or go to work, or have fun, but that all things are in their proper perspective because Jesus is first in your life.

"Forgetting what lies behind." Here is where we make another major mistake. We focus too much on the past. For some, the past represents the dark ages. I had too much sin, too much bad in my life. God could never forgive me. I can never be anything great. The good news is that Jesus forgives all our sin. Paul the apostle was at one time Paul the murderer. But God saved him, forgave him, and gave him the power to be the most famous apostle in the Church. If God can and did do that for Paul, God can and will do that for us. Paul forgot his bad past, his sin, his persecution of the saints. He accepted God's grace and got on with his new life in Christ, not letting his past hinder his present and future performance. What is in your past? Confess it to God. Accept his forgiveness and move on to God's glorious future for your life.

For others, the past represents the glory days, the good old days. This is even more dangerous, because we don't want to let the past go. Many churches, perhaps yours, have idolized certain traditions, programs, ways of doing things. To let them go may stir up conflict, but we live in an atmosphere of constant change. Nothing stays the same. When we don't change with our environment, we run the risk of diminishing the effectiveness of our mission. We must constantly evaluate the structures of the church so that the mission of the church can be carried out most efficiently. Jesus says that new wine must be put in new wineskins. The new wine is the life in the Holy Spirit that we share. The wineskins are the structures of the church and its programs. The Holy Spirit is constantly renewing the life of the church so that we can accomplish our mission in the world. If we don't renew our structures, we risk bursting the old as the life of Jesus moves within us.

"Straining forward to what lies ahead." Whether good or bad, we have to let go of the past in order to focus on our future. What lies ahead? Ultimately heaven. That is our goal, to be with Christ. That is not pie in the sky by and by. We can know Christ in the here and now and have heaven in the future. That is what Paul was aiming for. We must focus on the vision of the future that God has given us.

"I press on to the heavenly call." There it is again. "I press on." It connotes progress, movement, a continual process of growing and learning in Jesus Christ. It says we are on the way to knowing Christ in all his fullness. Can we forget the past, and make new wineskins for the present? Can we focus on that one precious thing, knowing Christ?

- **Over the last ten years, what shows that you have made progress in your relationship with Christ? Over the last five years? Over the last year?**

We tend to skip over Paul's next line, but it is instructive: "Let those of us who are mature be of the same mind and if you think differently about anything, this too God will reveal to you." At least in Paul's view, mature Christians will share his perspective. Mature Christians are focused on the goal of the future, not the days of the past. Mature Christians are focused on one thing, knowing Christ. They are not focused on earthly things. They are not distracted by forty things. Mature Christians are on the way to heaven, pressing onward to the heavenly call and prize of knowing Jesus Christ as Lord and Savior in a living relationship that deepens in this life and is fulfilled in the next life. We are on the way.

For Further Reflection

What past things would you like forgotten? Make a list on paper then tear it up and throw it away. Remind yourself that God casts our sins as far as the East is from the West.

What things do you consider your greatest accomplishments in life? Are you willing to consider those "rubbish" as Paul considered his past accomplishments?

What "one thing" will you focus on for the next year or two to deepen your relationship with Jesus?

Chapter 50

The Christmas Test: Jesus Has Come In The Flesh

1 John 4

It seems every year at Christmas, there are more towns and cities embroiled in legal disputes over holiday displays. Many have had to abandon traditional holiday displays such as crèches, crosses, and manger scenes because some group finds the display "offensive." We should not be too surprised. Jesus warned that people would persecute us. The Apostle John and his community were thoroughly familiar with this kind of harassment. Raymond Brown's theory is that the adversaries of the Johannine community were some who had seceded from the community over differing interpretations of the Gospel of John (Raymond Brown, *The Epistles of John,* Anchor Bible, vol. 30, [Garden City: Doubleday & Co., 1982], p. 70). John's letter serves to clarify the faith for his community, and it has insight for us as we come again to the holy season of Christmas.

> *Dear friends, do not believe every spirit, but test the spirits to see whether they are from God, because many false prophets have gone out into the world. This is how you can recognize the Spirit of God: Every spirit that acknowledges that Jesus Christ has come in the flesh is from God, but every spirit that does not acknowledge Jesus is not from God. This is the spirit of the antichrist, which you have heard is coming and even now is already in the world.* — 1 John 4:1-3 NIV

- **What spirits and false prophets can you identify in our world today?**

"Do not believe every spirit, but test the spirits." Many false prophets and spirits have gone out into the world. There are the spirits of other religions. There is the spirit of worldly thinking and attitude. There is the spirit of humanism. There is the spirit of hedonism, pleasure seeking. Many others could be named as well. We must test these spirits to determine if they are from God.

What is the test? Every spirit (or person, or group, or organization, or philosophy) that acknowledges that Jesus Christ has come in the flesh is from God. Maybe we should call that the Christmas test. That is precisely what we celebrate at Christmas, isn't it? Jesus Christ has come in the flesh. As we look around our world on this great day, how many are acknowledging that Jesus Christ has come in the flesh? Business people and merchants will be happy for all the money that comes their way. Many will exchange gifts, have parties, and celebrate with family, but their lives say, "Jesus Christ has not come in the flesh." A recent news article noted that many organizations now prefer "Happy Holidays" as the greeting for the season, rather than "Merry Christmas." This is preferred so that one can avoid saying "Jesus" or "Christ." John makes this a fairly dramatic test of Christian orthodoxy and practice. If you acknowledge that Jesus has come in the flesh, you are from God. If you deny that Jesus has come in the flesh, you are an antichrist.

- **What is your favorite part about Christmas?**

To celebrate Christmas truly in the Spirit of Jesus Christ we must acknowledge what this holiday means in the first place. God came to earth as a human in Jesus Christ. The baby in the manger was God in human flesh. Jesus Christ has come in the flesh. That is the message of Christmas. When God came to earth, He did not come in wrath, anger, and judgment. He came in love, humility, patience, gentleness. He came to reconcile humanity back to Himself. He came to die for our sins on the cross. He came to die so that we might live.

Sometimes the manger becomes disconnected from the cross, yet if we allow this to happen we will be telling only half the story. The cross was the main reason for Christmas in the first place. We find the cross in the Christmas story. It is in the gift of myrrh. It is in the prophecy of Simeon. The message of Christmas is a message of hope and salvation for the world. The God who came to earth as the baby in the manger became the Savior of the world dying on the cross. In the Johannine community's controversy with the secessionists, their denial that Jesus had come in the flesh was a denial of the importance of Christ's death on the cross. In John's view, the Christmas story is solidly linked with Good Friday (Raymond Brown, *ibid.*, p. 77).

If we really want to confess and demonstrate our conviction that Jesus Christ has come in the flesh, it must be done the other 365 days of the year. The rest of 1 John 4 tells us about how our lives are to be transformed by Jesus. For John, this transformation is evidenced by the Holy Spirit and love. In John's theology, one becomes the proof of the other. John's way of describing the Holy Spirit is by confessing that God lives in us:

> *We know that we live in him and he in us, because he has given us of his Spirit. And we have seen and testify that the Father has sent His Son to be the Savior of the world. If anyone acknowledges that Jesus is the Son of God, God lives in him and he in God. And so we know and rely on the love God has for us. God is love. Whoever lives in love lives in God, and God in him.*
> — 1 John 4:13-16 NIV

"We know that we live in him and he in us." Do we know this? Our victory and strength come from this reality, that Jesus lives inside us. Meditate and think about this and you will be awestruck. God, the living God, the creator of the universe, the baby in the manger, the Savior on the cross, the resurrected Lord — He lives inside us.

If you confess that Jesus is the Son of God come in the flesh, then the Bible is clear that Jesus is living in you as well. You can live out that belief by your Christian walk throughout the year. It is time to begin again with Genesis and read the Bible through. We need to communicate with the Spirit of Christ inside us through continual prayer. We need to worship Christ on a regular basis through faithful attendance at church. We need to serve Christ with our gifts and talents through service in the church. We need to support the work of Christ here and around the world through our faithful and generous giving.

According to John, there must be more than the mere confession of the mouth. There must be action in our lives to back up our wonderful words. John calls that action, love. Love is obviously important to John. It is the unique characteristic of Christ within us.

> *Dear friends, let us love one another, for love comes from God. Everyone who loves has been born of God and knows God. Whoever does not love does not know God, because God is love. This is how God showed His love among us: He sent His one and only Son into the world that we might live through him. This is love: not that we loved God, but that He loved us and sent His Son as an atoning sacrifice for our sins. Dear friends, since God so loved us, we also ought to love one another. No one has ever seen God; but if we love one another, God lives in us and His love is made complete in us ... We love because He first loved us. If anyone says, "I love God," yet hates his brother, he is a liar. For anyone who does not love his brother, whom he has seen, cannot love God, whom he has not seen. And He has given us this command: Whoever loves God must also love his brother.* — 1 John 4:7-12, 19-21 NIV

- **In what ways can we show love to others?**

According to Jesus, all people will know we are his disciples by our love (John 13:35). If we do not love, we show we do not know God. God showed His love by sending Jesus to die for our sins. How can we show our love and demonstrate that God lives in us? That is a compelling question if we really want to back our words with actions. Christmas is the time when some of the barriers come down and we show love more openly. Have you shown love this Christmas season? There were several opportunities. Did you buy presents for an underprivileged child? Then you showed love. Did you contribute to a needy family? Then you showed love. John is especially concerned that love be demonstrated by acts of kindness, generosity, and compassion to those who are not as fortunate as we are.

How else do we demonstrate love? Paul, in 1 Corinthians 13, gives us a very demanding list of qualities we continually need to work on if we want to be loving. Love is patient, kind, never jealous, never boastful, never rude. Love does not keep a record of wrongs but rejoices when truth wins out. Jesus' standards include, "Love one another as I have loved you" (John 13:34 NIV). "Do unto others as you would have them do unto you" (Matthew 7:12). "Forgive others when they sin against you" (Matthew 6:14-15). "Bless your enemies and pray for those who persecute you" (Matthew 5:44).

For John, love was just as much a test for true Christians as confessing that Jesus came in the flesh. You might say the confession is a test of orthodoxy, right thinking, while love is the test of orthopraxy, right practice. The two must go together or you cannot be a true Christian in John's eyes. Notice John continually talks about loving brothers and sisters. True love begins here in the community of faith. Those who confess Christ should be at the top of our love list. It is almost frightening to read that line from John, "If anyone says, 'I love God,' yet hates his brother, he is a liar. For anyone who does not love his brother whom he has seen cannot love God, whom he has not seen" (1 John 4:20 NIV). If you really love God, whom you haven't seen, then you need to love the people around you whom you have seen. This is the commandment we have from Jesus. If we love God, then we must love our brothers and sisters. There is no option.

John reminds us that while we celebrate Jesus' birth on one day of the year, the Spirit of Christ and the love of Christ must be demonstrated every day of the year. We need to help the poor in March, in July, and in October as well as at Christmas time. We need to confess Jesus in the flesh in March, in July, and in October as well as at Christmas. We need to love our brothers and sisters in March, July, and October as well as at Christmas. We need to demonstrate our commitment to Christ in March, July, and October as well as at Christmas.

This year, as we celebrate Christmas, the birth of the Savior, God come in the flesh, take these tests and see where you may need to improve over the next year. Do you need to improve your confession, your faith? Bible study and Sunday school can help you deepen your faith and knowledge. Do you need to improve your Christian walk? Make a plan for more prayer, regular church attendance, serving within the church, or for giving generously. Do you need to improve your love? Make an intentional effort to help those in need and to demonstrate your love for your brothers and sisters in Christ. Remember, greater is he that is in you than he that is in the world. Jesus lives inside us to give us the power to live a life of Spirit-filled love and commitment.

This year at Christmas, may you celebrate the birth of Jesus Christ, God who came in the flesh.

For Further Reflection

What year-round project could you or your church undertake to show the Christmas spirit at times other than Christmas?

Read through all of 1 John and discuss his emphasis on faith and love put into action.

Chapter 51

Full Circle:
God Has A Plan For You

Revelation 21 and 22

We began with the goal to read and preach through the entire Bible. Here we are. We have achieved our goal, but we are not really at the end, but at a new beginning. As we come to the end of the Bible we see the promise of a new beginning in a new heaven and a new earth for eternity.

Revelation is an awesome book, isn't it? Most Christians — scholars and preachers and lay people — can't fathom this book, so it is generally avoided. With the exception of those who expound on prophecy, most people never delve into Revelation because they can't understand it. Personally, I think the problem is that we want to make the various beasts and events of this book fit into our particular point in history. Another serious problem is the desire to take this book literally rather than symbolically. If we are trying to fit our modern situation into a literal interpretation of Revelation we are going to have a difficult time sorting things out. Let's be content with some broad strokes in the message of Revelation.

The broadest message of Revelation is that God's plan for the ages is still in motion and will be fulfilled. Though there are unfaithful churches, God's plan will be accomplished. Though there is misery and suffering in the world, God's plan will be accomplished. Though God's judgment falls on the wicked and they refuse to repent, God's plan will be accomplished. Though Satan does his best to persecute and annihilate the people of God, God's plan will be accomplished. Revelation is essentially a verbal comic book of what will happen before Jesus comes back.

- **Which part of Revelation gave you the most problem or confusion?**

In Revelation 2 and 3 we see that before Jesus comes back there will be churches with differing levels of faithfulness and commitment. Some have lost their first-love. Some are lukewarm. Some are persecuted. Some are weak. Some tolerate sin. But Jesus is the one who continually walks among the churches, encouraging them to holiness and faithfulness to their mission of witness. Those who need rebuke receive rebuke. Those who deserve praise are praised. We are encouraged to be faithful and holy because when the time of the end comes, we will need to stand fast.

In Revelation 6, we see the horsemen of the Apocalypse. We see war, famine, disease, and death roaming the earth before the time of the end. We sometimes wonder why these things happen. The Bible says that these are the result of our sin in the world. Here, they are the signs of the end to come. The seals are judgments of God. These judgments will increase in intensity and range as the subsequent judgments come. In Revelation 8 and 9 we see the trumpet judgments. Again, God's wrath is poured out in order to lead people to repentance, but we see in chapter 9 the wicked by this time are stubbornly wicked and refuse to repent. In Revelation 16-18 we see the bowl judgments and the judgment on the great harlot, Babylon. At a certain point, which only God can decide, there is nothing left to do but send complete judgment that wipes out nearly all the unrepentant sinners.

In chapter 19 Jesus comes back with all his saints and defeats the beast and his armies at Armageddon. The beast is judged. The dead are judged. Those who have not followed Jesus will be thrown into the Lake of Fire. I would call this the bad news of the Good News. God will judge those who refuse to repent of their sins and follow Jesus. The clear message of Revelation 1-20 is that God will judge.

- **Do you want to watch the rest of the world being judged? Why or why not?**

The crimes of the world demand that there be a righteous judgment. The Kennedy assassination cries out for righteous judgment and the guilty parties to be held accountable. The O.J. Simpson case cries out for truth and justice to prevail. The countless missing children throughout our land cry out for resolution, justice, and judgment. The assassination of Martin Luther King cries out for justice and judgment. The wrongful deaths of Jesus, Paul, Peter, James, and a host of other martyrs for the faith cry out for justice and judgment. People think they have gotten away with their sin, away with their crime. They may never be caught or prosecuted in this world. There must be a time and a place where someone more powerful than they will hold them accountable and make them tell the truth. There will be no high priced lawyers with jury studies and fancy tactics. There will be no bribes or blackmail or intimidation of the judge. There will be no getting off on a technicality because they weren't told their rights. There will be no plea bargaining. There will be no light sentences of probation and community service for horrible, heinous, vicious crimes.

Revelation 20 says God will get out the books and the books will tell all. The first book is the book of works. According to Hebrew tradition, God keeps meticulous records of all our works in His book. No detail is left unrecorded. Everything we have done, whether good or bad, is recorded. The second book is the book of life. In it are all those God has given eternal life. The only way to be written in that book is by putting your faith in Jesus Christ. The dead are judged. As the book of works is opened, everyone will be found to be guilty of breaking God's Law at one point or another. If the book of works were the only book in heaven, all of us would be thrown into the Lake of Fire. But Revelation 20:15 says that only those whose names were not found in the book of Life were thrown into the Lake. As long as we are faithful to keep our commitment to Jesus Christ as Lord and Savior, our names are in that book of life. That means that our sins are forgiven.

Up to Revelation 20, the theme is judgment. But beginning with chapter 21, the theme is restoration and renewal. God makes all things new, listen:

Then I saw a new heaven and a new earth, for the first heaven and the first earth had passed away, and there was no longer any sea. I saw the Holy City, the new Jerusalem, coming down out of heaven from God, prepared as a bride beautifully dressed for her husband. And I heard a loud voice from the throne saying, "Now the dwelling of God is with men, and He will live with them. They will be His people, and God Himself will be with them and be their God. He will wipe every tear from their eyes. There will be no more death or mourning or crying or pain, for the old order of things has passed away." He who was seated on the throne said, "I am making everything new!" Then he said, "Write this down, for these words are trustworthy and true."
— Revelation 21:1-5 NIV

Here is God's plan! He wants to make everything new. We are being made new through our faith in Jesus Christ. When the judgments are done, God will make the whole earth and heavens new. The Greek word for new here means new like there has never been one like it before. It is not a rehash or remake of the old. It is totally new. This earth and heaven are rolled up and trashed. The brand new is rolled out and tacked down and ready for use. Our relationship with God is complete. "The dwelling of God is with people and He will live with them." God will live with us.

The old order has passed away. There will be no more death or mourning or crying or pain. Can we even imagine what that will be like? Every day of our lives we live with death, mourning, crying, and pain. Loved ones who have gone before us leave that certain empty spot that is never quite filled. We live in a certain awe and fear of death. We are ready to die, but not desiring to die. We live with pain. Whether it be the twinge of arthritis, the cloud of a cataract, the old football injury, or car accident or allergy, we all live with a certain amount of pain, a certain amount of disability and limitation. Very few people are blessed with perfect health. Most of us count ourselves blessed when we have functional health. Pain, death, mourning, crying is all part of this old order of things. When all things are made new, these things will pass away as well.

- **What limitation or disability do you live with that you look forward to getting rid of in heaven?**

That the old order has passed away also implies that sin and evil are no longer present. John makes this perfectly clear.

> *He said to me: "It is done. I am the Alpha and the Omega, the Beginning and the End. To him who is thirsty I will give to drink without cost from the spring of the water of life. He who overcomes will inherit all this, and I will be his God and he will be my son. But the cowardly, the unbelieving, the vile, the murderers, the sexually immoral, those who practice magic arts, the idolaters and all liars — their place will be in the fiery lake of burning sulfur. This is the second death" ... "Blessed are those who wash their robes, that they may have the right to the tree of life and may go through the gates into the city. Outside are the dogs, those who practice magic arts, the sexually immoral, the murderers, the idolaters and everyone who loves and practices falsehood. I, Jesus, have sent my angel to give you this testimony for the churches. I am the Root and the Offspring of David, and the bright Morning Star."*
> — Revelation 21:6-8; 22:14-16 NIV

The unholy things are outside of heaven and their influence cannot be felt inside of heaven. John describes this new world in some detail, but again, we must guard against literal application. How can you describe an entirely new reality with words that belong to the old order of things?

> *One of the seven angels who had the seven bowls full of the seven last plagues came and said to me, "Come, I will show you the bride, the wife of the Lamb." And he carried me away in the Spirit to a mountain great and high, and showed me the Holy City, Jerusalem, coming down out of heaven from God. It shone with the glory of God, and its brilliance was like that of a very precious jewel, like a jasper, clear as crystal. It had a great,*

> *high wall with twelve gates, and with twelve angels at the gates. On the gates were written the names of the twelve tribes of Israel. There were three gates on the east, three on the north, three on the south and three on the west. The wall of the city had twelve foundations, and on them were the names of the twelve apostles of the Lamb. The angel who talked with me had a measuring rod of gold to measure the city, its gates and its walls. The city was laid out like a square, as long as it was wide. He measured the city with the rod and found it to be 12,000 stadia 1,500 miles in length, and as wide and high as it is long. He measured its wall and it was 144 cubits [75 yards] thick, by man's measurement, which the angel was using. The wall was made of jasper, and the city of pure gold, as pure as glass. The foundations of the city walls were decorated with every kind of precious stone. The first foundation was jasper, the second sapphire, the third chalcedony, the fourth emerald, the fifth sardonyx, the sixth carnelian, the seventh chrysolite, the eighth beryl, the ninth topaz, the tenth chrysoprase, the eleventh jacinth, and the twelfth amethyst. The twelve gates were twelve pearls, each gate made of a single pearl. The great street of the city was of pure gold, like transparent glass.*
> — Revelation 21:9-21 NIV

We don't often consider this description except to sing about the pearly gates and the streets of gold. Again, time won't permit detail, but in general, what John is saying is that this is a beautiful new city. The interior decoration specs call for precious metals and jewels as the construction materials. What is interesting is that if we take this literally, the city is 1500 miles high, wide, and long. Can you imagine a city 1500 miles high? The biggest skyscraper today is about 120 stories high. This is 1500 miles high. When the space shuttle orbits the earth, it is 200 miles above the surface. That can give you some perspective.

The message is that God has a plan. We who have faith in Jesus are part of that plan. And we will be there when this new heaven and new earth come into view. So what is our job until that day?

Invite people to come to the heavenly city by putting their faith in Christ. The Spirit and the bride say, "Come!" And let him who hears say, "Come!" Whoever is thirsty, let him come; and whoever wishes, let him take the free gift of the water of life (Revelation 22:17 NIV).

Come. That is the invitation of God. Come to Jesus. Come in faith. Come to the new heaven and the new earth. The message of the Bible is that God's plan for our lives and for our afterlife is good. It is worth everything we endure now to be there then. Come, enter the kingdom prepared for you from the foundation of the world.

For Further Reflection

Looking at the churches in Revelation 2 and 3, which best describes your own personal walk with Jesus? Which describes the church you attend?

What "unsolved mystery" or crime do you want to see solved in heaven?

Chapter 52

The Story Continues

As we come to the end of this book, we also come to the end of the Bible. But as we near the end, we need to ask, has the story really ended?

Revelation presents the end of history in the style of symbolism and vision. But the end has not come yet. We are still in the "in-between" time. We are part of the continuing story of God's action and interaction with the people of earth. We are part of the sequel to Acts. It is a sequel that has been written for the past 1900 plus years and continues to be written until Jesus comes back.

What will the heavenly Bible, the final copy, say about us who lived in this generation? Will it record our individual acts and accomplishments in the power of the Holy Spirit? Will we find our names written in the final version of the Bible? We could. I believe all of God's faithful servants, who do God's will and do their part to fulfill God's mission, will earn a place in that final version of the Bible.

You are saying to yourself, "But I'm no Paul, I'm no Peter." But think of all the "ordinary" Christians and saints we have met in the Bible. There is Ananias in Acts 9 who lays his hands on Paul. There is Simon the tanner, where Peter stays for a visit. There are all the people in Romans 16, who are mentioned only there. These are regular saints that Paul knew and greeted. We don't have to be Paul or Peter. We only have to be ourselves and faithful to the task God has called us to accomplish.

During the Christmas season, we must remind ourselves that Jesus came especially to the ordinary people. He was raised by Joseph and Mary. They were ordinary Jews who were faithful to God's call. Jesus' birth was announced to shepherds, the most ordinary of ordinary people. Jesus came to be one of us, not to seclude himself in the stratosphere of the superstars, nobility, filthy rich, or world famous. Jesus was an ordinary guy, doing an ordinary job. He was a carpenter up until that day when he obeyed God's call to him to be the Messiah.

I sometimes think that God will honor the ordinary saints before He honors the superstars, in keeping with the teaching that the last shall be first. Ordinary saints who were faithful in prayer, faithful to serve in their church, faithful in their giving, faithful to help other people, are just as important, maybe even more important than the "big name" Christians. Ordinary saints are being written into the final version of the Bible by their deeds and their words.

So now you have the plan God has for you. It was a plan that began long ago and is still being fulfilled. It will be entirely fulfilled when we get to heaven. The last question of this book is this: Do you want to be part of God's plan for you?

The first step to be in God's plan is to put your faith in Jesus Christ as your Lord and Savior. You can do this in prayer as you confess your sins, ask Jesus to forgive you, and ask Jesus to come into your life as your Lord and Savior.

The second step is to be obedient to the commands of Jesus. You have read the whole Bible. You know what God requires of you. Go out and do it. Let God work His plan in you.

Index Of Referenced Scriptures

A
Acts 4:32-35	238
Acts 4:36-37	239
Acts 5:1-2	239
Acts 5:3-10	240
Acts 19	194
Acts 19:11	194
Acts 19:13-16	194

C
1 Chronicles 10:13	79
1 Chronicles 15:15, 19-22	101
1 Chronicles 25:1, 6-7	102
2 Chronicles 5:11-14	111
2 Chronicles 7:14	186
2 Chronicles 20:6, 7, 12	108
2 Chronicles 20:12	108
2 Chronicles 20:15	109
2 Chronicles 29	118
Colossians 3:16	102
1 Corinthians 3:12	32
1 Corinthians 10	190
1 Corinthians 10:20	168
1 Corinthians 11:26	87
1 Corinthians 12	190
1 Corinthians 12:26	139
1 Corinthians 13	271
1 Corinthians 15	190
1 Corinthians 15:3-8	250
1 Corinthians 15:12-18	251
1 Corinthians 15:19	252
1 Corinthians 15:22-26, 51-53	255
1 Corinthians 15:29-34	252
1 Corinthians 15:35-50	253
1 Corinthians 15:58	255
2 Corinthians 5:17	44
2 Corinthians 5:20	117
2 Corinthians 5:21	140

D
Daniel 7:9	198
Daniel 7:17	197
Daniel in 7:18	200
Daniel 9	186
Deuteronomy 6:13	55
Deuteronomy 6:16	55
Deuteronomy 8:3	55
Deuteronomy 18:14-19	55
Deuteronomy 18:17-19	56

E
Ecclesiastes 12:13	166
Ephesians 3:10	17
Ephesians 4:12	209
Ephesians 5:19	102
Esther 4:6-17	123
Esther 4:16	125
Exodus 3:7	33
Exodus 3:10	33
Exodus 14:11	37
Exodus 20:15	203
Exodus 22:18	76
Exodus 32:4	37
Exodus 32:10	38
Exodus 32:11-14, 24	40, 185
Exodus 32:30-34	40
Exodus 33:11	58

Exodus 33:18	41	Isaiah 44:12	170
Exodus 34:6-7	41	Isaiah 44:13-16	170
Ezekiel 3	196	Isaiah 44:14	171
Ezekiel 8	193	Isaiah 44:18	168
Ezekiel 9:10	193	Isaiah 46:10	169
Ezekiel 10-11	193	Isaiah 55	173
Ezekiel 18:2	203	Isaiah 55:8, 9	173
Ezekiel 18:4, 30	45, 204	Isaiah 55:9	135
Ezekiel 18:22	204	Isaiah 56:4-8	177
Ezekiel 18:23	204	Isaiah 57:20	197
Ezekiel 18:24	204	Isaiah 58:3	173
Ezekiel 18:32	204	Isaiah 58:6, 7	175
Ezekiel 22:30	185	Isaiah 58:8	175
Ezra 9	139	Isaiah 58:9	175
		Isaiah 58:13	175
		Isaiah 66:13	71

G

Galatians 4:4	257
Genesis 1	15
Genesis 2	16
Genesis 3:1	16
Genesis 3:15	17
Genesis 6	19
Genesis 12	19
Genesis 12:1-2	20
Genesis 15:5	20
Genesis 15:6	20
Genesis 32:28	44
Genesis 41:51	26
Genesis 41:52	26
Genesis 45:5	28
Genesis 50:20	28

J

James 4:7	130
James 5	190
James 5:16	186
James 5:17	94
Jeremiah 15:1	183
Jeremiah 29:11-13	11
Jeremiah 29:13	263
Jeremiah 31:35-37	246
Jeremiah 36:20-26	188
Job 1:1	128
Job 1:5	128
Job 1:13ff	128
Job 2:10	129
Job 4:12-21	133
Job 5:17	134
Job 8:5, 6	134
Job 8:8-10	134
Job 11:1-6	134
Job 11:5, 6	135
Job 13:15	131
Job 19:25-27	131
Job 42:7-9	136

H

Hebrews 4:16	41
Hebrews 9:22	45
Hebrews 11:32	67

I

Isaiah 40:29-31	262
Isaiah 44:6-8	168

Job 42:10	137	**K**		
Job 42:7-9	136	1 Kings 3:3	86	
Joel 2:28, 29	207	1 Kings 4:29-34	87	
John 3:30	220	1 Kings 18:16-17	90	
John 6:5	233	1 Kings 18:19-21	90	
John 6:7	234	1 Kings 18:22-24	91	
John 6:8-9	234	1 Kings 18:27	92	
John 6:10-13	234	1 Kings 18:30-35	92	
John 10:18	98	1 Kings 18:36-37	93	
John 11:25-26	97	1 Kings 18:38	93	
John 13	190	1 Kings 18:39	93	
John 13:34	271	1 Kings 19:15-16	113	
John 13:35	270	2 Kings 2:9	114	
John 14:13	108	2 Kings 13:20-21	96	
John 14:23	224	2 Kings 14:25	211	
John 14:30	129	2 Kings 16:3	117	
John 14:6	162	2 Kings 22	55	
John 16:8	144	2 Kings 22:8-10	119	
John 20:18	72	2 Kings 22:14-20	72	
1 John 4:1-3	267			
1 John 4:7-12, 19-21	270	**L**		
1 John 4:13-16	269	Levitcus 1:4	45	
1 John 4:20	271	Leviticus 19:31	76	
Jonah 1:4	212	Leviticus 20:6	76	
Jonah 1:17	212	Luke 1:37	212	
Jonah 3:4	212	Luke 6:35	238	
Jonah 3:10	213	Luke 7:15	97	
Jonah 4:4	213	Luke 7:27	220	
Jonah 4:6	212	Luke 12:15	238	
Jonah 4:7	212	Luke 12:16-21	238	
Jonah 4:11	214	Luke 17:21	201	
Joshua 1:5	58			
Joshua 1:7-8	58	**M**		
Joshua 1:16-17	60	Malachi 2:16	217	
Joshua 7	139	Malachi 3:1	218	
Joshua 9:14	82	Malachi 3:10	217	
Judges 2:10	61	Malachi 4:1	219	
Judges 13:5	62	Malachi 4:5	218	
Judges 14:4	63	Mark 8:34	126	
Judges 21:25	62	Mark 10:17	223	

Mark 10:18-19	224	**P**	
Mark 10:20	224	1 Peter 1:6, 7	131
Mark 10:21-22	224	Philippians 1	254
Mark 10:43	65	Philippians 3:12	262
Mark 12:41-44	226	Philippians 3:13	263
Mark 16	190	Philippians 4:8	156
Matthew 3:7	221	Proverbs 1:7	159
Matthew 3:15	220	Proverbs 3:5	162
Matthew 4:4	51	Proverbs 3:5, 6	67
Matthew 4:7	51	Proverbs 3:5-8	159
Matthew 5:23-24	27	Proverbs 13:1	160
Matthew 5:44	271	Proverbs 13:24	160
Matthew 5:45	151	Proverbs 14:12	161
Matthew 6:14-15	271	Proverbs 16:32	162
Matthew 6:26	151	Proverbs 17:9	162
Matthew 7:7	41	Proverbs 19:15	163
Matthew 7:12	247, 271	Proverbs 22:13	163
Matthew 7:21	181	Psalm 51	143
Matthew 10:29	152	Psalm 51:1-2, 5-6	146
Matthew 11:11	220	Psalm 51:3	144
Matthew 12:39-41	211	Psalm 51:4	144
Matthew 13	263	Psalm 51:7-20	147
Matthew 14:4	221	Psalm 51:11-12	145
Matthew 16:19	108	Psalm 51:13-15	147
Matthew 17:11-12	220	Psalm 51:16-17	146
Matthew 24:24	134	Psalm 53:1	144
Matthew 25	22	Psalm 81:1	102
Matthew 25:41	130	Psalm 95:1	102
		Psalm 121:1	149
N		Psalm 121:2	149
Nehemiah 5:14	140	Psalm 121:3-4	150
Numbers 13:31	51	Psalm 121:5-8	150
Numbers 14:2-3	51	Psalm 121:7	152
Numbers 14:13ff	41	Psalm 121:8	152
Numbers 16	50	Psalm 127:3	218
Numbers 16:3	52	Psalm 139	154
Numbers 17	50	Psalm 139:1-4	154
Numbers 32:23	147	Psalm 139:5-12	155
		Psalm 139:13-18	156
		Psalm 139:23-24	158

R

Revelation 1-3	22, 199, 274
Revelation 4:1	105
Revelation 4:10	105
Revelation 5	105
Revelation 6	274
Revelation 8-9	274
Revelation 12	129
Revelation 12:9	16
Revelation 16-18	274
Revelation 20:15	275
Revelation 21:1-5	276
Revelation 21:6-8, 14-16	277
Revelation 21:9-21	278
Revelation 22:17	279
Romans 1:18	180
Romans 8:20, 21	145
Romans 10:9	251
Romans 11:1-6	246
Romans 11:11-16	244
Romans 11:25-27	244
Romans 11:28-32	245
Romans 12:1-2	117
Romans 12:2	156

S

1 Samuel 1:10-11, 20	71
1 Samuel 8	186
1 Samuel 28:3-7	76
1 Samuel 28:8-15	77
2 Samuel 11-12	144
2 Samuel 21	82

T

2 Thessalonians 3:10	163
1 Timothy 2	190
1 Timothy 2:1-2	186
1 Timothy 3:16	190

www.ingramcontent.com/pod-product-compliance
Lightning Source LLC
Chambersburg PA
CBHW070725160426
43192CB00009B/1325